W9-CFJ-171

Service Oriented Architecture Demystified

A pragmatic approach to SOA for the IT executive

Girish Juneja, Blake Dournaee, Joe Natoli and Steve Birkel

INTEL
PRESS

Copyright © 2007 Intel Corporation. All rights reserved.

ISBN 1-9340530-2-3

No part of this publication may be reproduced, stored in a retrieval system or transmitted in any form or by any means, electronic, mechanical, photocopying, recording, scanning or otherwise, except as permitted under Sections 107 or 108 of the 1976 United States Copyright Act, without either the prior written permission of the Publisher, or authorization through payment of the appropriate per-copy fee to the Copyright Clearance Center, 222 Rosewood Drive, Danvers, MA 01923, (978) 750-8400, fax (978) 750-4744. Requests to the Publisher for permission should be addressed to the Publisher, Intel Press, Intel Corporation, 2111 NE 25th Avenue, JF3-330, Hillsboro, OR 97124-5961. E-mail: intelpress@intel.com.

This publication is designed to provide accurate and authoritative information in regard to the subject matter covered. It is sold with the understanding that the publisher is not engaged in professional services. If professional advice or other expert assistance is required, the services of a competent professional person should be sought.

Intel Corporation may have patents or pending patent applications, trademarks, copyrights, or other intellectual property rights that relate to the presented subject matter. The furnishing of documents and other materials and information does not provide any license, express or implied, by estoppel or otherwise, to any such patents, trademarks, copyrights, or other intellectual property rights.

Intel may make changes to specifications, product descriptions, and plans at any time, without notice.

Fictitious names of companies, products, people, characters, and/or data mentioned herein are not intended to represent any real individual, company, product, or event.

Intel, the Intel logo, Celeron, Intel Centrino, Intel Core, Intel NetBurst, Intel Xeon, Itanium, Pentium, MMX, and VTune are trademarks or registered trademarks of Intel Corporation or its subsidiaries in the United States and other countries.

† Other names and brands may be claimed as the property of others.

This book is printed on acid-free paper. ∞

Publisher: Richard Bowles
Editor: David J. Clark
Program Manager: Bruce Bartlett
Graphic Art: Kirsten Foote (illustrations), Ted Cyrek (cover)

Library of Congress Cataloging in Publication Data:

Printed in the United States of America

     10 9 8 7 6 5 4 3 2 1

First printing Version 1.0, October 2007

Contents

Preface

When in doubt, predict that the present trend will continue.

—Merkin's Maxim

In our age of rapid technology development, any technology book must be considered a stake in the sand against the rapid tide of innovation. Soon the stake will be buried and overrun, but hopefully not too soon. Realizing the situation as such, which is no doubt similar to the thousands of other authors of technology books, we have a strong desire and commitment to make a lasting contribution.

Unfortunately, this desire fades when we realize that the speed of technology innovation cycles through new paradigms faster than they can be fully absorbed by any normal person. This leaves little room between the continual arrival and onslaughts of new trends, all fighting for the coveted position of 'the next big thing.'

We are pleased to announce, however, that in writing the preface near the end of the production of this book, SOA remains as relevant as it did when we began this project nearly a year earlier. We believe that SOA will make a lasting contribution, but in a unique way. SOA is more than just a singular technology trend, and while SOA does have some measure of sheer innovation, it is not innovation that defines its importance. Instead, it is the combination of technology and business enablement *taken together* and furnished at the proper time that gives it prominence. As we will see throughout the book, the core tenants of SOA are not new, it is their combination and application that is new. Time and time again we have seen the term *SOA* used as a flexible label within organizations. Rather than criticize the loose definition, it should celebrated due to the inherent power it provides in making *better software* in the long run.

This book bears a practical title in an effort to show the pragmatic side of SOA. To this end, the reader will notice a dichotomy present in the book. This dichotomy is the familiar split between business and technology, or more specifically, between business stakeholders and technology stakeholders. Naturally, each has their own agenda taken separately, but taken together the synthesis is what makes SOA important today. We are firm believers that not everyone knows everything (despite their best beliefs!), so for those readers with a technology background we recommend the organizational and vertical market chapters (2, 5, 6, 7, 8, and 9), and for those readers with a business background, we recommend a focus on the technology chapters (1, 3, 4, and 10). In terms of specific readers, we are writing at the CIO and CTO level. The book doesn't contain code samples or design-pattern architectures, but a combination of SOA applied to business problems and a thorough description of SOA technology concepts, which are hopefully written at the right level to remain upright in the sand for some time to come.

You should briefly read our "metadata" concerning each chapter. We have tried to include important qualifications and suggestions to keep in mind.

Chapter 1 (Introduction): This chapter gives an introduction to SOA, and lays out our definition as SOA as a *design practice* with XML as a foundational component. We go through the OASIS SOA-RM model in order to ensure that readers have exposure to at least one attempted definition of SOA. In the review period, there were some suggestions that this Chapter was too abstract; we have tried to counter this by calling out specific features of the SOA-RM model and show how they might be practically applied as well as comparing this model to existing real-world software use cases. You should keep in mind that SOA-RM is used as an example to bolster our main point, that a standard for SOA defined without a consideration of XML is too broad to be meaningful.

Chapter 2 (Organizational Considerations of SOA): This Chapter drives home the point that SOA is not just a technology consideration. We go through how IT operates as a manufacturing function of applications and infrastructure within an enterprise and how the prevailing models of IT design, development and sustaining operations is insufficient to implement SOA at scale. The chapter goes through a pragmatic explanation of how to structure projects, resources and investments to implement and realize the substantial benefits of SOA.

Chapter 3 (SOA Technology Concepts): This Chapter is a bit unique as we try to call out foundational technology concepts that are part of SOA. To be sure, it may be argued that these concepts are "not new", especially ideas like service reuse and loose coupling. However, we try to define the concepts such that they stand on their own and we try to give the reader a deeper understanding that answers "why" questions about SOA rather than "how" questions. We believe that this conceptual framework leads to a greater understanding of why SOA considered a valuable trend.

Chapter 4 (SOA Technology Infrastructure): This Chapter builds on Chapter 3 and turns concepts into practical technology investments. Here we get into the details of standards and required infrastructure investments, including a treatment of SOA security. This is one of our most technical Chapters and assumes a CTO type of reader throughout. The reader should follow the development of the "big-bus" / "little-bus" concept as it forms the basis of the architectures present in the vertical market chapters. Lastly, we cover how SOA can be applied to the management of computing infrastructure (SOI), enabling transformation to services based computing utility.

Chapter 5 (SOA in Government): This chapter takes a look at SOA usages in the government IT infrastructure. A significant departure from many other chapters is the focus on data interoperability as a baseline in order to create and deploy enterprise class services that can be used outside of silos of specific government sub-groups. The chapter highlights how by starting to address the data interoperability through problem domain-specific canonicals, significantly increases the ability to create SOA-based flexible, reusable services that can be used by other government agencies and even by private sector.

Chapter 6 (SOA in Financial Services): This chapter begins vertical-specific look at usage scenarios, business value, constraints both technical and otherwise, for SOA, starting with financial services. Specifically, it highlights the reasons and benefits of SOA in specific investment banking and retail banking usage scenarios. It uses the concepts introduced in the Chapter 3 and Chapter 4 and analyzes how these concepts can be applied in these usage scenarios. It also points out the missing technologies critical to financial services in deploying SOA in this vertical market.

Chapter 7 (Healthcare): This chapter describes the application of SOA to clinical systems in the healthcare market. Specifically we cover how the use of SOA can improve delivery of important information at the point of care for making critical treatment decisions, how SOA can make the sharing of clinical information across a community of care practical from a cost, security and risk of deployment point of view, and finally how it can be used to increase the adoption rate of electronic medical records.

Chapter 8 (SOA in Manufacturing): This chapter delves into how SOA can be leveraged to assemble and manage data from many sources on the manufacturing floor, which often requires integration from many suppliers. It identifies how services can lead to decreased cost to deploy manufacturing automation systems in a distributed environment, and SOA options that can enable increased availability. The use of data services is explored, with SOA enabling more effective dissemination of critical highly shared data such as customer, supplier, and item. It also addresses how federated identity, applied to enable services that operate between enterprises, can streamline business communications with suppliers and customers and reduce operational costs.

Chapter 9 (SOA in Telecommunications): This chapter examines the telecommunications industry, and analyzes two radically different usage scenarios of SOA. First, it addresses the ability and limitations of SOA based architecture to support service delivery capability across networks and applications in order to offer users integrated services. Second, it takes a look at the architecture required for telecommunications service providers to become service delivery networks of choice for enterprise and web-based services.

Chapter 10 (SOA and Future Trends): This chapter tries to deal with a few of the emerging technology trends that have XML as a common component. More specifically, we examine the entire SOAP versus REST debate and we attempt to relate SOA to Web 2.0. During the review period it was called out that we should have tackled other trends, such as semantic web services or aspect-orientation. There is no doubt that we do think these trends are important, but it was simply a matter of chapter length and timing considerations.

We hope you find this mix of technology, business, and industry-specific content to be beneficial as you consider how SOA can best be applied in your situation. Enabling SOA to be practical and realizable is the principle objective of this book, as making SOA technology, processes and skills effective in the enterprise is increasingly important to the foundation of enterprise IT.

Acknowledgements

This book is the result of a substantial amount of work of not only the authors but many others who provided inspiration, insight, support, and review. Many thanks to our reviewers who provided thoughtful feedback:

To Jorgen Thelin of Microsoft for his enthusiastic support, advice and foreword.

To David Sprott of CBDI Forum for the insightful foreword and inspiration behind Chapter 2.

To Michael Bridges, Ron Ribitzky, and Alan Boucher for content and expertise on the application of SOA to healthcare.

To Aslam Handy and his team at Johnson & Johnson for their input and support on the manufacturing chapter. Thanks also to Don Michie for his feedback and support on that chapter.

To Jim Hobbs and Rob Sullivan for their expertise and contributions to the SOA technology infrastructure chapter.

To Wayne Chemy of Symcor for encouragement, support, and review of several chapters of this book.

To Craig T. Hughes from Department of Justice, Wisconsin for encouragement, support, and review of several chapters of this book. To June M. Krbecek for her words of encouragement.

To Ravi Kumar and Alan Honey for their strong words of encouragement, as well as their timely and painstaking review of several chapters of this book.

To Mark H. Davis, Shi-Wan Lin and others associated with Sarvega Engineering for significant portions of the telecommunication chapter that were done as part of their painstaking research.

To Michael Weintraub, Alex Tserkovny, and Sandi Jones for support and review of the telecommunications industry SOA usage scenarios.

To John G. Chirapurath and Sunil Gaitonde for support, encouragement, and humor throughout the writing of this book.

To Neerja J. Bajaj for her encouragement, and timely feedback on several chapters of this book.

Finally, we would like to thank the team from Intel Press. Stuart Goldstein got the book started and then Bruce Bartlett assumed duties as the program manager, shepherding it to completion. Wayne Jones provided solid operational support. David Clark was the editor of the project, performing the essential task of taking our engineering prose and turning it into a finished book. Ron Bohart created the cover art, making it look like a real book.

For anyone that we may have missed, please accept our apologies and appreciation.

Dedications

In particular, this book owes its existence to significant patience, encouragement and support from the spouses and children of the authors.

(GJ) Thanks Lakshmi, Nishant and Rishi.

(JN) Thanks Rachel, Madison, Aidan and Reagan.

(BD) Thanks to Mary Phillips and Jeremy Crisp.

(SB) Thanks to Debbi, Kristina, Elyse, Naomi, Brianna and Jake.

Foreword
by Jorgen Thelin

Service Oriented Architecture (SOA) and web services offer great potential to connect people, data, and information—both within and between organizations—but many times IT projects in this area fail to deliver on that potential because of the particular approaches and mindsets used in these SOA projects. This book advocates a pragmatic approach to service orientation and enterprise architectures that helps to ensure that SOA and web services projects contribute to long lasting organizational effectiveness and agility.

Service Oriented Architecture provides the design framework to integrate siloed applications so that their functionality can be accessed as services on a network. Most commonly implemented through standards-based and technology–neutral web services, SOA breaks down monolithic applications into a suite of services implementing functionality in a modular, reusable fashion.

The ultimate goal with Service Oriented Architecture is to create a set of reusable business IT assets that can be combined and consumed in flexible ways to support business agility. Those reusable IT assets are connected through a virtual "service bus" spanning the enterprise or extending out to external partners and customers through Internet-scale interconnectivity. This book explores the various approaches and parameters for achieving that. There are many problematic approaches that could be taken to SOA projects, but this book identifies a better way to approach the SOA challenge based on pragmatism and practical reality.

It is very encouraging to find a book about Service Oriented Architecture that deliberately tries to avoid the hype currently surrounding SOA in the industry and, in particular, avoids the pitfall of equating SOA with any one individual product. Instead, this book tries to get beneath the surface to find the nuggets of gold from among the terminology, concepts and approaches, and in so doing helps you to build a solid architectural foundation for an enterprise.

At Microsoft, we use the phrase "middle-out" to describe the pragmatic approach to SOA development; driving projects from an overarching strategic SOA vision matched to business needs, but combined with incremental, iterative SOA projects that are designed to deliver on business goals one business need at a time. The framework and approach described in this book is a perfect example of such a "middle-out" approach. Rather than trying to "boil the ocean" with an all encompassing top-down SOA framework approach (which risks a project being out of date by the time it is delivered), or using a bottom-up SOA approach without organizing principles and guidance (which risks creating a chaotic implementation that has no business relevant), the pragmatic approach blends both to ensure SOA projects deliver against focused business goals.

By rounding out the book by investigating how to apply the pragmatic SOA approaches described in this book to some key vertical application domains such as healthcare, financial services, and public sector the authors help to ground the exposition in practical real-world examples, and help readers cement their understanding of the concepts and application of those ideas into realistic situations.

If you want to deliver IT and business value for your organization through SOA projects, then this book will help you avoid many of the potential problems that can derail SOA projects, and will help cut through the hype curve to deliver lasting, pragmatic business value from your SOA projects.

Jorgen Thelin

Senior Program Manager for Interoperability Standards

Connected Systems Division

Microsoft Corporation

Foreword
by David Sprott

Architecture is a discipline that determines style and behavior of domains ranging from buildings to software systems. By definition architecture is a somewhat imprecise discipline, positioned somewhere between science and art. Consequently it can be a difficult and confusing subject. However whether we are thinking about buildings, bridges, semiconductors, middleware or software applications, architecture is always a very important subject that we should expect to have a major influence on IT practices and business outcomes.

Changes in architectural style are very often the result of new technology. Gothic cathedrals became the de facto style back in the 12th Century initially stimulated by the invention of the pointed arch—a design that provided greater load bearing using lighter materials. This together with new building methods and materials enabled the development of a series of new design patterns including greater expanses of glass, ribbed vaults, clustered columns, sharply pointed spires and flying buttresses. We can also see good examples of technology led architecture in the strongly artistic 20th Century art deco style that was strongly based on the use of new, manmade materials such as glass and stainless steel often adopting modern aerodynamic designs.

Most changes in architectural style do not emerge fully finished. Quite the reverse—architectural styles generally go through a period of development before they stabilize. Gothic cathedral design went through four distinct phases of development—early, high, rayonnant, and late. Sometimes the development of style and technique can be very protracted, as in the case of the Egyptian pyramids that continued to evolve over several thousand years.

The concepts underlying Service Oriented Architecture have been emerging for years. Some practitioners, myself included, can somewhat proudly report using service concepts in early mainframe systems to specialize and reuse functionality. More recently the more formal technique of encapsulating a capability behind an interface has been universally accepted in object oriented methodologies. Distributed object architectures took these ideas much further forward in technologies such as CORBA and DCOM, however with less widespread acceptance. Early efforts to enable greater separation of concerns with more comprehensive encapsulation were also explored in pioneering component based development methods and tools over ten years ago. But SOA really came of age as XML-based web services standards were formalized by the W3C and OASIS after 2000 and the realization of platform independent services became reality.

It's characteristic of many types of architecture that in the early stages of deployment the concept and particularly the enabling technology is used to enhance current practices. We can observe this in web systems architecture where early implementations were focused on replacing client server systems providing a very useful benefit of eliminating client layer intelligence, but nonetheless representing a linear evolution from mainframe based green screens to client server to web based transaction processing. It's only relatively recently that we have started to realize the real power of the Web by embracing collaborative architectures in Web 2.0, and this process is still very much work in progress.

This same characteristic can be seen in the way SOA is being adopted. Early exploitation of SOA has been largely focused on enabling better application integration. More recently services are being used to enable process orchestration, but in many cases the service architecture is simply providing better loose coupling between the application and process layers. Important and useful benefits, but small steps towards the broader SOA vision. It seems that while there is widespread acceptance of SOA, there remains considerable confusion and misunderstanding over how to harness the concepts for business advantage.

Realistically we can expect SOA will develop through a number of distinct phases. We can expect the next phase will enable a higher order of benefit as shared services enable very high levels of reuse with appropriate customization. In this phase services will be delivered and managed using a manufacturing and assembly model, with a massive reduction in the application and code base substantially reducing complexity resulting in dramatic improvement in business process agility.

SOA is a paradigm shift that has not yet been fully understood, primarily because the strategic use of SOA requires substantial change in practices. Those enterprises that deliver on the real promise of SOA will realize dramatic reduction in cost base and time to market that will enable significant competitive advantage.

This book is a very useful addition to the literature about SOA. It provides practical and realistic answers to the question of how to move SOA to the next stage of maturity. It provides detailed guidance on how to plan, manage, organize and design for effective service usage, supporting the twin objectives of business process improvement and architecting for agility. It deserves to be widely read, not just by IT architects, but especially by IT executives who must engage with this crucial subject.

David Sprott, CBDI Forum

Cork, Ireland

June 2007

Chapter **1**

Introduction

An undefined problem has an infinite number of solutions.

—Robert A. Humphrey

One popular argument states that SOA is not a technology per se, but that it stands alone and can be implemented using a wide range of technologies. The authors believe that this definition, while attractive and elegant, doesn't necessarily pass pragmatic muster. The evolution of service-based software design is driven by technology. While theoretically attractive, it is a mistake to consider SOA as completely distinct from its very real technology forerunners. But perhaps we are getting ahead of ourselves, for there is another argument that claims that SOA is just a new name for an old concept: "It's all been done before" goes the saying, with a generic appeal to a host of predecessor technologies such as DCOM, CORBA, EJB and COM. What are we to make of this statement? The authors believe that the mere existence of a predecessor technology is no final test. SOA isn't important because it is wholly new, it is instead important because it combines older ideas in the right way at the right time to provide business value. While many consider SOA to be just hype we must not forget the practical force it has in causing *change* within organizations. Whether we are considering new software investments within an enterprise datacenter or an ISV, SOA is the leading design practice for lowering software costs. If you are new to the SOA concept, we will dispense quickly with our definition. Before we get this, however, we should mention that this chapter may seem a bit abstract given our practical claims, especially with our treatment of the general SOA definition. Keep in mind that we use a general definition and explain it piece by piece so we can remain systematic, leaving no possible part of SOA untouched. We believe that exposure to a bit of the elegant definition will be useful when contrasted with the practical considerations in each of the vertical market chapters.

What Is SOA?

The term *SOA* stands for service oriented architecture and this is where the consensus over the definition stops and the debate begins. Numerous standards organizations such as W3C, DMTF, and OASIS have all made an attempt to own the definition of SOA, with varying amounts of success. Large enterprises such as IBM, HP, and SAP now offer SOA products and services along with a host of smaller ISVs. Finally, IDC estimates that the total market for SOA software and services combined will be over USD 31 billion[1] by 2009. With so much potential, how is it possible that the definition of SOA remains a contentious battleground?

The ultimate aim of this section is to delve into the reasons why the SOA concept has many stakeholders and many definitions. Rather than exhaustively comparing and contrasting the existing definitions, we investigate the underlying foundations of the *service* concept and try to understand the motivations behind SOA as well as the debate around properly defining it.

The core of the debate over the definition of SOA can be characterized by its degree of reference to specific technology. General definitions of SOA are abstract and devoid of concrete technology, while specific definitions are technology-laden. The position we take in this chapter is that *SOA is a software design practice with strong technological considerations*. Although we will elaborate on this simple statement, it forms the opening premise of the first half of the chapter. In addition to the basic idea of a *design practice,* we attempt in Chapter 2 to frame SOA in terms of a manufacturing model. As such, two main components form our concept of SOA: first that it is a design practice with technology considerations, and second that the full value of SOA is realized at the organizational level through a manufacturing model.

The remaining part of the chapter moves from considering the definition of SOA to pointing out the necessary investments that an organization must make to adopt SOA, including both organizational and

---

[1] See *IDC WorldWide SOA driven software market 2005-2009* and *Worldwide SOA-Based Services 2006-2010 Forecast: Demand for Services Continues as Adoption Expands Across Industries and Geographies*

technological considerations as well as a word on how to assess the value of SOA. The final part of the chapter introduces the practical viewpoints as defined by different vertical markets that have adopted SOA. Overall, the focus of this book is a practical one; the viewpoints presented in the vertical market chapters are all taken from real-world deployments and in these sections we hope to show the gap between the theoretic SOA definition and the details of how it is realized for each of the vertical markets we consider.

The remainder of this section is organized as follows. First we consider the *service* concept in practical business terms and what this means for software, second we look at one of the most general definitions of SOA and show that it fails to meet the practical test, and third, we present *the* specific technology consideration, namely XML, and expand on the general definition.

Why Services Matter

Today's economy is becoming more and more service based rather than manufacturing or even purely product based. In the technology sector specifically, this manifests itself in companies offering more services and customization along with products. Trends like standardization, commodity products, and educated consumers make services the cornerstone of the new economy.

Services themselves, however, aren't necessarily new. What is new is their increased importance in a business context. It may be useful to think of services having increased value in the new economy as product values are threatened by increased commoditization and consumer choice.

The connection made here is between business and technology. More specifically we can think of software and related technology assets designed in terms of the business context or prevailing business trend. In this specific case, designs should be service based. This concept is what is referred to when SOA is described as providing "business agility."

Once the reader considers the service concept in business terms, the debate becomes immediately apparent. Business-focused stakeholders would think of SOA in terms of services for business, while technology focused stakeholders would think of SOA in terms of software concepts or specific technologies for designing software with services in mind. Business stakeholders would see their definition polluted with technology components, and even technology or theoretical stakeholders would see an abstract service framework sullied by mentioning specific technology. While there is inherent value in considering existing workflows and business practices in a service context, only with specific technology considerations can SOA provide its intended value.

In the next section we consider the definition of SOA given by OASIS, the SOA Reference Model. The authors believe that this is one of the most abstract and generalized definitions of SOA and provides a useful conceptual model. To this end it serves an explanatory purpose; we are not necessarily endorsing this specific model, but merely using it as a tool to explain why SOA should be considered in terms of specific technology considerations, specifically XML. Because the model is especially general, we refer to it as the *general SOA definition*, or the *general definition*. We are also aware that this definition is a little abstract because it is a very hierarchical definition. We will try to provide some color along the way and point out practical considerations in light of some of the more abstract statements.

You should notice that there are two common complaints about the general definition. First, some argue that the general definition is overly broad and potentially incomplete by not mentioning XML, and second, the stronger statement, which is that the general definition of SOA *only* makes sense when XML is specifically referenced. The viewpoint taken here lies in the middle of these two statements. We acknowledge the possibility of *another* format that could replace XML, but note that from a practical standpoint, XML is the only real choice that derives full value from SOA. The purpose here is to get you to think about the meaning of a general SOA definition when it is put forth divorced from specific technology.

The General SOA Definition

The OASIS Service Oriented Architecture Reference Model (SOA-RM) TC represents a group of companies with a common goal of defining a *reference model* for SOA. The goal of such a definition is to provide "a minimal set of unifying concepts, axioms and relationships within a particular problem domain, and is independent of specific standards, technologies, implementations or other concrete details."

SOA-RM makes it a point to declare that their reference model to be "at least three levels of abstraction away" from concrete technology details. They intend to provide a "higher level of commonality, with definitions that should apply to all SOA." It is due to these considerations that we consider this model to be one of the most general.

SOA-RM does an excellent job of defining the service concept for software in terms of capabilities and needs. The definition they give is "Service Oriented Architecture (SOA) is a paradigm for organizing and utilizing distributed capabilities that may be under the control of different ownership domains." For SOA-RM, capabilities are provided to service consumers via the service concept. Other key concepts that define the boundary of SOA include visibility, interaction, and effect. SOA-RM uses the concept of real-world effect as the end purpose to using a capability (exposed through a service). The reader should pay close attention to the three concepts of *visibility, interaction*, and *effect* as we will return to these concepts throughout this chapter to frame the general definition.

The general definition has two important aspects. First, it considers the service concept as fundamentally derived from capabilities and needs, and secondly, the definition is general enough to cover any conceivable service-based software case, and even cases outside of the software domain.

For example, when I take my laundry to the dry cleaner I am utilizing the dry cleaning *service*; my *need* is having my shirts pressed and their *capability* is the set of workers that clean and press the shirts without damaging them. The service is offered to me by the person who either picks up my clothes or by the person tending the front counter at the dry cleaner's brick and mortar store. The real-world effect here is the fact that my clothes are cleaned and my bank account is lighter. If the service delivers my clothes to me personally, there are the effects of the delivery person driving a car to my house and me possibly offering a tip.

One could also think of buying a book from an online bookseller in terms of the definition offered here. That is, the service the online bookseller offers is providing the book I want at the lowest price. The *capability* they have is the means to search many suppliers and the *need* I have is to buy a cheap book. The case of the online bookseller also includes the aspects of different ownership domains, as it is effectively searching different supplier bookstores and traversing many domains to find the lowest price. Again, the real-world effects here are numerous as well: I receive a book, my bank account is lighter, a delivery service has delivered me a package, and the bookseller has reduced the inventory of one or more of its suppliers and may possibly have altered the state of its ordering system to order more books.

Given the definition offered by SOA-RM, does the local dry cleaner have an SOA? What about the online bookseller? Does Amazon.com have a service oriented architecture for users of its Web site? Surely SOA-RM must eventually offer us more in its definition of SOA. Clearly, the dry-cleaner example isn't relevant because SOA-RM explicitly considers only software architecture (but what if the dry cleaner had a software tracking system?).

In the next section we approach SOA-RM systematically as a general definition and show that without mentioning XML as a foundational technology, SOA-RM is simply too broad. What we hope to show is that a general definition of SOA formalizes existing modes of service interaction without providing anything new—that is, it doesn't capture technological considerations that brought SOA to bear. In other words, SOA conceived without reference to XML is incomplete.

Again, keep in mind that throughout the next section when we use the term *general SOA definition* or *general SOA model* we are referring to the reference model and SOA definition as defined by the OASIS SOA-RM TC.

A General SOA Model

The basic model defined by SOA-RM can be described in terms of a *service consumer* accessing a *service* via a *service interface* for the purposes of fulfilling a need. The service then produces a real-world effect either in the form of message exchange or modifying some shared state. Figure 1.1 shows the basic model provided by SOA-RM.

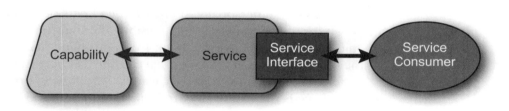

Figure 1.1   Basic SOA Model

In Figure 1.1, it is important to note that the service and the underlying capability are considered distinct, but in practice these may in fact be combined (that is, the service and the capability are one in the same).What is described in Figure 1.1 is the service consumer and service *interaction*.

As mentioned before, the interaction results either in messages passed back to the client or in the modification of shared state. What precedes this interaction is *visibility*. These visibility criteria are considered to be prerequisites for the service interaction shown in Figure 1.1. The next three sections try to describe each of these components in some detail for the purposes of understanding the general SOA definition.

Service Visibility

The general SOA definition breaks the visibility concept into *awareness, willingness,* and *reachability.* Awareness implies the knowledge or existence of the service and further implies service description and policy. In other words, before the service consumer accesses the service, the consumer must be aware of the service and have a good enough idea of what it does in order to properly interact with it. The general definition notes that such policies may be pushed or pulled by the service itself, or the client may even request a service by broadcasting a proposal or offer. The general definition makes a strong attempt, however, to define *service description* with some extra precision, noting that the hallmark of an SOA is the large amount of associated documentation and description. The service description should contain the information needed for a consumer to use the service. If we were to mention a specific technology here for the purposes of concreteness, we might mention an XML-based description, such as WSDL along with other XML-based policies.

One interesting point offered by the general definition is the suggestion that descriptions can be used by consumers to construct systems that use services. Such usage is not required, however. We return to this concept when we discuss service metadata near the end of this section.

The service description concept is further decomposed into four sub-concepts: service reachability, service functionality, service policies, and service interface. The *service reachability* concept implies that the service description should contain enough information to allow the service consumer and service provider to interact with each other. Further, service reachability may also include meta-information such as status, location, or availability information. Note however, that the general definition of SOA doesn't say if this description is atomic; it could be information available in various places that must be pulled together by the consumer. It is useful to observe here the elegant manner in which the service reachability concept is defined, and we will note that in practice very few enabling technologies really fulfill the entire concept. Most of the time, the lofty concept of reachability is simply conflated into the bindings and protocol definitions in a standard document such as

WSDL, or even just represented as a predetermined HTTP endpoint. Service reachability as defined by SOA-RM is larger-than-life when compared to practical implementations.

The *service functionality* concept states that a service description be clear in expressing the available service functions and corresponding real-world effects. It is liberal in its assumptions about whether or not these descriptions are written in human language or in some machine-processable language or format. Also included in the functionality description are the functional limits based on the type of user. For example, a service may give different levels or types of service based on the type of user. From a practical standpoint, *service functionality* captures useful information about service functions in principle, but also tries to include access control and by implication, an association of identities to available functions. While such information is useful, and there are even standards to capture access control information and identities (such as OASIS WS-Security and XACML), there is no official way of tying it all together.

The *service policy* concept simply defines a generic policy to be associated with a service that describes its operating constraints. The general SOA definition distinguishes between policies and contracts. A policy is broken down into three concepts: the assertion itself, the owner, and the enforcement of the policy. Policy assertions should be measurable statements about the way in which a service is realized, such as "all users must be authenticated with a user name and password." Policies have owners, and the general definition defines a policy owner as the person who is making or stating the assertion. Policy enforcement simply means the attempt to ensure that the policy assertion is consistent with the real world. For the general SOA definition, policies are considered broad and can cover diverse aspects of a service including manageability, quality of service or even business-level policies. The only constraint given on policies is that they should be understandable and processable by the intended recipient of the policy.

A *contract* differs from a policy in that it is an agreement by a two or more parties rather than a statement or point of view of one of the participants in the service interaction. Contracts are likely to cover legal agreements, but may also cover how some services are used by another. The general SOA definition makes it a point to say that contracts may be arrived at by out-of-band mechanisms (outside of the service context) or by an in-band process as well. That is, it does not mandate one form or another.

The *service interface* is described by the general SOA definition as the means of communicating with the service. In this context we are still considering the definition of a service description, so what is described here is really the description of the service interface. This description should include specific information, such as protocols, messages, and commands that produce a real-world result. The general SOA model claims that having interfaces and accessible descriptions of these interfaces is fundamental to the SOA concept. The remaining parts of visibility also include willingness and reachability. The former implies a willingness of the service to serve the particular consumer (or any consumer) and the latter property captures the fact that a suitable (or available) communication mechanism operates between the consumer and the service.

Let us stop for a moment and contemplate these additional parts of the general definition. Figure 1.2 shows a hierarchical breakdown of the parts of service visibility. Clearly, there are many sub-concepts to consider.

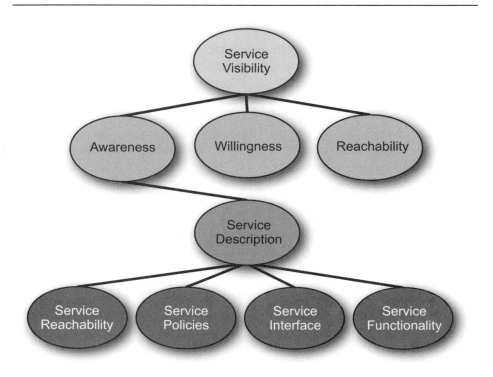

Figure 1.2   Service Visibility Concepts

In Figure 1.2, the reader should keep in mind the relationship between the *awareness* criterion and the service description, noting that a large part of the SOA definition rests on the various types of information *about* a service. This is also referred to as *service metadata*. We will use this term in the future to refer to the totality of information (description, policies, interface, functionality) about a given service.

Service Interaction

As soon as a consumer is aware of a service, interaction can begin. The general SOA definition breaks the *interaction* concept into two sub-concepts of *information model* and *behavior model*. Interaction between a service and consumer is defined in terms of messages sent and received. While it is possible for service consumer to interact via some shared state (imagine two people communicating on a shared whiteboard), the general SOA definition puts a focus on message-passing paradigms.

The *information model* covers the information exchanged between the service and the service consumer. The parts of the information model include the format, structure, and meaning of messages. The important pieces of the information model include *structure* and *semantics*. Structure is defined by the general SOA definition as including encoding, message format, and data types associated with the information elements in the message format. Semantics refers to how units of information are interpreted, especially across ownership boundaries. The general SOA definition refers to the optional use of an *ontology*, which can be used to specify alternate ways of referring to a piece of information to ensure its consistent meaning. Notice that all of these concepts are referred to in the abstract; no specific format type or technology is mentioned. The only constraint provided is stated in a general sense; messages must be *consistently* and *correctly* interpreted for structure and semantics between a service consumer and a service.

In addition to *visibility*, the concept of the *behavior model* between the service and service consumer is also required for successful interaction. The behavior model covers the actions and temporal constraints for the messages passed between the service consumer and the service. That is, the general SOA definition is referring to specific actions, their responses and any temporal dependencies around these actions. The parts of the *behavior model* include the *action model* which is the message-exchange pattern itself, or the order of messages and their expected responses, and the *process model* which singles out the time based properties of actions and events. If the reader is finding these descriptions extremely general, this is intentional.

The general SOA definition doesn't single out or constrain the types of messages exchanges for an SOA or prohibit any type of behavior model. It does, however, note that services may have properties such as idempotent, long-running, or transactional. An *idempotent service* is one in which repeated messages have the same effect as a single message. That is, repeated messages don't *further* alter the result or real-world state. An example of this would be a balance check command at an ATM machine. Repeatedly checking the balance has the same net effect as checking it once, unlike an action such as a cash withdrawal or deposit. Another example of an idempotent service is one that can identify duplicate messages that are received due to message reliability mechanisms. A *long-running service* would be one that may take extra time to complete, or one that requires repeated queries over time. One example of this is would be a delivery service that picks up a package for delivery; the tracking number could be used at a later time to check the status of the package. This would be considered a long-running service as the context of the service is held for a long period of time and permits re-handling based on further user requests.

Finally, a *transactional service* is one that involves the ability to rollback or commit a specific action, such as a financial trade. All of these properties are listed as possibilities for the general SOA definition, but no one specific property is mandated or even necessarily expected.

Similar to the previous section, we would do well to stop and get a visual picture of the concepts that comprise the *interaction* portion of the general SOA definition. Figure 1.3 shows a hierarchical breakdown of the parts of interaction in terms of the general SOA definition.

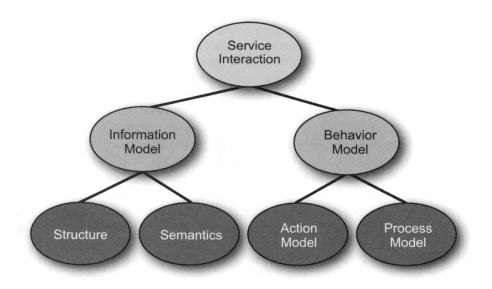

Figure 1.3 Service Interaction Concepts

Figure 1.3 shows the concepts that have just been discussed. The reader should carefully consider the *information model* concept, especially the structure and semantics concepts. As we will argue in the next section, a generalized, portable data format such as XML is one of the only practical candidates for these considerations.

Real-World Effect

The final portion of the general SOA definition is the real-world effect. We have already alluded to this concept as the result of the service consumer accessing some capability through a service.

For the general SOA definition, the real-world effect is defined in terms of some message passed back to the consumer or in the modification of some shared state about the requested action. The general definition takes care to emphasis that the real-world effect need not include information about how a service provider or service consumer maintains its private details. For example, in an online ordering system, the service consumer may order a product but doesn't need to know how the service keeps track of the order; just that it is managed somehow. Similarly, the service consumer may keep track of its order privately, but this detail is stored independently of the service.

XML and SOA

At this stage, the reader should have a good understanding of the general SOA definition. We have tried to cover it systematically, leaving no part untouched. The next question to ask is, given our new understanding, is the online bookstore example *still* an instance of an SOA? Have we been given enough new information to make a distinction, and if not, what does the general definition offer us over the formalization of existing *service* concepts?

If we consider SOA-RM as just presented we are making the argument that the general definition is *incomplete;* that is, there are many software systems that meet this general definition, and the unique significance of SOA isn't mentioned. Our cards are on the table here: we believe that what is important about SOA is a fundamental reliance on a portable cross-platform data format. Further, because we are approaching SOA from a *practical* perspective, we argue that the only feasible choice in this case is XML. What we will show here is that rather than XML being derived from the SOA concept, the practical reality is the exact reverse— SOA when taken in its entirety derives most of its inherent value *from* XML.

The Online Bookseller

Let us return to the online bookstore example. We have already established that in the basic sense, a Web site offering books for sale meets the general SOA model of a *service* being offered to exploit a *capability*. In the bookseller example, the service consumer (web browser) can access the *service interface* (web server) to produce a real-world effect (order a book). It may be useful to return to the *visibility* and *interaction* components to determine if there are additional components that disqualify the bookseller from being an SOA.

Visibility and Interaction for the Online Bookseller

In a previous section we defined the term service metadata to refer to the totality of information about a specific service. This includes all of the components of the service description such as the service reachability, service policies and contracts, service interface, and service functions. The general SOA definition says that the hallmark of an SOA is the existence of this information—but this statement as phrased is much too weak.

If we consider the online bookseller carefully, we can see that in fact it too has service metadata for each of these components. For example, I can examine the HTTP specification to build a client that interacts with the service; I could even build a custom client that just has a few HTTP commands that interact with *just* this one online service. I could do this by examining the various HTTP endpoints available on the website and pass the proper query parameters and HTTP authentication information in response to various expected messages from the web server. The service interface is well defined, and while the set of possible functions aren't explicitly documented in one place, most are based on HTTP request and request paradigm and can be determined by experimentation. In terms of the interaction requirements of an SOA, the general definition states that the structure and syntax of the messages must be commonly understood, but it doesn't offer any more constraints. The same is true of the behavior model; an SOA must define a message exchange pattern that is understood between the service and the service consumer. In this case, there is in fact a well defined request/response pattern as identified by various HTTP commands such as GET and POST.

It is important to note that the general SOA definition doesn't put temporal, dynamic, or static constraints on the visibility criteria. It takes a general stance and says services and their descriptions can be accessed either dynamically or statically, manually or automatically, via push or pull mechanisms. To this extent it is complete in what it allows, but the careful reader will also see that it does little to distinguish itself from existing service functions that involve software.

Further, policy and contract information is also documented in the online bookseller example, mostly in written language on the Web site itself. There are clear policies about which specific security protocols are used and under what circumstances they are required. There are also clear business policy descriptions, such as how returns are handled and what to do in case of a damaged or missing product. You might object that for the online bookseller to *be* an SOA, this information must all be documented in a single place, but the general SOA definition doesn't mandate this constraint. We could even counter this objection by constructing a single document that contains all such information. The closest that the general definition comes to mentioning a specific technology is its general statement about the service description itself:

> Best practice suggests that the service description *should* be represented using a standard referenceable format. Such a format facilitates the use of common processing tools (such as discovery engines) that can capitalize on the service description.

The key missing part of the general SOA definition is why such a format is useful and what it offers over the example just given. Clearly the online bookseller cannot be an instance of an SOA—for if it were, there wouldn't be anything new or innovative when comparing existing Web-based applications or Web sites to a new paradigm like SOA. Table 1.1 lists the explicit conformance criteria from the general SOA definition and shows that even our online bookseller could be considered an SOA.

Table 1.1   General SOA Conformance Criteria

Criteria	Online Bookseller
Have entities that can be identified as services	The bookseller offers a service for its capability of finding a low priced book among its suppliers.
Be able to identify how visibility is established between service providers and consumers	Service awareness is provided by advertising or word of mouth; interfaces are specified by TCP/IP and HTTP protocols.
Be able to identify how interaction is mediated	Interaction is mediated by the use of HTTP commands such as GET and POST.
Be able to identify how the effect of using services is understood	Real world effects such as delivery and charges are outlined explicitly on the Web site.
Have descriptions associated with services	The service functions are described in written language (e.g. its purpose). The description for the communication interface is defined by HTTP.

Criteria	Online Bookseller
Be able to identify the execution context required to support interaction	The interaction requires an HTTP connection (or set of such sessions) within a given time limit over a potentially secure connection. The user is authenticated by the bookseller and is actively using the service for its intended purpose.
Be possible to identify how policies are handled and how contracts may be modeled and enforced.	Business level policies (such as returns) are described in English on the Web site.

Source: OASIS SOA-RM, Section 4, Conformance Guidelines

When considering Table 1.1, you should mentally add the prefix *"A system that adopts the SOA approach will..."* before each of the conformance criteria. In a literal sense, the online bookseller is a type of SOA and meets the loose constraints offered by the general definition. If this is the case, then, what is *missing* for the general definition? We have already alluded to this many times over the past few sections. In this case, the missing component is a standard, referenceable, portable cross-platform data format. Further, aside from such a format simply being standard (there are many standard formats), it should also be machine processable and be capable of representing service metadata as atomic units—even in cases where service metadata is split across many physical locations—that is it should provide linking capabilities as well. The next section outlines the properties of XML that are important for SOA and tries to outline how these properties provide a major portion of the value of SOA.

The Power of XML

This section assumes that you have some basic exposure to XML. If not, many great books and articles on the subject are available, many for free on the World Wide Web. At the very least, you should know that XML is a portable syntax for representing structured data and have a general idea of basic XML concepts such as elements, attributes, and namespaces.

For service oriented architecture the central role XML plays is its ability to represent different service artifacts using a single syntax, as well as the fact that XML is self-referenceable. The self-reference property is the ability that XML has to refer to parts or portions of its own substructure as well as ways to easily link to and refer to external XML documents. This allows the easy composition of XML documents together such that they can be processed in a logically atomic way.

The earlier discussion of the online bookseller provided plenty of available service metadata. That is, if you consider all of the service description components such as service reachability, service policies, service interface, and service functionality, all of these details are available to the service consumer in one way or another. The obvious problem with the metadata in the online bookseller case is that the information scattered and doesn't permit automated processing.

What would happen if you could describe the totality of the service metadata in XML? Without mentioning any further standards (which will be considered in Chapter 4), imagine the service metadata in a portable, machine-processable form. This could be in a single logical file or split among many XML subdocuments, but the key point is that the entirety of the service metadata, all of the endpoint information, interface (API) definitions, service policies and expected messages and patterns, are all available and described in XML. To take this to a more practical level, a service may be described by a service description that identifies basic API information that then links to other XML documents that contain additional policy information. The number of links and the depth and complexity of the linking is specific to how much service metadata is offered. This implies that anyone who can process XML can ostensibly interact with the service after processing the service metadata.

Why does it matter if XML is used or not? In this case, the bar for XML processing is set very low; XML is an extremely simple text-based syntax that permits easy understanding and has natural mappings to software programming languages and methods. On a practical level, standard XML processing tools are available for nearly any conceivable platform, and due to the structural nature of XML, it can represent any sort of data. That is, the same basic XML syntax can be used to represent service definitions, interface definitions, policies, messages, or even audio and video information.

Notice here that, in addition to the service metadata concept, other areas of the general SOA definition stand to gain by the use of XML. The interactions have already been alluded to in terms of messages being passed back and forth between the service consumer and service in XML, but shared syntax and semantics also come into play. XML can also be used to represent ontologies in a standard form, helping to alleviate the semantic mapping problem across different ownership domains, and further, business process can be represented in XML format. The totality of the service metadata, actual messages, and behavioral patterns for a service all can live in one common format that can be made to easily linked together, providing a logically atomic view of a service that isn't really possible in the online bookseller case without using XML.

Finally, service consumers can be statically or dynamically constructed against this service metadata. A statically constructed consumer example would be very close to a web browser, or even a web browser constructed especially for a specific Web site, but dynamic construction is impossible without XML. Speaking of dynamic service orchestration or service choreography only makes sense when the service metadata and processes are expressed in a machine-processable format that permits a degree of automated processing. For example, a service consumer could use a new service very quickly if it had all of the service metadata readily at its disposal. Essentially, a client would process this service metadata in XML and be able to resolve new endpoints, new message exchange patterns, and policies all in one logically atomic action. There is no substitute for this type of dynamic behavior without using XML.

If you consider the valid instances of an SOA, as defined by the general definition, only those with XML as a foundational technology will realize additional value. SOA conceived without specific technology references to XML may not necessarily derive any additional value over and above process or increased business alignment.

A Word on Standards

At this point we have argued that XML must be a foundational part of the general SOA definition, and conceiving SOA outside of the scope of XML negates much of its value. Simply choosing XML, however, is not enough. XML alone is a meta-language; a language for defining other languages. By itself, XML brings syntax portability and basic structural features, but no semantics. In this case, well defined standards are needed, in the form of XML languages, which describe enough of the pieces of SOA definition to be useful. But precisely which parts of the SOA framework or definition have additional value when expressed in XML? XML has its own drawbacks in terms of wire processing and verbosity, so simply using XML blindly across all aspects of the SOA infrastructure may not be the most optimal approach. The value in SOA standards lies in their ability to permit automated processing, with clear semantics and a minimum amount of extensibility points, or a bounded profile over those extensibility points. A good XML standard should be as close to the problem statement as possible, with a minimum amount of variability in the syntax. To make this more concrete, if you consider an XML standard for describing a service interface but then allow an unbounded, extensible number of ways of specifying how the service functions are defined, you have simply moved the problem, so to speak. Anyone with previous exposure to XML and SOA standards will immediately recognize that the nature of XML suggests extensible languages designed to address future concerns, but very rarely are enough specifics tied down to permit real-world implementations. If you add to this rampant vendor positioning in a new space, the number of standards to address every aspect of SOA explodes. Further, this situation also needs to be remedied, but not by reducing the number of standards. Instead independent interoperability consortiums exist that write profiles on top of SOA and XML standards. Now we not only have an explosion of standards, but we have and explosion of profiles upon standards. XML itself is partially to blame here—it simply defines syntax for encoding a logical tree, nothing more. This means a tremendous amount of work must go into molding and constraining XML for real-world use cases. The reader should be suspicious of standards that are too extensible and attempt to generalize other data structures in XML with little or no concrete details; these types of standards are likely to be far away from real-world implementations without further profiles or details added.

Important pieces of the SOA definition that demand good standards would be the totality of the service metadata, including the description, policies, interface, and functionality. Other important pieces that require an XML definition are the information model, especially the syntax and meaning of the messages, and enough of the behavior model, especially the expected message patterns and means of transporting messages between the service and the service consumer. In Chapter 3 we spend more time on the practical issues surrounding standards, including our views on the important issues from a practical viewpoint.

Assessing the Value of SOA

Now that we have established a workable definition of SOA as a software design practice, the most common next question is "why should I care?" The most common cited value proposition of SOA stems from the agility and cost benefits generated from establishing an inventory of reusable services that build common solutions to common problems.

Establishing reusable code assets is not a new concept, but doing so in a manner that reuses an instance of a software service on a scale that spans applications, business processes, and companies is a new evolution in software development. This new evolution in reusable software is made practical by XML as well as directly related maturing technologies and standards such as SOAP Web Services.

A key motivating factor for increasing the level of reusable code assets and using standard integration technology such as XML and component-based design practices like SOA is to change the cost economics that plague most IT organizations and ISVs. Software organizations that maintain a legacy of applications often find themselves in a state where the vast majority of available budget is spent maintaining and integrating existing applications leaving little to no room for incremental innovation. Each new application and each new interface that is created adds to the sustaining cost burden since more often than not each application or interface is either built or procured from scratch.

Highly-reusable software services that are implemented through XML provide for a material shift in those cost economics. Instead of starting anew for each application or interface, established services are reused to provide things like shared implementations of security authentication, order processing, and review/approval workflows. Each time a service is reused, time and money are saved. The more functionality that can be provided to multiple business processes with a core set of shared services, the easier it is to integrate data across those business processes and provide sustaining technical support.

The details regarding how this value is achieved from an organizational and technology point of view are the topics of Chapters 2, 3, and 4, along with specific examples by industry throughout the rest of the book. For example, in Intel IT we did time studies and financial evaluation models through a number of SOA proof-point projects. What we found consistently was by using SOA design techniques anchored by XML that the time savings to implement a new application or interface drop by approximately 50 percent when reusing services that manage shared data (for instance employees, suppliers, customers, products, contracts, and so on). When applying this technique across the entire portfolio of applications and interfaces we could decrease our sustaining support costs thereby increasing our budget for innovation by approximately 40 percent.

SOA Investments

In order to implement a service oriented architecture several key investments are required to achieve the agility and cost benefits described above. This is not a trivial task and it requires careful coordination of investments in the following areas:

- Organizational structure and skills development
- Services inventory
- Services infrastructure

The details of what these investments should consist of and the key considerations of each investment are the topics of discussion in Chapters 2, 3, and 4. Chapter 2 focuses on the organizational structure considerations and Chapters 3 and 4 cover the technology aspects of the services inventory and the services infrastructure.

These will most likely be incremental investments to what currently exists in your enterprise landscape so we also describe an iterative, phased adoption model in the last section of Chapter 2.

Practical SOA Viewpoints

Throughout the remainder of this book SOA is characterized in terms of different vertical markets. For each such market, achieving SOA means something different and involves different transformational shifts. The vertical markets we cover include healthcare, government, manufacturing, financials, and telecommunications. We find that SOA considerations are quite different across these vertical markets, and that in some cases, the required organizational shifts and technology shifts are highly divergent and context dependent.

Summary

- SOA is a design practice with strong technological considerations and the full value of SOA is realized though a combination of organizational and technology changes.

- SOA is a methodology and approach and does not predicate any one approach in design. It's based on modular software architecture concepts that have been used for decades, but takes on new prominence due to wide application of industry common standards and accepted practices.

■ SOA is differentiated from prior incarnations of modular programming approaches by the use of XML as a foundational component. Without neutrality and simplicity of XML, SOA would be too broad to be practical.

■ Because XML documents can link to themselves as well as other XML documents (that is, they are self-referencable), XML adds considerable power and flexibility to SOA. And because of its text form, XML enables SOA to be readily extended across many technologies and frameworks, utilizing any operating system.

■ XML can bring about performance challenges due to the verbose nature of its textual format. Technologies that boost the performance of XML may be needed in areas of parsing, transformation, routing and security—wherever large numbers of SOA/XML messages must be processed.

Chapter 2

Organizational Considerations of SOA

It isn't the incompetent who destroy an organization. It is those who have achieved something and want to rest upon their achievements who are forever clogging things up.

—Charles Sorenson

In Chapter 1, we discussed that SOA is not a technology that you can buy from your favorite packaged software vendor, but that it is a design and engineering technique which is applied to the architecture and implementation of information systems. In order to practically implement those design and engineering techniques on a large scale, you must re-examine the way enterprise IT and software function as a business.

SOA as an Evolved "Manufacturing Model"

By now few would debate that IT is a business within the enterprise and like all businesses has a model (sometimes consciously defined and sometimes not) of revenue, costs, supply chain, and an investment portfolio. Specifically, software development organizations and IT departments are manufacturing businesses, and like all manufacturing businesses they make "stuff." The finished good might not be discrete physical widgets but when they are well developed and supported, a satisfied end-user will find it equally tangible.

The realm of manufacturing has many models, but they all effectively derive from three base models:

- Build-to-order
- Made-for-order
- Assemble-to-order

Build-to-Order

A build-to-order manufacturing model is one in which all new business is effectively treated as completely new. The key characteristics of this model are that new orders are viewed as a new problem for a new customer with very unique needs that demand a customized and specialized solution. Each finished good is developed from the ground up, as if drawn on a blank sheet of paper. Custom homes are an easily recognizable example of this model in action, as well as most departmental and enterprise applications that are developed entirely from programming languages (popular examples include Java, .NET, and so on). For the most part the design and implementation of the finish good is done from scratch with only the historical learning's of previous projects and maybe some left over raw material (like maybe some drywall in the custom home example or a small set of reusable code fragments or libraries in the custom application example). The key advantages of the build-to-order business model are that it requires less startup capital to take on a new customer, the timing of the costs and revenue are often directly correlated, and, when well executed, the customer gets exactly what they asked for. The key disadvantages are the time and cost associated with delivering each new order, which limit the scalability of this approach. For instance, you can only take so many orders at the same time. Also, a single customer bears the all of the initial and sustaining costs of the resulting product. Figure 2.1 shows a graphical depiction of the build-to-order model.

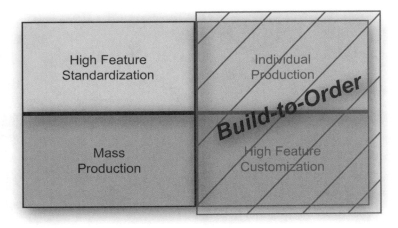

Figure 2.1   Build-to-Order Manufacturing Model

Made-for-Order

A made-for-order business model is the opposite end of the spectrum from the one described above. The key characteristic of this model is a highly standardized product with a specific set of features, which, for the most part, are universally defined for all customers. A great quote that illustrates this model comes from Henry Ford, who said "You can have any color car you want as long as it is black." Examples of this model in practice are commodity consumer goods and packaged software that is rigorously deployed without customization. Effectively, these products are designed once and then high-volume repeating production is used to create finished units that are put in inventory stores. Product is then sold and delivered to customers from those inventory stores. This business model achieves economies of scale since the cost of a single design is spread across the revenue from multiple customers, often reducing the initial and sustaining cost of the finished good. In the case of software, this method often reduces the time it takes to deploy the software and make it usable in an IT environment. Cost and scale of delivery are the clear advantages of this model, while feature flexibility and extensibility are most often the resulting disadvantages. Figure 2.2 shows a graphical depiction of the made-for-order model.

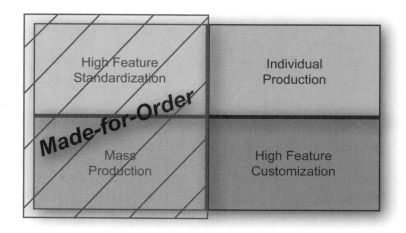

Figure 2.2   Made-for-Order Manufacturing Model

Why Build-to-Order and Made-for-Order Don't Fit SOA

Build-to-order and Made-for-order have been the dominant manufacturing models used to date in enterprise software development and present inherent obstacles in actually achieving the definition of SOA discussed in Chapter 1. They have fundamental barriers in delivering the agility, time-to-release and resulting cost benefits that can be realized by SOA. When implementing a built-to-order or made-for-order business model, it is necessary to organize capital and people investments around vertical channels that deliver the application and directly related infrastructure to the end user. We have seen this time and again where organizations have dedicated teams focused on deploying, sustaining, and continuously improving specific applications per business process. For example, entire organizations separately dedicated to order management, procurement, financials, and business planning/forecasting. Each application is either built from scratch or acquired by a favorite software vendor and custom-configured. In the worse case the application is acquired from a packaged software product and has been so highly customized that it is no longer recognizable by the software producers as their own.

Over time, as the enterprise IT or independent software vendors' application portfolio grows, so does the need for inter-application integration. This eventually results in runaway sustaining costs, as well as continuously rising support complexity that eventually makes both of these models unsustainable over the long term. For many IT organizations that now exist in an environment where budgets are flat or shrinking, the dollars required to sustain the existing applications far exceed what is available for materially new or improved business capability. Many organizations spend approximately 70 percent or more of the budget on sustaining operations and less than 30 percent on new business capabilities. The sustaining costs and rising support complexity often become so severe that the implementation of entire application portfolios are abandoned and the portfolio becomes re-implemented or "re-platformed" in an attempt to optimize the mix of where applications are built versus bought and what suppliers are used (commonly every 7 to10 years). Figure 2.3 describes this trend.

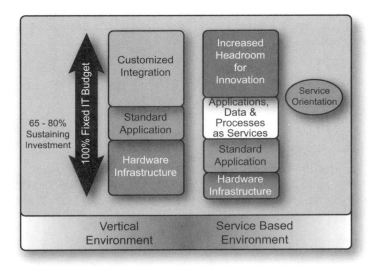

Figure 2.3   Reasons for SOA, Assemble-to-Order

SOA: Assemble-to-Order

SOA is based on applying the third listed manufacturing model; assemble-to-order. In this model you neither treat every need for information technology as a blank sheet of paper nor a black car. Instead the investment portfolio is structured by rigorously and proactively identifying those elements for which there is a feature and cost advantage to standardization and where there is material competitive business advantage to customization. In each case those elements are componentized into discrete units so that they can be mixed and matched into various configurations during the finished good assembly process. The most recognizable current example of this is car manufacturing. Today, the components and subassemblies of cars (like engines, dashboards, wheels, seats, body frames) are standardized and put in inventory stores like in the made-to-order model (and are often provided by third-party suppliers). Then the manufacturer offers base models, like the minivan, SUV, sedan, and sports car, which are configured and assembled through option packages that result in the final instance of a finished good. The key advantage is that it is possible to achieve the flexibility and scalability advantages of both the built-to-order and made-for-order models while minimizing much of the associated disadvantages. Figure 2.4 shows a graphical depiction of the assemble-to-order model.

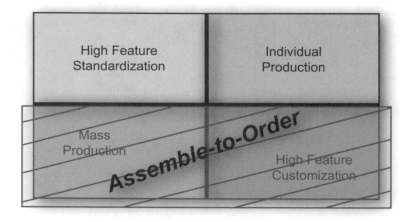

Figure 2.4   Assemble-to-Order Manufacturing Model

When the assemble-to-order manufacturing model is applied to information technology, the funding and organizational models that are based on monolithic "applications" are no longer sufficient. Finished good assembly depends on pre-assembled functional modules—services—that are readily taken off the shelf and rapidly made part of a new finished good or subassembly. This requires a shift in IT development focus; the fundamental piece parts of software solutions must be decomposed in a way that leads to identification of re-usable parts.

This is not a new concept in software development; systems have relied on decomposed piece parts for decades, in the form of subroutines and the methods of modular programming. However, extending the modularity beyond the confines of a single application/solution has previously been difficult to coordinate and sustain in a large scale over time. Figure 2.5 illustrates at a high-level how factoring of reusable functions happens in SOA.

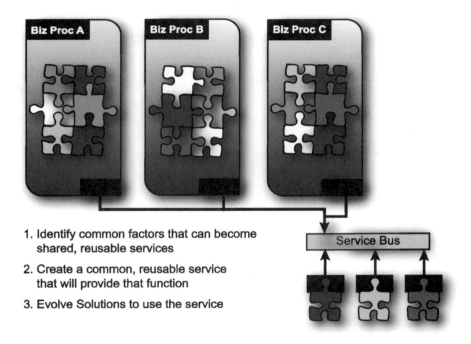

1. Identify common factors that can become shared, reusable services
2. Create a common, reusable service that will provide that function
3. Evolve Solutions to use the service

Figure 2.5   Factoring Services in Assemble-to-Order

SOA, through the use of standard practices and software-system-neutral integration standards, overcomes previously insurmountable integration difficulties. So decomposition and reassembly become a practical reality, yet the technical considerations of implementing SOA are often less complex than the organizational challenges associated with changing the direction and momentum of the build-to-order or made-for-order organized software factory. Existing organizational models and culture can be a considerable resistive force that can limit or even scuttle attempts to successfully implement SOA. To successfully establish the standardized, shared components that are put in inventory stores and used to assemble various finished good configurations, you need not just new technology, but also new organizational models.

Key Organization Shifts Required to Deliver SOA

IT organizations that are optimized for build-to-order or made-to-order software deployment are ill-equipped to take on the challenges of SOA assemble-to-order production. The key difference lies in their reliance on vertically organized development and sustaining teams that are matched to key business solution domains. Each enterprise solution domain, such as human resources or the supply chain, has captive development resources exclusively focused on delivering solutions to address that vertical domain's needs at nearly all levels of the technology stack. Priorities are set and resources allocated based on the solution most needed at the moment.

But creation of an SOA assemble-to-order model requires that a foundational set of services be created that is independent of any one business domain and that can be leveraged for assembly. As an enterprise IT organization is making the shift to SOA, the resources needed to develop foundational services can be perceived as competing for resources that otherwise could be delivering the build-to-order or sustaining the made-for-order solutions. If priorities used to allocate resources are set exclusively based on short-term time-to-delivery of solutions, foundational services creation will never materialize. This can create a great deal of tension and conflicting priorities, especially if nothing is done to change the organization and investment funding model in order to establish a beachhead in creation of SOA foundational services.

Therefore, organizing capital and human resources around an investment portfolio driven almost exclusively by applications is insufficient to implement an assemble-to-order software development model. Yet no organization can turn on a dime to reorganize from exclusively one of the first two models to exclusively assembling-to-order. If an IT organization were to attempt to do so, solution development would be delayed for what would most likely be an unacceptable amount of time as the SOA foundational services were constructed. Instead, an evolutionary approach to shifting both organization resources and priorities is needed to build out for SOA while still delivering needed business solutions. A balanced portfolio of mixed solution and service creation priorities must be maintained, both serving immediate organizational needs for solutions and the need to build out the SOA foundation. The remaining sections of this chapter cover how to setup this balanced portfolio and how to set a practical pace of transition.

The SOA Organizational Blueprint

To understand how an organization evolves towards SOA, it's important to understand the completed blueprint of a fully implemented SOA organization model. The main organization roles required to implement SOA include:

- Enterprise Architecture
- Service Procurement
- Operations
- Solution Assembly

Figure 2.6 depicts these main organizational roles and their relationships.

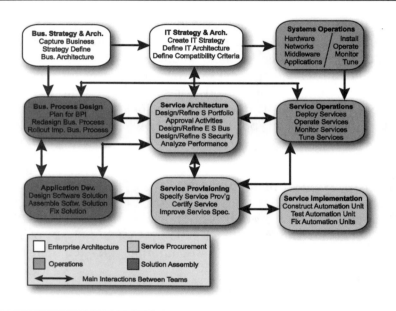

Figure 2.6   Functions and the Relationships in an SOA organization. Source CBDI Forum

Role of Enterprise Architecture

Enterprise Architecture is the anchor-point of the SOA-based, assemble-to-order manufacturing model. The need to implement Enterprise Architecture precedes the other roles, as this command-and-control function sets the implementation and transition plan to SOA. Specifically, the Enterprise Architecture function's primary charter is to:

- **Define the Service Portfolio:**   What does the long-term investment portfolio in services look like? How many services will there be? What are the categories/features/interfaces of the services? What capabilities of services should be standardized versus customized, and what is the supply strategy of the service portfolio? (For instance, when do we build versus buy versus outsource services?) You will find guidance in answering these questions later in this section.

- **Define the Service-Oriented Infrastructure:**   What are the investments that should be made in shared infrastructure to stand up, assemble, monitor and manage services once they are ready to be assembled into solutions? What foundational services must be installed to enable a secure, managed, and efficient SOA implementation? Recommendations regarding how to identify and evaluate these investments are primarily the scope of Chapters 3 and 4, but key considerations are covered later in this section.

■ **Define the Service-Oriented Adoption Roadmap:** What is the evolutionary roadmap to move from the current manufacturing model to Assemble-to-order? Specifically, what business domains and sections of the current investment portfolio would achieve the largest and/or most immediate benefit from the time-to-release and sustaining cost potential of SOA? Pointers to what we have seen as those high-value areas are in the last section of this chapter.

■ **Define the SOA Governance Processes:** Finally, what funding and corporate governance models will be put in place and managed to ensure to delivery of the strategy and roadmap established by the other three functions Enterprise Architecture? This is a program management, policy compliance, and investment risk mitigation function discussed in more detail later on.

Clearly this is a broad strategic scope, which is used to consciously and concretely define the new organizational assemble-to-order business model and architecture. Most often this function aligns directly with the CTO and/or CIO in order to be effective, because organization changes prescribed by the transition to SOA impact almost all IT functions. Enterprise Architecture can't simply be an advisor function—it needs to be the driver of the balanced investment portfolio and be accountable for the results associated with the architecture, investment, and governance decisions.

Our findings from benchmarking through our IT@Intel program have revealed a number of best-known methods regarding how to staff and successfully deliver on the charter of an Enterprise Architecture function as described above.

Enterprise Architecture – Define the Service Portfolio

In order for the Enterprise Architecture function to effectively define the service portfolio, it requires both a broad and deep understanding of the current business and technology environment, as well as where the material trends are headed that will change the current state of affairs. There are no crystal balls here, but what we have found is that undiscovered insight can be gathered on the current environment as well as future trends when using multiple views of architecture. That is, when documenting the current environment or developing the vision of a better future state, it is important to use and integrate four different perspectives described in Figure 2.7[1].

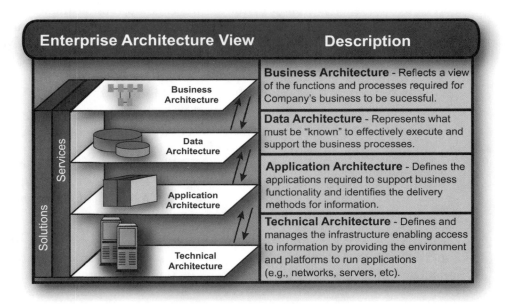

Figure 2.7   Four Views of Architecture

- ■ **The Business Architecture:** This is the business process model of the architecture: describing, decomposing, and codifying business process so that it can be mapped to services through assemble-to-order. Business Architecture identifies the tasks that

[1] Chapter 2 Enterprise Architecture Structure - "A Framework for Information Systems Architecture." John   A. Zachman. *IBM Systems Journal*, vol. 26, no. 3, 1987. IBM Publication G321-5298. 914-945-3836 or   914-945-2018

need to be accomplished to deliver a business result (such as "take an order"). For each task: determine what is required information, describe what decisions or actions are to be taken, and detail what overall business-process result is produced.

- **The Data Architecture**: This is the information model that includes the data provider and data consumer view of the architecture. Data necessary to make each decision or progress through each process step is identified as consequence to demands identified in the business architecture. Data is structured and standardized to provide reliability and quality to decision-making. Systems and business process are identified for data origination and delivery.

- **The Application Architecture**: This is the software capability and associated integration architecture. It describes the software functions needed to enable automation of the business tasks, as well as associated data input, transformation, and output steps. Each software function's purpose, scope, interface, and technology are described.

- **The Technology Architecture**: This is the infrastructure foundation required to host application and data architecture, and enable capabilities such as scaling, quality of service (including leveraging distributed infrastructure), and service/data recovery. It describes the client, server, storage, and network topologies required to host the enterprise environment.

By performing complete assessments of the current and future state from all of these points of view provide substantially more clarity regarding what functions of the applications and IT infrastructure can and/should be decomposed into reusable services, as well as where standardization of functionality is required and customization is really needed. At Intel, we developed a process we refer to as the Service Portfolio Planning process as the means to define and evolve our list of core enterprise services. A graphical description of that process can be found in Figure 2.8.

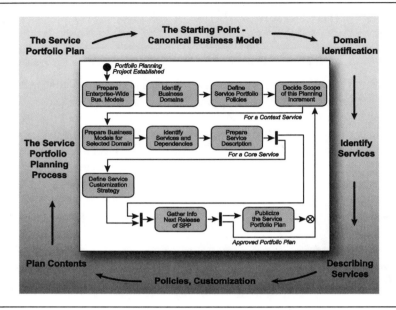

Figure 2.8   Process Steps in Service Portfolio Planning.

Detailing all steps of the Portfolio Planning Process is outside the scope of this book, yet there are some key highlights to discuss. First, the most reliable way to identify services that provide reusable functionality at the highest levels is to perform decomposition starting with the data architecture. Then, for each data entity, validate its applicability for reuse across business processes that will create, update, and reference that data. The vast majority of the benefits that are derived from SOA come from the ability to share services that manage data that span the boundaries of business processes. Figure 2.9 is a visual example of identifying potentially shared services to manage data and its applicability to various business processes.

Mapping Data Types to Business Process

Business Types (grouped by domain)	SUPPLY					HUMAN RESOURCES	
	Supplier	Purchase Order	Forecast Demand	RFQ	Supply Contract	Worker	Worker Request
Value Chains or Sub-Processes							
Inventory & Demand Management			Create				
Supply Planning	Read		Read				
Logistics Execution							
Requisition to Settle	Read	Create	Read	Create	Create		
Compliance & Control							
Cash & Risk Management							
Hire						Create	Create
Retain						Update	
Build Strong Organizations						Update	

Figure 2.9   Identifying Reusable Data Types for Services. Source CBDI Forum

Studying recurring patterns in application and technology architectures also provides indicators for reusable components. However, they will mostly be those horizontal technology functions that are already available in code libraries of various forms (like authentication, logging, general purpose database access APIs, and so on).

Second, not all services are created equal. A properly formed service portfolio provides a tiered architecture from which horizontal, business-domain–independent functions (like messaging, logging, and security) are leveraged as discrete components. Those discrete components are then consumed by higher-level services that manage shared enterprise data (like customers, suppliers, and orders). Finally, services that define business processes consume the shared data services and apply appropriate business rules as required (like for order taking, hiring employees, and approving purchase requests).

A graphical description of this proposed service taxonomy relative to a few business domains can be found in Figure 2.10 for healthcare and Figure 2.11 for manufacturing.

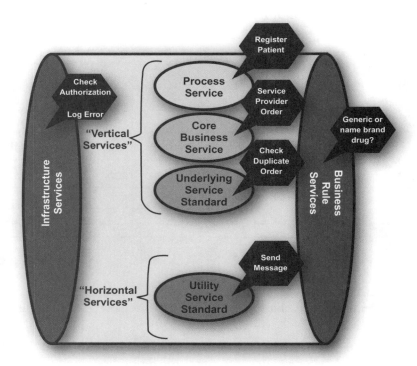

Example of Core Healthcare Business Services

- Service Provider – organization & affiliation relationships, plus roles & groups.
- Patient – including MPI
- Scheduling and Appointments
- Service Provider Order – labs, treatment, pharmaceuticals
- Encounter – including clinical results and recommendations
- Health Record – summary or full history
- Insurance – claims and referrals
- Accounting – hospital GL
- Document – scanned paper or DICOM image
- Location
- Material
- Event
- ACL – security access control list

Figure 2.10 Example Service Taxonomy for Healthcare

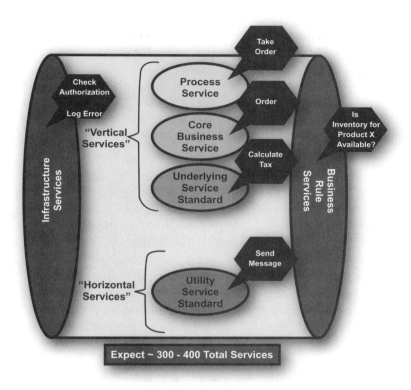

Example of Core Manufacturing Business Services

- Employee –internal, contingent, organizational relationships, plus roles & groups
- Customer
- Order – purchase, sales, service
- Location
- Physical Resource (non-people)
- Product
- General Ledger
- Incident – structured task record requiring disposition and holding history
- Document
- Event
- ACL – security access control list

Figure 2.11   Example Service Taxonomy for Manufacturing

Finally, when defining this taxonomy, a key decision needs to be made by the Enterprise Architecture organization. That is, for each service, should the service:

■ Be built by wrapping, or "fronting" existing application(s) or infrastructure?

■ Be built by creating a new service from scratch?

■ Be bought from an existing or new supplier either by landing the implementation of the service inside the data center or through outsourcing?

This is a crucial set of decisions for any organization seeking to adopt an SOA strategy. It is likely that for most organizations, identifying the reusable services in the taxonomy will be obvious. The harder decision will be how to source the implementation of those services, as this is a "rubber meets the road" action in adopting a tangible SOA strategy. Existing organizational momentum will attempt to assign a default answer to this difficult question; meaning that if the current business model is predominately built-to-order that the push will be to build the services and if it is predominately made-for-order then an attempt will be made to buy and then integrate services from one or many software suppliers.

Our experience to-date tells us that the right answer to this difficult question is not a simple one, and that it requires taking a conscious and specific strategic posture on three main points:

■ **Competitive Differentiation:** Where is the root of your overall business's corporate competitive advantage in the market? Specifically, what are those things that your company does or features your software products have that must be done better than anyone else to sustain and extend your market position?

■ **Industry Best Practices:** What are those things that your business must do to meet government regulations or what are established as an industry best practice or norm? That is, what are the minimum set of business functions and quality levels of those functions in order to even be in business?

■ **Boundaries of the "Glass House":** What are those business processes and associated systems in the current application portfolio that just simply cannot be subjected to any form of re-implementation risk? Specifically, what systems, if an attempt to re-implement or upgrade in a substantial way fails, could stop the operation of your business?

Taking a strategic position on these three issues and implementing guiding principles the organization can follow drives the decision-making regarding how to source your service taxonomy. Specifically:

- For reasons of intellectual property protection and maintaining market differentiation, those capabilities that represent a competitive differentiation should be built. Algorithms, business rules, and process workflows that represent unique intellectual property can readily be packaged as independent services and be composed into final solutions alongside services supplied by other means. For most companies, this will be a small handful of services in the order of magnitude between 10 and 100. If you find yourself defining hundreds of services this way, it is likely that your built-to-order organizational legacy is still at play.

- For the reasons of "keeping the business running," the best strategy is to "wrap" or "front" your glass house applications with service interfaces so that they can be an essential part of your evolving SOA landscape, enabling continued leverage of the application investment and providing value over a longer period of time. Most often these are financial, human capital, or other core operational systems from which a substantial advantage can be gained by exposing the data they manage as services, but for which too much risk is associated with a full re-implementation. It is also common to first front these applications with service interfaces and then iteratively migrate the implementation of those services from the legacy application code and database to a re-platformed implementation in the future. This is an effective means to migrate highly shared data (like product definition codes, financial general ledger, customer master files, and so on) from a built-to-order or made-for-order model to SOA. Again, for most companies this is a small handful of services in the order of magnitude between 1 and 100. If you find yourself defining hundreds of services this way, it is likely that your existing organizational legacy is also still at play.

- For reasons of cost relative to value it almost always makes sense to either outsource or acquire those services that define industry best practices and are expected to provide standardized functionality across companies either due to regulatory requirements or established industry norm. Key examples in this space are things like regulatory auditing and reporting requirements, expense reporting, order capture, as well most low-level application functions such as messaging, logging, basic workflow, and data access. In this case it almost always makes the most sense from a time-to-release and cost standpoint to provide these services from market leading suppliers from which you establish a strategic licensing agreement. For most enterprise IT organizations, heavy use of this sourcing model provides the greatest cost-of-ownership benefit. For independent software providers this can still work well for commodity product functions for which there is a clear market leader in providing that application component as a service.

The task of defining the Service Portfolio is the first and most important responsibility of the Enterprise Architecture team. It will be an ongoing process that works iteratively with the other tasks described here.

Enterprise Architecture – Define the Service Oriented Architecture enabling infrastructure

In the previous task, the Enterprise Architecture team defines the discrete software components and subassemblies that will be built or acquired to provide the inventory stores of software functionality that will be drawn upon to assemble resulting information management solutions. However, in order to actually assemble services into running solutions, a shared hardware and software infrastructure is required. This task is where the Enterprise Architecture team decides:

- What are the components that will provide the service oriented infrastructure? Specifically, will an ESB, Enterprise Portal, and/or Service repository be deployed? If so, when?

- What messaging patterns will be supported (pub-sub, request-reply), and will infrastructure support higher level functions such as caching, guaranteed delivery, and message routing to enable endpoint virtualization?

- What standards will the service oriented architecture support and align to? Specifically, what level of WS* standard support? UDDI 2.0? What about JSR standards for portlets and ESB containers?

- What topology will be used in the deployment of the infrastructure? Will server or storage virtualization be used? What infrastructure management and security standards will be applied?

■ Will there be one centralized enterprise infrastructure instance or some manner of departmental or regional distribution, or a mix of both?

■ What will be built versus bought? For the infrastructure components, which are purchased from a supplier and which supplier?

This is a very deep and important topic so the next two chapters of this book are devoted to covering these and more questions in detail.

Enterprise Architecture – Define the Service Oriented Adoption Roadmap

This task is where the Enterprise Architecture team determines what services to define and implement first and what resulting business processes will be supported via the SOA, assemble-to-order model in what order. The pace of the adoption roadmap should be aligned to the maturity model described in the final section of this chapter, so that investments in technology, organization, and process progress in sync with each other.

In terms of identifying where to start first, priority should be given to those services and associated business processes where change, data integration, and customization are prevalent requirements. Often these are systems to provide customer and/or supplier facing portals, business-to-business e-commerce integration gateways, and ERP-like application modules for sales, marketing, and supplier management functions.

Also, it is prudent to focus on highly shared data for which a common definition and shared instances of records are required across applications and business processes. Most often these are highly reusable lists of "master data" or reference data that are used by many transactions to conduct business. Good examples of "master data" include things such as:

■ Employees

■ Customers

■ Suppliers

■ Product codes and characteristics

■ Material codes and characteristics

■ Physical resources (such as capital equipment and facilities)

■ Security roles and privileges

Finally, highly shared functions in applications that can be effectively abstracted and configured to support multiple data types, business processes, and compute algorithms are also good candidates for implementing in early phases of the SOA adoption roadmap. Key examples include:

- Security routines for entitlement, provisioning, authentication, authorization, and auditing
- Application status, warning and error logging
- Database and persistent storage create, update, read, and delete functions
- Business rule ("if-then-else") definition and execution
- System-to-system messaging (such as JMS and other forms of message-oriented middleware)
- System-to-person messaging (such as e-mail, SMS, and so on)
- Workflow ("do task A, then B") definition and execution

To build an effective roadmap you must identify needs and opportunities that have manageable scope for success and that do not require years of development to achieve the first measurable business results. SOA design techniques are geared towards applying iterative development techniques for both the services and resulting assembled solutions. You will find more often than not that the most effective iteration technique is to focus on a segment of the existing application portfolio (either by business or technology domain) and then replicate throughout the portfolio.

For example, if starting with a technology domain like e-commerce integration, establish the service infrastructure and portfolio on new transactions and then once measurable success is achieved apply the SOA technique across all e-commerce transactions. Or, if starting with a business domain like sales and marketing, establish the service infrastructure and portfolio around leads, customers, product, and orders for the newest required application. Once measurable success is achieved, apply the SOA technique across all sales and marketing applications. Once a beachhead of starter services and the associated infrastructure is put in place, it becomes practical to expand its adoption to the next phase.

You will find most roadmaps require more than two to three phases to establish a rich service portfolio and a mature service infrastructure. Current experience tells us that common, well-developed service portfolios contain in the scale of hundreds of services (approximately 100–700). Building out those services from greatest reuse potential to marginal reuse potential will yield the greatest return and offer the least risk of adoption failure.

Enterprise Architecture – Define the SOA Governance Process

The final key task of the Enterprise Architecture team is to define and manage an SOA governance process. Specifically, what this means is to:

- **Ensure Standards Compliance:** Put standards in place and communicate broadly to technical staff and non-technical project management the minimum requirements of service creation and use. Document best practices and require that proposed service creation or acquisition be rationalized against the established roadmaps. Reduce service proliferation (and resulting sustaining burden) by staying true to the planned and roadmap-documented portfolio. You also need to develop decision-making criteria and associated review mechanism to decide when exceptions should be granted to the solution assembly team to not use an established service or piece of infrastructure.

- **Measure Progress:** Establish metrics that are reported periodically and are used to define the success of the overall SOA program, to measure its impact on the overall business, and to provide indications that the strategy and roadmap defined by Enterprise Architecture is taking shape in production systems.

- **Enhance Roadmap:** Institute a process for gathering real-time input from Service Procurement, Operations, and Solution Assembly regarding the effectiveness of deployed services and the infrastructure and what, if any, changes to the strategy and roadmap are required.

These three functions and there relationships are illustrated in Figure 2.12.

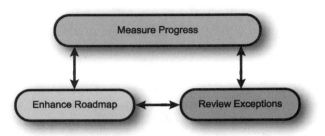

Figure 2.12   Activities for Governance

Our experience to-date has shown that the most tangible metrics to measure progress of SOA is based on:

- The number of services available
- The level of adoption of those services into the portfolio of production systems
- The number of failures/incursions a service faces in production
- The time savings that solution development teams are realizing when consuming that service in their production system.

With these metrics, the enterprise architecture team can measure proliferation and adoption of services, as well as the quality and business value that individual services and the portfolio in aggregate is providing to the company overall. Target goals regarding service performance and investment models can be tied to metrics as a planning function. Through this planning function, the metrics can be used to project the expected benefit and required investment to deliver a particular number of services at an agreed to level of quality. Then a monitoring process can track the actual realization of those planned metrics to determine if the built and/or bought services are at the right cost, delivering the right quality and value, and are actually being leveraged by systems in the production portfolio.

Regular, iterative communications between the Enterprise Architecture organization function and the others (Service Procurement, Operations, and Solution Assembly) will be required to establish the metric goals and to gather the data in which the planned vs. actual results are obtained. This communication will then support course correction in the metrics (for instance, was something too aggressive or too conservative?) and to understand such things as why certain services have more prevalent adoption than others. This is a critical operational function of the assemble-to-order software factory that should be established early in the formation of the organization and whose function should be continuously reviewed and fine-tuned as the adoption of assemble-to-order is proliferated in an organization.

As the service portfolio grows, it's likely that it will need to be segmented into domains so that the right level of communication occurs and minimum levels of red tape exist in getting work done. This domain segmentation will be industry- and company-specific, but effectively it involves taking logically related sets of services in the portfolio and grouping them in such a manner that they are managed as a set with only the necessary level of dependencies on other sets of services in the portfolio. A visual example of domain segmentation can be found in Figure 2.13.

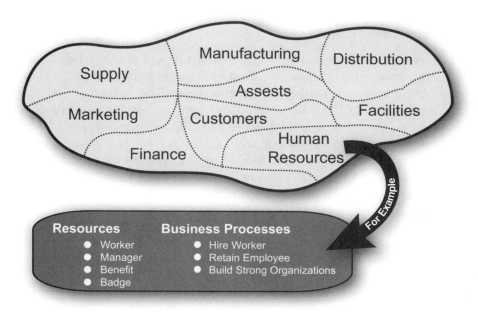

Figure 2.13   Example Domains to organize SOA teams. Source CBDI Forum

Finally, with the metrics and domain segmentation established the enterprise architecture team sets the criteria and decision-making forums. The criteria and forums drive decisions upon which planned services are implemented, implemented services are to be adopted, and exceptions to the roadmap are granted. This is a very difficult function to execute well. You will find this especially hard if there is not funding as well as a reward and recognition tied to the decision-making process. What we have found time and again is that unless developers are personally rewarded for reusing existing services in the portfolio they will not do so naturally. If funding for a production system is not tied to a commitment to use services on the roadmap or in the portfolio, project managers will not do so naturally. Therefore, it is extremely important in the foundational stages of your transition to the SOA assemble-to-order software factory to implement reward and funding mechanisms that encourage and recognize consumption of the service portfolio investments you make.

Role of Service Procurement

Service procurement plays a key role in support of SOA; this involves the choice and associated engineering to acquire, build, or integrate in order to bring a service on-line in the enterprise. The need to bring a service on-line will have been identified through the service portfolio planning process, where future demand is identified in the form of a roadmap, dependencies are identified, and priority for service deployment is set. The use of the service in assembly to multiple solutions will come after procurement, in Solution Assembly. The procured service will align with the services taxonomy definition and standards for implementation set forth by Enterprise Architecture. Figure 2.14 provides a graphical depiction of the scope of Service Procurement. The key functions of Service Procurement are the acquisition, solution support and maintenance of the service inventory.

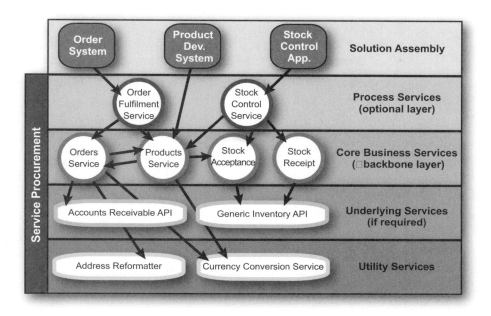

Figure 2.14   Example Mapping of Service Procurement Teams to a Taxonomy. Source CBDI Forum

Service Procurement - Acquisition

The taxonomy and roadmap of the service inventory (that is, what services, their features, and so on) is set by the Enterprise Architecture function and acts as the target which drives the day-to-day operation of Service Procurement. Through that taxonomy and roadmap, the Service Procurement function establishes each service either through construction or purchase as defined by the taxonomy. The establishment of a service when constructed involves the usual software-engineering best practices of requirements, design, and testing. One fundamental difference regarding a service is that at the time of development it is not definitively known the usages that the service will ultimately take part in as the solution assembly teams consumes the service. Therefore, great care needs to be taken in the definition of the data structures and the functions the service so that it remains a reusable component. Specifically, this means:

- Wherever and whenever possible, use established industry standard definitions of data types and data structures.

- If technically feasible, provide a means to safely extend the data representation managed by the service through configuration.

- Use the business rules engine (discussed in detail in Chapter 4) to configure decision-making algorithms that are most often determined by end-user preference/policy (such as identifying a preferred customer or supplier) rather than by some other more permanent definition (like referential integrity rules or long-standing legal requirements).

- If technically feasible, provide a "plug-in" means to safely extend the functions offered by the service through configuration and solution assembly customization. This can include things such as custom event handlers, pre- or post-processing insertion points in the service's methods, or providing for a certain number if incremental methods to be added to the service interface.

When acquiring services from a supplier, the key decision that needs to be made is whether or not the definition of that service's interface from the supplier should be reused as-is by the Solution Assembly team or should be "wrapped" by the Service Procurement team. Theoretically, "wrapping" could provide a level of abstraction for future functionality as well as establish an architectural layer of independence from the supplier's implementation of the service. For many of us, the first initial reaction will be to say "...absolutely provide the wrapper", and in some cases that will be the best answer. However, our experience has shown that for enterprise IT organizations, the fastest and most cost-effective way to implement a services inventory is to buy it from a limited number of strategic suppliers. If what you finally decide upon is putting a code layer on top of every single service those vendors supply, then what you are doing is adding a incremental layer of complexity that will likely yield a limited return over both the near and long term. In enterprise IT, the better bet is to implement the service portfolio process to define your services inventory from the point of view of your business and data needs then select those suppliers with the best fit. From there you add wrappers on those services that clearly have lacking functionality or where they directly intersect those services you plan to build. For independent software vendors, there is substantially more business incentive to "wrap" the services you acquire, however middleware technology in your service infrastructure might provide a most cost-effective means to provide that encapsulation and supplier independence (such as through ESB service endpoint definitions; refer to Chapter 3 for details).

Service Procurement - Support

Whether a service is built or bought, the sustaining solution support function of Service Procurement is common. One key capability that Service Procurement needs to provide as an organization is reliable delivery to SLAs (Service Level Agreements). Specifically, this means:

■ Service Procurement needs to hit deadlines and milestones for adding services to the inventory or enhancing existing services.

■ Services available in the inventory need to deliver to specific quality metrics regarding their availability, performance, scalability, and code/data defects.

■ Requests from Operations and Solution Assembly for technical support on services should be addressed and resolved in mostly predictable and universally agreed-to timeframes. There should be clear escalation procedures when these timeframes are missed.

The reliability of a SOA enterprise will be heavily dictated by the service procurement team's ability to cleanly define and deliver to these SLAs. Unpredictability on service delivery, support, or execution will yield insurmountable distrust for nearly any SOA program. Providing this predictability will be the result of dedicated focus by small engineering teams on individual or a small set of services which have a properly defined and well understood scope from Enterprise Architecture. As you build the service inventory, additional teams are brought on to cover those additional services. Also, there should be a distinct organizational separation between the Service Procurement and Solution Assembly functions. They both represent engineering skills, but they need to be motivated and rewarded differently. That is, Service Procurement teams need to be rewarded for supporting the most amount of functionality with the least amount of services that can meet SLA and cost metrics. Solution Assembly teams need to be rewarded for fast delivery of solutions to satisfied customers.

Service Procurement – Maintenance

In addition to providing quality implementations that are delivered at a reliable beat-rate for releases and call support, the Service Procurement team has the difficult responsibility of handling version control for service interfaces. What inevitably happens as the service inventory is constructed is a solution requirement comes up that requires an enhancement to the definition of the service interface. Then the question faced is "How do we improve the service without breaking all the other deployed solutions or forcing them to upgrade"?

Effectively there are three main options to address this problem:

- Revise the definition of the service interface and require all consumers to use that new definition. This is necessary for horizontal functions that cannot support the existence of more than one service definition for reasons of data integrity, security, and so on. Depending on the technology implementation of the service interfaces this may or may not require consuming solutions to re-compile, test and re-deploy.

- Support the side-by-side deployment of more than one version of the service interface. There are certain appealing advantages of this technique for shared services that have some varying capabilities in different business contexts (like an order), but care needs to be taken that there are not so many versions that it becomes overly complex to determine what version is the right one to use for a solution or support burdens become too costly like in the build-to-order model.

- Provide a new interface definition for each new version. This is a variant of the side-by-side model where each new version is treated as an entirely new service. This is useful when you are looking to provide a limited amount of backward compatibility but still want to drive a clear departure for future iterations of the service definition. In this approach a mediation technique can be used to dynamically select the right version of the service interface based on the incoming request from the solution.

Which choice is the best of the three options will depend on a number of factors such as the maturity of the service inventory, the budget available to support differing versions and the number of total deployed solutions. However, the key guidance is to keep your service inventory appropriately lean—more services are not always better. In fact, fewer services that are reused more frequently are the ones that yield the largest time-to-market and cost of ownership benefits.

Role of Operations

Effective SOA Operations requires significant changes in methodology, as compared to operations resulting from Build-to-Order or Made-for-order models. Most changes can be traced to the fact that services, used to assemble solutions, are not bound to any single vertical business solution; rather, services are consumed by two or more solutions, and possibly by other services in the case of a composite service assembly. This difference reflects significant changes in operational approach as shown in Table 2.1.

Table 2.1   Differences Between Traditional and SOA Operational Approaches

Traditional Application Operations	SOA Operations
Application designed to meet specific vertical business need in a solution stack including applications, data, and infrastructure.	Services meet data and application services needs of diverse consumers, which may be business processes or other services.
Applications most often scaled up on custom platform designed for peak capacity.	Services leverage scale-out for capacity increase; capacity can be adjusted based on demand.
High availability achieved through redundant infrastructure, both local clusters and remote disaster recovery.	Availability assured through service redundancy, both in local scale and remote location.
Operations specializes in support of many solution stacks; cross-training and coverage can be issues.	Operations is tuned to ensure that service levels of many SOA services are maintained.

Each of these consequences are explored both here from an operations organization impact, and in Chapters 3 and 4 with respect to technical impact. Due to the nature of Operations in the SOA organization, it is best aligned to function as a corporate-wide support function for all services and resulting solutions in the portfolio.

Solution Stack versus Service Assembly

When applications and data are custom developed or configured to meet a specific business process purpose (Build-to-Order or Made-for-Order), Operations will reflect the vertical organization through the designation of operations specialists in those stacks, as illustrated in Figure 2.15.

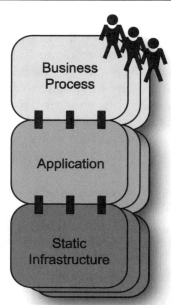

Build-to-Order and Made-for-Order Results in Many Tightly Coupled Solution Stacks

Figure 2.15   Application Solution Stacks

This is a natural byproduct of establishing an operational "defense" against possible interruption to business systems. Staffing levels are often directly associated with both the complexity and criticality of the specific stack, and often an operations manager (and even the solution's customer) could identify names of individuals that are mapped against specific stacks and the business functions they provide. Also in this operations sustaining model, the operations support staff is often familiar with the entire stack, specializing in applications, embedded data, and even the hardware deployed in the stack.

While this is simple and straightforward, it can be both inefficient and can be risky—loss of a single individual can impact the sustainability of a stack and thus the operations integrity of a solution (and its associated business process). Cross-training and redundancy is often advised, and so increases the relative inefficiency of the approach.

An operations model servicing an evolved SOA deployment must be configured differently. While operations staff will still need to be familiar with the solutions in play in the environment, this affinity takes a very different form. The assembly of services into solutions most often will involve codified business processes affected in business process automation (BPA) or business process management systems (BPMS) capability. The flow of business process steps is codified at a high level— invoking the function and data encapsulated in discrete services. Expertise in the Business Process Automation systems and familiarity with the codified processes is a needed skill—but those individuals need not be familiar with operations of the underlying services. That expertise—horizontal in focus in contrast to the vertical focus of the application solutions stacks, is another critical skill in support of SOA, as illustrated in Figure 2.16. The focus is in the operation of a service, and the integrity and quality of underlying data. However, unlike the broad focus of the solution stack operations support specialist, the service operations specialist can afford laser focus on a more limited scope, and can take on support of many services.

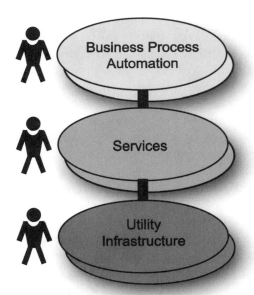

Assemble-to-Order With Loose Coupling Results in a More Horizontally-Focused Support Model

Figure 2.16   SOA Solution Stacks

The advantages of this horizontally focused support model are many. Less specialization can lead to reduced dependency on specific individuals. Maintaining a loose coupling between services and the service infrastructure can further enhance this model, as software and data specialists no longer need to have expertise in underlying infrastructure. Instead, they depend on generic hosting infrastructure for their service hosting needs. The concepts around abstracted and loosely coupled infrastructure are covered in more detail in Chapter 3.

High Availability and Disaster Recovery

An operations benefit that is often overlooked when considering a move to SOA is assurance of service levels and availability. This benefit is rooted in the stateless nature and loose coupling of services themselves. This is in contrast to a stateful, tightly bound solution stack that creates vulnerabilities due to need for nonstop operation of a single application server or data source.

Before discussing this, it helps to describe a typical support model for a vertical solution stack that is custom designed to support a critical business process. Such stacks are typically comprised of an architecture that includes multiple tiers of capability, such as web, application, and database services. Tightly bound to one another, failure of any of these layers can result in functional loss of the system. And the stateful nature of communications both between the layers of the system, and between the system and its consumers (often web browsers) results in a no-compromise requirement for continuous operations of the system's layers.

Engineered solutions to this challenge often involve clustering of systems to decrease the risk of failure. Yet the increased complexity of the resulting systems—with clustering or other often propriety technology to ensure uninterrupted operation—can itself make the systems difficult to sustain, requiring additional operations expertise in the clustering systems technologies. Often, systems are not engineered with this form of fault tolerance in order to avoid the added complexity—and systems "fly without a parachute."

In addition to clustering and other fault tolerance systems, disaster recovery (DR) systems are often deployed in separate facilities to further assure the integrity of solution stacks. DR facilities contain local operations staff and additional operations expertise to provide continued operations of key applications if they are interrupted in the primary site. Often the systems are functionally idle, passively waiting to be engaged in the case of emergency. And while the operations staff maintaining DR may be trained for other tasks, the skills and training to assure operations in case of failure of the primary site adds considerable overhead to the organization.

In contrast to this, an SOA implementation can substantially reduce the complexity and cost, as compared with the fault-tolerant, tightly coupled solutions stacks. SOA services are typically architected to rely on stateless message flow, each message conveying an atomic step in executing a business process. The stateless nature of the communications means that any instance of the service that is present can serve the message's request and fulfill the task. Multiple instances of services can be assembled side-by-side to increase the scale of a service, referred to as *scale out* architecture. These multiple instances can be load balanced either through a services directory, or through other infrastructure-based load balancing methods. In addition to the ability to add local instances of a service to increase capacity, instances of a service can be added remotely, in data centers that are widely separated from one another.

This is the key to SOA's ability to hedge against infrastructure systems failure; the loss of any single instance of a service is of little consequence as long as other instances of the service are available to serve the requesting load. If instances of a service are lost due to a site failure (the scenario that in the prior example may have caused DR site to be activated), services that are actively servicing requests at another site dynamically pick up the load. The primary concerns in architecting the balanced SOA system are that sufficient capacity be on-line at any moment, compensating for either system or site failure.

This is very different scenario from the vertical solution stack architecture that required substantial constructs of redundancy to assure system continuity. In addition, the balanced SOA system has all functional instances of a service actively participating in serving requests at any time. The integrity of the infrastructure is continually assured because the infrastructure is "exercised" continuously. This is in contrast to the vertical stack scenario, where cluster failover must be tested and DR facility failover drilled both with respect to infrastructure and personnel.

While the simplified operations model of SOA is very attractive, distributing services and the underlying data across remote installations presents its challenges. These are more thoroughly covered in Chapters 3 and 4.

Service Level Monitoring and Assurance

The prior mentioned ability to operate multiple services in parallel in a scale-out architecture yields yet another benefit—that of run-time dynamic response to changing service level needs. SOA enables benefits in dynamic response that were never before practical with application solution stacks.

It's instructive to look at how capacity is managed in integrated solution stacks. Because of the stateful, relatively inflexible nature of most vertically integrated solutions; capacity decisions are typically made at design time, before systems are deployed to production. The capacity prescribed is often more an artful guess than a data-based prediction, and results in system capacity judged up in order that there's reserve capacity beyond actual estimated peak demand. On implementation, actual utilization of systems is woefully low; often well below 20 percent (as measured by CPU and/or I/O use). Peak utilizations—conservatively set at design time—most often do not come close to challenging the capacity of the infrastructure.

Why is this done? Because the systems—tightly coupled and bound together—are inflexible at runtime in terms of changing capacity, an extra measure of conservative judgment is added so that systems will be sure to keep up with production loads. It is this inflexible, natural conservative response to design requirements that leads to vastly underutilized infrastructure resources. SOA has the ability to change this—but only if a balanced SOA system is teamed with both service monitoring and service level assurance capabilities.

Consider a balanced SOA system, where each service monitored to track its current state performance. For example, an SOA service monitor may directly observe system loading (CPU or I/O), or it may empirically evaluate the performance of the service with respect to message response times or queue size (increasing queue size indicating an overburdened service instance). Service monitoring will be explored more in later chapters; however, for now we can summarize by stating that many attributes of service and SOA systems can be instrumented and used to indicate service health.

Service monitoring—dynamic in nature—can enable dynamic capacity adjustments. If a monitored service is seen to be approaching it's service level limits due to load, another instance of that service can be brought on line to balance the load and maintain service levels to the agreed upon levels. Likewise, if multiple service instances are running but load is running light—instances of the service can be stopped and their resources returned to a pool of available resources.

However, if services are installed and initiated manually, the dynamic service capability has less appeal; if a substantial amount of human effort is required to install and configure a system to operate a service (and then again to release the resources for reuse), the conservation of resources is less; one could envision an environment where the churn of continual capacity adjustments is more trouble than it's worth—with a natural outcome that services would be scaled out with sufficient capacity to meet peak demand (and perhaps beyond). This bears resemblance to vertical stack situation, where infrastructure runs at a fraction of its potential capacity due to conservative deployments aimed at peak capacity availability at all times.

Enter the advantage of Service Oriented Infrastructure, or SOI implemented by the Operations team. With appropriate automation interfaces and infrastructure itself exposing service interfaces, the provisioning (and release) of capacity can be controlled with the same types of messages that provide for business process automation. In fact, the processes to monitor, provision capacity, and otherwise control SOA service levels can be viewed as IT processes that equally benefit from SOA implementation.

With an SOI implementation, messages from service monitoring indicating the need to scale up a service can act directly on the infrastructure, triggering actions that directly invoke additional capacity; service functions can include:

1. Identify available resource and configure

    a) Select resource from available pool

    b) If resource is not already in desired configuration, configure it for use

    c) If the service (to be capacity increased) is not installed, install it

2. Run service on the provisioned resource

3. Register additional capacity in directory

Service 1 is a compound service that encapsulates the function of several subordinate services (a–c), however, those services could be encapsulated and used by other compound services, for example one that would configure newly installed equipment for initial use. The sequenced, orchestrated steps 1–3 above could be executed through an SOA-interfaced by a business process automation capability.

And that is why you really, really want an Operations team implementing SOI.

The efficiencies realized through this automation increase in proportion to how dynamic the environment becomes. If provisioning and release of resources occur frequently, benefit can be greater than in a static environment. However, considering the earlier discussion of SOA potential to provide fault tolerance—an SOI controlled infrastructure can provide some essentials of fault tolerant infrastructure management. For example, if service monitoring detected that one of two instances of a critical service had failed (say, due to hardware failure), the automation system could (through a programmed rule) identify that the service level minimum threshold of two instances was not met, and trigger the above provisioning sequence. In this way, SOI automation could maintain a service pool at a predetermined level. Fold in dynamic capacity increase if service levels lag due to load—and this becomes a self-sustaining, self-healing autonomic system. Normal operational sustaining for such a system would be focused on ensuring that the pool of resources was healthy and spares were at a level so that the autonomic system will have enough capacity; in fact, one could even imagine where an SOI system could place orders with suppliers to increase its own capacity!

Role of Solution Assembly

The Solution Assembly function in an SOA organization is the finished good manufacturing arm of the software factory. Where the Service Procurement function establishes the software components and sub-assemblies as services per the definition and roadmap established by Enterprise Architecture, Solution Assembly draws on that inventory of services to assemble specific automation solutions for customers.

Solution Assembly is a vertical, business process facing function of the factory software as opposed to the primarily horizontal and technology facing functions of Service Procurement and Operations.

Fundamentally, what the Solution Assembly team is focused on is working directly with system end-users to determine business process automation requirements and then mapping the appropriate services from inventory to the tasks in the business process the service supports. Given this focus it most often makes sense for this organization function to be most directly aligned to the other product management or customer engagement functions of the company. A graphical example of this high-level process is shown in Figure 2.17.

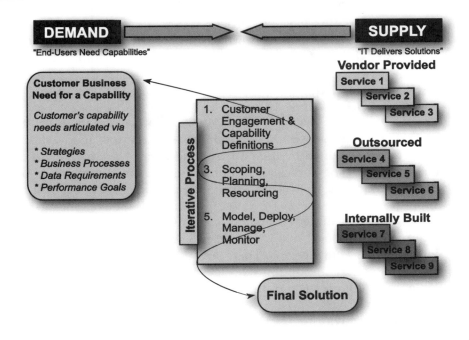

Figure 2.17   High-Level Solution Assembly Process

The fundamental operating concept of the Solution Assembly function is "model, deploy, and improve".

Solution Assembly – Model

In the model task of Solution Assembly, what the analysts and software developers are focused on is modeling the business process and information needs of the system end-user. What we mean by modeling is not sitting down in front of the end user with a blank, white sheet of paper and asking "so what do you want ...." Doing so would be an implementation of the built-to-order manufacturing model with a few more reuse opportunities. In the assemble-to-order manufacturing model, the developer or analyst focuses on identifying the following:

- What business domain(s) are relevant to meet this need (for instance is this a sales/marketing need, a finance one, human resources? Or some combination)?

■ What are the services in the portfolio which would be required to support this business process? Are there existing processes in the portfolio that this business process needs to connect to? Can an existing process simply be enhanced or customized?

■ Are there any gaps in the interface definition of the identified services in the portfolio to meet this need?

Effectively, the modeling process in solution assembly is a "fit-gap" processes which focuses on determining what services in inventory meet the need as identified by the end-user and what if any gaps exist. This is analogous to going and visiting your favorite car manufacturer when you have a need for transportation (time for a new car). When you go into the dealership, you don't sit down with the salesperson and bring out a whiteboard and design your new car. Instead you have a conversation about your high-level needs and desires which helps the sales associate narrow down your options. Then once you have selected a base model, you then look at the option packages which can be applied to the car. Sometimes, the car with all the features you really want is already on the lot and you drive away a few hours later. Sometimes it's not and you place an order with the factory. And sometimes the car comes close but there are still some additional features that you want which you end up going to an after-market customization shop to add them. A very similar process will happen when modeling by the Solution Assembly function, as illustrated in Figure 2.18.

Figure 2.18 Customizing Services for Solution Assembly. Source CBDI Forum

Demonstrating what services are available and what their capabilities are to end-users by the Solution Assembly team is a fairly straightforward rapid prototyping function. A robust service catalog, enterprise portal, and enterprise service bus is needed to effectively do this rapid prototyping, but when in place time studies we have done internally to Intel show that a few hours of need discussion can be represented in a functional prototype in hours-to-days of time.

Once the end-user interacts with the prototype, they will effectively be presented with a decision: Is the prototype good enough or do you really need more functionality, and if so are you ready to wait for it? This is a very similar decision you make when you see a car in the dealership that is close to what you want but not a 100-percent fit (maybe you wanted leather instead of cloth seats). Do you drive away today with the car that does over 90 percent of what you want or do you wait another two or three months for leather to be shipped from the factory?

Software development and car manufacturing aren't exactly the same, but when using the SOA, assemble-to-order methodology the prototype presented to the end-user is using tested and production worthy services drawn from inventory. Those services used by Solution Assembly don't need to be re-designed, coded or tested again. What are being developed by Solution Assembly are some unique user interfaces, some specialized business rules / workflows, and configuration settings of the underlying services. It does not completely eliminate the need for doing engineering by Solution Assembly, but reduces it dramatically. Therefore, prototypes can move to production solutions in hours-to-weeks and not weeks-to-years (as is common in the built-to-order and made-for-order models).

The most complex issue to deal with by Solution Assembly is when a service does not support the data or function insisted by an end-user and the time estimate provided by Service Procurement to enhance the service is deemed as unacceptable by that end-user. In those cases Solution Assembly needs to determine how best to customize the existing services in assembling the desired solution. This is complex, because the right answer is not straightforward and if the wrong decision is made too many times, then the quality and integrity of the service portfolio will degrade significantly as it becomes burdened with a legacy of user specific enhancements.

There are effectively four ways to deal with service customization by the Solution Assembly function:

- If the service supports it, configure the service to support the additional data fields and/or plug-in rules, functions, validations or workflows needed. Architecturally, providing a means for this level of customization by each service is highly desirable but not always practical, especially for services which are acquired from vendors which do not support this capability.

- Wrap the service in a middleware or user interface function. Reuse the service functionality that fits, and add the missing functionality in the middleware or user interface. This works for implementing things such as workflow, validation, and incremental operations, but is not that effective in supporting additional data fields or data types.

- Wrap service in a higher-level, customer specific service / application component. Again, reuse the service functionality that fits and add the missing functionality to the customer specific service. This is only effective in creating incremental process services and should not be used on core business, utility or underlying services as doing so could corrupt the integrity of your service inventory if other users started reuse those added functions without a comprehensive validation process done by the Service Procurement team. This can be used to support additional data fields, however care will need to be taken to ensure transactional integrity and query performance.

- Setup the business process to either ask for the data or perform the additional function in the resulting solution before or after the service is invoked. Again, reuse the service functionality that fits and outside of the service infrastructure do what is needed and call into the service infrastructure either at the very start or very end of the business process. This only works in situations where an existing or packaged application is performing much of the required business functionality and the service infrastructure is tied into to perform some focused incremental capability (like messaging from a supplier systems to financials).

A well run solution assembly team will be highly effective at mapping user needs to the service inventory, will rapidly produce prototypes which demonstrate that fit and if appropriate material gaps, and finally will work smoothly with the end-user, Service Procurement and Enterprise Architecture to establish customizations which are absolutely required.

Solution Assembly – Deploy

In the deploy task of the Solution Assembly function, the configuration and customizations need to be deployed in production and documented so that the Operations, Service Procurement and Enterprise Architecture teams now know what services are being used to support what new or modified business process and what customizations were necessary. The sharing of information regarding customizations is an important piece of information to drive continuous improvement to the services inventory. A key goal of the service inventory should be to support as much reusable functionality as possible, so that Solution Assembly teams are only engineering for truly unique needs. The deployment process is a configuration and release management task like other forms of software deployment; however the testing requirements might be lower for solutions which implement a minimum amount of customization above the standardized capabilities of the services in inventory.

Solution Assembly – Improve

Since Solution Assembly is a fit-gap process, it naturally leads to an iterative process of improvement. As services in a deployed system are enhanced with new capabilities (data and/or functions) there becomes a natural opportunity to take advantage of those capabilities in existing production solutions or to remove previously defined customization with the capabilities now standardized in the service. Additionally, since the release cycles in an assemble-to-order architecture are reduced end-users will seek to take on less functionality in earlier releases which then necessitate more, shorter releases to achieving a full set of capabilities for a mature solution. The net effect is more frequent, smaller releases which provide the "completed" application in a shorter overall time frame.

SOA for Solution Assembly fits naturally with agile and spiral development techniques like Extreme Programming. The more comprehensive the service inventory and stable the service infrastructure, the better agile / spiral development techniques work. It is even possible to create what we call "throwaway applications", where a Solution Assembly team works with an end-user to create a production solution with a life span of a few days or so to do things like unique business analytics (such as an audit) or to support a short-term change in a business processes (for instance created by an unsuspected supply or demand problem).

"Crawl, Walk, Run" ... the SOA Maturity Model

As we have discussed time and again throughout this chapter, you won't likely be able or want to move to an SOA, assemble-to-order manufacturing model in one step. Instead, an incremental approach will most often work best.

What we have discovered is that a "crawl, walk, run" evolutionary model which is based on achieving phased maturity milestones is the most reliable way to adopt SOA. Figure 2.19 graphically describes the maturity model.

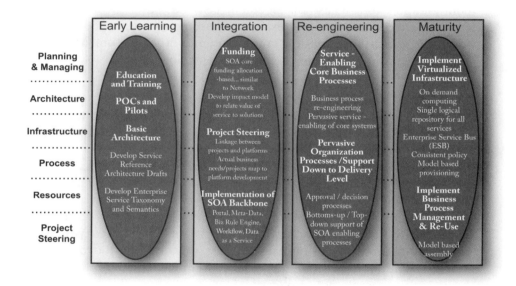

Figure 2.19 Phases of a SOA deployment roadmap. Source CBDI Forum

The phases of the maturity model include:

- Early Learning
- Re-engineering
- Integration
- Maturity

The remainder of the chapter will cover the key deliverables, transitions as well as associated entrance and exit criteria for each maturity phase.

Early Learning

In the early learning phase is where an organization begins the journey to adopt SOA. During this phase is where the Enterprise Architecture function is founded and staffed with the leaders of the SOA definition and adoption program. Also, small cores of service procurement and operations resources are assembled. In Early Learning is where the first revision of the service taxonomy, roadmap, and foundational architecture decisions are made. Success metrics are defined along with a working financial model to project the investments and associated financial returns expected from the SOA roadmap. Finally, in early learning an appropriate number of hands-on proof-of-concept and pilot projects should be completed to demonstrate the viability of the services, service infrastructure, and associated architecture. As part of these pilot projects, documentation regarding key learnings and shifts in operational policy should be delivered to the organization in preparation for the ramp into the Re-engineering phase.

Re-engineering

Re-engineering is the phase where the SOA adoption roadmap gets out of the lab an into the software factory. At this point the Enterprise Architecture team will have completed the definition of the first generation services inventory, the architecture for the services infrastructure, and have defined an approved roadmap for solution adoption. The starting team of Service Procurement and Operations will have established a "pilot light" of services and infrastructure that provide real working examples for additional engineering and project manager resources to handle and understand the shift to SOA. During re-engineering a shift of resources from the built-to-order or made-for-order teams will migrate to the Service Procurement, Operations and Service Assembly teams. At this point there should a number of production solution development projects underway which leverage the services inventory and infrastructure to deliver the application functionality. During re-engineering the beach-head of the assemble-to-order software factory is definitively established.

Integration

Once re-engineering is completed, the integration phase will begin. Integration starts when a mature service inventory and infrastructure is established and the first phase of identified solutions on the Enterprise Architecture roadmap have transitioned to SOA. The Enterprise Architecture and Service Procurement teams are fully established and at a reasonably mature state of operation. At this point, multiple and simultaneous teams will address the remaining targeted business domains on the roadmap and initiate the transition to SOA. Integration will involve continuous improvement to the service inventory and infrastructure as well as a substantial rise in the Solution Assembly and Operations teams. At this point, the established metrics and associated communications processes should be driving adjustments to the future roadmap.

Maturity

Once re-engineering and integration phases are completed, then you enter the maturity phase of the roadmap. Maturity is a state where that the material defined aspects of the service inventory, infrastructure and organizational shifts are completed and work going forward is primarily focused on continuous improvement from the foundation established by the Integration phase. At this point the full shift to an assemble-to-order manufacturing model is completed.

It is important to pace technology investments, organizational shifts and new funding/reward policies in alignment with one another. You do not want to be crawling in one area while running in another ... doing so will cause you to trip in the execution of the SOA transition.

Summary

- More than just a technology investment, SOA is an investment in your organization to create a "software factory"—providing an assemble-to-order manufacturing model enabling rapid creation of business solutions.

- Retooling the organization for SOA is necessary to be able to effectively build a reusable portfolio of software assets, as line-of-business application oriented organizational structures have insufficient funding and incentive structures to create these common assets.

- Organizing for SOA creates a forward thinking and agile organization structure that matches the agility benefits inherent in the technology of SOA.

- To successfully implement, the four main organizational functions of Enterprise Architecture, Service Procurement, Operations, and Solution Assembly need to be established.

- Implement a phased adoption roadmap based on a "Crawl, Walk, Run" methodology where you incrementally make aligned investments in technology, organizational roles, and new investment policies.

Chapter 3

SOA Technology Concepts

Technology is dominated by two types of people: those who understand what they do not manage, and those who manage what they do not understand.

—Putt's Law

Software complexity is a zero-sum game. Core software logic can be moved around and shifted, but never eliminated. Any real reduction in software complexity results in reduced functionality or ability. To be sure, we are making an idealistic statement here and assuming that software, either within the data center or at an ISV, is written with a baseline amount of efficiency and reasonable design choices. This being the case, the goal of any new computing paradigm is to provide flexibility and malleability of software resources (programs and infrastructure) to bring about increased business value. This can be done by reducing the periphery costs of software. This includes everything but the initial development: the maintenance, repurposing, extensibility, and malleability of software. In essence, this represents the new computing paradigm's ability to adapt to changing business circumstances easily and efficiently. This is part of the promise of SOA, but there is always a question of *degree*—is it prudent to rip and replace every asset in the data center with a "service oriented equivalent?" Is there enough value in just using SOA for integrating applications in a piecewise manner? Precisely where does SOA reach the golden mean of efficiency?

These are no doubt difficult questions, and to reach an answer we will build on the core assumptions put forth in Chapter 1, specifically the idea that the value of SOA *begins* with XML. We will move from XML to the general technology trend which we call *decoupling;* the authors believe this underlying theme bounds the scope of the more detailed technological investments described in Chapter 4. It should give the reader an idea of how to gauge just how much value SOA will bring to an organization, whether it be an ISV or IT data center. As you shall see, decoupling leads directly to some of the open questions about SOA, specifically the value and feasibility of *service reuse*, *loose coupling*, and the balance of between SOA as an integration mechanism or pure software design paradigm. This chapter also develops the idea of SOA as a *universal communications tunnel,* which drives many of the actual technology investments, especially around SOA security and messaging, described further in Chapter 4. Along with fundamental concepts, this chapter also introduces some of the prevalent SOA myths and gives a big picture view of one of the central holistic concepts we present for heterogeneous software architectures, which we call *big bus, little bus*. At the end of the day, as clear and elegant as SOA seems, it still has to bring about value in world of mixed technology stacks, and is still subject to performance and QoS (Quality of Service) concerns.

Dumb Clients, Smart Data

It can be argued that the precursor to XML-based SOA is the gradual trend of *decoupling* within the context of distributed software. There are two types of decoupling to mention here: *functional decoupling* and *interface decoupling*. As a side note, when SOA is described as "loosely coupled," this generally refers to *interface decoupling*. Some authors (Krafzig, Banke, Slama, 2005) describe *interface decoupling* with two terms that describe each end of the spectrum. When the messages bear the function to be executed, they call this *payload semantics* and when interfaces are bound at compile time, they call this *interface semantics*. The entire issue of *interface decoupling* is key to a conceptual understanding of SOA. We will explore this notion further in this chapter to clarify our meaning. In short, both types of *decoupling* trends have a profound impact on how SOA is implemented and the value it ultimately provides

The term *functional decoupling* is the separation of generalized software functions away from traditional clients or software systems *into* the communication path itself. Examples of *functional decoupling* include the gradual blurring of traditional network and application boundaries. For example, by taking a historical perspective, we can follow examples of IP routing becoming decoupled from servers into the network, SSL/TLS functionality becoming decoupled from web servers into purpose-built appliances (SSL accelerators), and even XML processing itself moving away from application servers into purpose-built software or appliances (XML Accelerators). In each of these examples some piece of generalized functionality has broken away from software in the traditional sense and moved closer to the communication path, blurring the line between the network and the application itself.

The term *interface decoupling* is part of a larger trend of *data-driven software design*. It refers to the movement of function calls into the data itself. That is, interfaces used for distributed communication between software systems would become more generic and the specific functions to be executed would be represented *in* the data itself. In this case, we are talking about function call representations, complete with arguments and data types, specified within an XML document that participates in a service-oriented exchange, rather than specified at the endpoints and bound at compile time. As mentioned previously, this type of decoupling is related to data-driven software, where the data itself (and in this case, usually XML) is becoming ever richer, while the clients themselves are becoming less complex. To be sure, because software complexity is a zero-sum game, the problem is moved away from the *software* into the *data* itself—the overall system-wide view didn't actually become simpler; the complexity was just moved.

If we then combine this with *functional decoupling* where we can generalize functions away from the client software, we can have software systems that can now in effect be *shielded* from many of the traditional software problems, such as maintenance, repurposing, extensibility, and malleability.

A Human Communication Example

Communication between distributed software or computer networks is often modeled after intuitive human-to-human communication. For example, basic concepts in computer networking like *sending messages, receiving messages, requesting a message, responding to a message*, and ideas like the *communication handshake* are all based on human-centric models. If this is the case, what does the communication model look like after we apply the ideas of *decoupling?* To get there, we need to examine in some detail the breadth of communication schemes used today. We will move from this heterogeneity to a simple human-centric communication scheme that underlies the promise of SOA.

Figure 3.1 shows an idealized "universal server" that communicates through different network ports and different transport middleware, all at different levels of *interface decoupling* depending on who is listening on the other end. This is an idealized example because many more variables could be mentioned, such as message exchange patterns (synchronous or asynchronous) and reliable application-level message delivery. Further, this depiction only shows one side of the communication. The reader will instantly recognize the universal server is simply an off-the-shelf replica of any standard operating system (this could also be thought of as a "universal client," depending on the orientation of the communication).

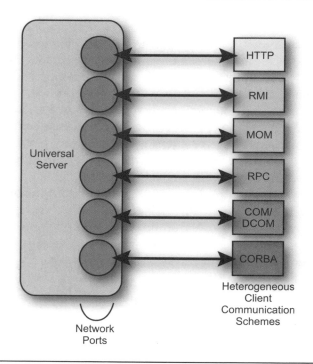

Figure 3.1   The Universal Server Concept

Figure 3.1 introduces a large number of new acronyms that demand some explanation. On the right side of the figure are heterogeneous client communication schemes, identified by common acronyms that place them in the context of specific distributed computing technologies. Generally a *client communication scheme* as shown in Figure 3.1 is comprised of three general parts: a commonly used communication port, a transport protocol structure, and the placement or treatment of the *operation* or *function* being requested or invoked (its level of interface decoupling). In some cases, the communication port can overlap for each of these services, but we will leave out this additional fact for the sake of brevity.

The salient details of each of the distributed computing technologies shown in Figure 3.1 are as follows:

■ HTTP (Hypertext Transport Protocol): Stateless, request/response protocol generally run over port 80 with functions represented in the payload such as GET and POST. No compile-time dependencies on the endpoints.

■ RMI (Java Remote Method Invocation): Distributed remote procedure calls with object support. Generally runs over a configurable port using a wire level stream protocol called JRMP or Internet Inter-ORB Protocol (IIOP). Function interfaces must be bound and defined at compile time.

■ MOM (Message Oriented Middleware): This wide technology category includes messaging and queuing technologies, mostly based on asynchronous delivery of messages between applications. Runs over configurable ports and messages have a high degree of interface decoupling; That is, the messages themselves have no compile time dependencies, although MOM implementations require homogeneity of technology on both sides to work properly.

■ RPC (Remote Procedure Call): Scheme for invoking functions remotely using a blocking (request/response) paradigm. RPC runs over a configurable port, and function interfaces must be bound and defined at compile time.

■ COM/DCOM (Distributed Component Object Model): Object-oriented remote procedure call (RPC) mechanism. DCOM generally runs over port 135 and requires compile-time binding of object interfaces.

■ CORBA (Common Object Request Broker Architecture): Distributed object architecture based on a common, programming-language–neutral IDL (interface definitions language). Communication between servers and clients is done over IIOP (Internet Inter-ORD Protocol) using a configurable port based on the CORBA object reference.

The important points you should keep in mind for each of these schemes include the communication port, the transport protocol structure, and the level of interface decoupling used. You should also keep in mind that Figure 3.1 is not a comprehensive list of distributed computing technology, just a sampling of common schemes found within a data center or ISV. Table 3.1 summarizes the three variables for each of the three distributed computing schemes.

Table 3.1 categorizes these technologies across these three variables.

Table 1.3   Distributed Computing Scheme Properties

Scheme	Port	Transport Structure	Interface Decoupling
HTTP	80, Generally	Request / Response	Low
RMI	Variable	Request / Response	High
MOM	Variable	Varied	Low
RPC	Variable	Request/Response	High
COM/DCOM	135	Varied	High
CORBA	Variable	Varied	High

So what is important about Table 3.1 and how does this help us understand SOA? First, let's make a primary assumption that a real-world data center or ISV actually deals with this heterogeneity of communication schemes—perhaps not all of them, but a significant subset. Next, let's return to our human communication model we alluded to earlier, which ultimately appears to be a useful model for communication in computing. What would human communication look like if we modeled it after this multitude of schemes?

Making SOA Human

Let's take an example of Alice and Charlie, where Alice wishes to tell Charlie to run three errands, pick up milk from the store, take the clothes to the dry cleaner's, and take the dog to the vet. In human terms, we communicate over a single *port* and the functions or operations are self-contained *completely* within the data (or message itself). If we formalize this interaction the way it occurs today, we can break it down into the following steps:

1. Alice: < *Gets Charlie's attention, usually with body language and name declaration* >
2. Alice: <*Begins speaking, using a common language*>
3. Alice: "Go to the store and get milk."
4. Alice: "Take the clothes to the dry cleaner's."
5. Alice: "Take the dog to the vet."
6. Alice: < *Awaits acknowledgement* >
7. Charlie: "OK."

Surely there is more to formalize in the previous example, like error handling (what if Charlie yells "no" in the middle), or intermediate acknowledgments but this set of steps roughly matches a basic human interaction. Let's look at this same interaction and apply the assumption about heterogeneity of communication schemes and see *why* the existing situation in a data center or ISV is overly complex. Let's assume Alice and Charlie communicate over three different communication schemes, one resembling HTTP, one resembling RPC or RMI, and one resembling CORBA or COM. Further, for the purposes of the example, let's assign one scheme to each of the three distinct commands Alice gives Charlie. That is, we'll use HTTP for the milk request, RMI/RPC for the dry cleaner's and CORBA for the dog. To be sure, we are not going to follow the protocol specifications here, just the basic ideas behind each interaction.

1. Alice: < *Opens a communications path with Charlie on specific port 80* >
2. Alice: < *Sends the equivalent of an HTTP GET message to Charlie, with the milk being specified (somehow) in the request header* >
3. Charlie: < *Sends an OK response back to Alice, then stops talking to her (closes port)* >

   (Notice now that if Alice wishes to use RPC for her next request, she must meet with Charlie and define the TakeClothes() function, which ostensibly must be bound to each side a priori.)

4. Alice: < *Runs a program that calls the TakeClothes() function using two arguments: the clothes to take, and the dry cleaner's to which Charlie must take them.* >

   (Notice that if she decides she'd actually rather have Charlie take the car for a wash, this would have to be a different function.

Also—Charlie is also probably using a different communication port here as well.)

5. Charlie: < *Receives request of invoked function (returns true, perhaps) and takes clothes to the dry cleaner's* >

(Next, to use a distributed technology like CORBA, Charlie would have to create some objects that involve the dog, the veterinarian, and some action to relate them together as in Charlie driving the Dog to the Veterinarian. Let's say there is a member function on Charlie himself that Alice calls to accomplish this. Again, if Alice wished for Charlie to do something else, this would also have to be defined using some set of objects as well.)

6. Alice: < *Find out how to get access to the Charlie "object," get remote object reference* >

7. Alice: < *Create call Charlie.GoToVet(theDog), with the Dog as the argument* >

(Note that Charlie is probably also using a different communication port here as well.)

If the previous example seems bizarre or counterintuitive, this is largely the fault of the varied communication schemes used in practice today. Why can't it all be simpler? The previous example leaves us with some illuminating questions: First, is it more natural to communicate on a port-by-port, function by function basis or by simply using a general communication mechanism over a single port? And second, what is the benefit of tightly coupled interfaces if we are expecting communication to change rapidly?

If human communication is any model to strive for, the concept of a *universal communication tunnel* is what is needed and part of the underlying *value* of SOA, at least in a theoretical sense, is the creation and maintenance of the universal tunnel idea along with rich, self-describing XML data for all distributed communication.

The Universal Tunnel

One way to understand SOA is in terms of a universal communication tunnel built around an accepted set of protocols and standards. That is, we currently have a myriad of protocols and technologies operating over disparate communication ports; why not consolidate this? Is there a compelling reason to have this heterogeneity? Moreover, is there an advantage to the consolidation? The *universal tunnel* concept argues that there is increased business value and a reduction in ongoing software costs with a universal, data-driven distributed application communication scheme.

From a conceptual point of view, the universal tunnel idea is central to the ultimate vision of SOA—the updated picture is shown in Figure 3.2. This is of course an idealization, as vendor lock-in, a myriad of security issues, and legacy concerns will keep the distributed application landscape in a state of heterogeneity for some time to come.

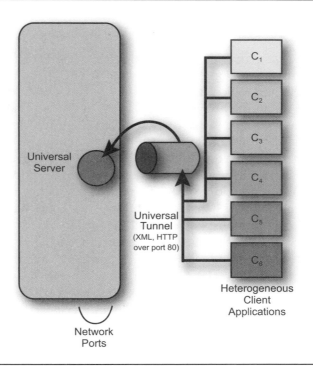

Figure 3.2   The Universal Tunnel

Figure 3.2 shows a disparate number of client applications all using the same communications tunnel. You can think of any protocol or application used in a data center today, whether it is proprietary and custom built or COTS (commercial off-the-shelf software), and imagine it using just *one common communication port* and *data format*. This is the essence of the universal tunnel idea. As more services are built and exposed and more vendors offer web services interfaces to their software, the need to disambiguate between communication ports will decrease—why not just one port and one common format for all interactions? This of course frames some of the most important problems with widespread SOA adoption, which include *security, performance,* and *manageability*. Many of the issues that bound the applicability and success of SOA can be derived from the universal tunnel model and we will spend a good deal of time examining technology investments required due to this new vision of distributed software.

Service Reuse

Reuse is an overloaded term in the context of SOA, and as such, it demands a thorough explanation. If we step back from SOA for a moment and look at the landscape of proponents and opponents, we will find that most proponents of SOA show its value by touting some argument around *service reuse*. That is, one should implement an SOA over some other ostensibly alternative technology because an SOA saves money over the long term and one way this is accomplished is through the reuse of services. This general statement, however, requires a great deal of clarification, and like many statements that ride the fine line between business and technology, this one has shades of meaning depending on the specific stakeholder.

To start, there are two divergent arguments around *reuse* within the context of SOA: a business argument and a technical argument. Moreover, within these arguments, even further dissension exists. This confusion around an allegedly simple term like *software reuse* is a symptom of different, traditionally conflicting stakeholders looking at the value of SOA from different perspectives. The two arguments we will discuss here include *reuse as business agility* and *reuse as software reuse*. Because this is a chapter focused on technology, we will spend most of the time explaining the concepts around *software reuse* as the first argument tends to pull us away from technology and into business process discussions. As we will see, *reuse as software reuse* will be described in relation to four important concepts around reuse within SOA: *static binding, dynamic binding, opaque services,* and *data-dependent services.*

Reuse and Business Agility

Most business-level stakeholders look at reuse from a top-down perspective in terms of a *dynamic business process*. That is, the value of the SOA is the fact that a business process is configurable and is merely an expression of a different set of uses over relatively static enterprise services. For example, a business process comes into existence, uses *services* as part of a workflow or orchestration, and then ultimately dies or morphs into a new process. The hope here is that this dynamic business process can change along with the needs of the business—the business and the technology layers need not be "tightly coupled." This, of course, is the idealized approach. The reality of this *reuse as business agility* argument is that it is heavily dependent upon organizational aspects of the business—that is, services are not shared cleanly or even shareable across different business units, and technology aside, political bickering may prevent services from being shared at all.

An example of this type of business agility can be conceived if we return to the online bookstore example from Chapter 1. Figure 3.3 shows a fictional business process for an online bookseller and some possible *web service* calls that the online bookstore might make if they were designed around an XML-based SOA. For the sake of brevity, exception conditions or error cases are not shown, just the positive sunny-day case for the workflow; you should assume that each response or step in the workflow reaches a successful outcome.

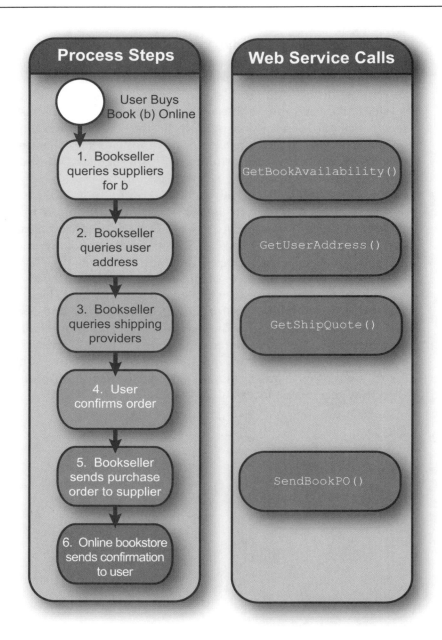

Figure 3.3   A Sample Online Bookstore Business Process

In Figure 3.3, we can summarize each of the six steps as follows:

1. It is assumed that the user has sent a query for a specific book, *b* through a web interface. At this stage, the online bookseller *may* use a web service call to check with its suppliers to determine whether the book is available, and at what price and condition (if used books are part of the query).

2. The online bookseller queries the address of the current user who is identified through some local authenticated session. Here the online bookseller may use a web service call to get the address of a specific user.

3. The online bookseller would use information about the destination address and number of books ordered to query various shipping providers for a shipping quote. In this step, the online bookseller may use a web service call to obtain a shipping quote.

4. The user confirms the order based on the selection of a shipping method.

5. The online bookstore sends the purchase order to the supplier with information on where to ship the book and through which shipping provider. This could be done with a web service interface between the bookstore and the chosen supplier.

6. The online bookstore receives confirmation from the supplier and sends a confirmation e-mail to the user.

The process flow depicted in Figure 3.3 is a basic one, but it illustrates a very important point about XML web services in the context of SOA: a one-to-one mapping between process actions and web service calls doesn't necessarily exist. That is, it may be possible to augment the process flow on the left side of Figure 3.3 to bring about increased business value, while keeping the core services on the right side of Figure 3.3 static, or simply used in a new way. This can be best illustrated by considering a change in the business context. For instance, if we assume that the bookstore is looking to capitalize on current external factors we might assume a scenario as follows: perhaps it is around the holiday season and a significant number of books have been overprinted and there is extra supply. One way a business could merge these two events into a profitable plan would be to offer a limited-time-only gift program for customers who happen to have purchased the books that are currently in oversupply. To implement this, the bookseller could ask the customer for the name and address of a friend that they would like to have the oversupply book sent to. That is, we could envision a new business process step that adds to business agility and business value, but simply *reuses* an existing web service call. This example is shown in Figure 3.4.

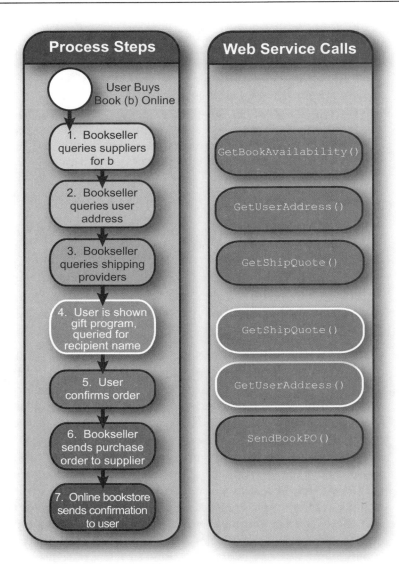

Figure 3.4 Modified Online Bookstore Business Process

The main difference between Figure 3.4 and Figure 3.3 is the additional of a new process step, called the *gift program*, shown in bold. In this step, the user is given the option of sending a copy of one (or more) of the books as a gift to an identified recipient. Perhaps the recipient is already part of the online bookstore's local database and the address can be queried locally based on a customer name or first and last name. Further, the gift recipient's address must also be factored in to the shipping quote with a second or an update query to shipping providers. In this case, the technology is helping to meet the changing needs of business: the bookstore can capitalize on its oversupply problem in conjunction with external factors such as high demand in the holiday season to quickly adapt and overcome external business factors.

You should notice that the idea behind this sort of reuse with an SOA is the fact that the services are static (or mostly so) and only really used in new ways. The reality of this type of business agility is that in fact new code and new logic must be integrated into the overall architecture and design of the augmented gift program option— it isn't *pure* reuse where an instant connection between a new business landscape and a new set of services is instantly re-orchestrated. The services are an important architectural component, but they don't define the totality of the software architecture for the online bookstore—many other systems such as databases, security stores, web servers, transaction support, and a myriad of other considerations are left out of this scenario. The purpose of this example is to show how *service reuse* is conceived by the business-level stakeholder in the context of an XML-based SOA. The next section on *reuse as software reuse* tries to consider the reuse concept from the technical stakeholder's viewpoint.

Software Reuse

In this section we consider some of the technical concepts surrounding the reuse of web services. There is no consensus about the value of *software reuse* in general. Some point out that software reuse is a noble goal, but in practice intractable. This section describes some of the common objections to service reuse and then gives the reader conceptual tools to understand the limits of service reuse. To clarify, we are using the word *software reuse* to speak of the general problem of software reuse and *service reuse* as specific to SOA. As mentioned previously, we will use the four concepts of static binding, dynamic binding, opaque services, and data-driven services to understand the landscape for service reuse. We will begin, however, with an initial example for SOA that casts the concept of *service reuse* in a new light based on the idea of "reuse as use."

Reuse as Use

Imagine for a moment that you are going to invoke a web service that is part of some service oriented architecture. If we follow the normal set of steps, you might envision something as follows:

1. A search through a centralized directory of services for a particular *service description*

2. Consumption of the *service metadata,* which includes the totality of information about the service such as the policies, description, interface and functionality description (recall this from Chapter 1)

3. Invocation of the service itself based on the *information model* and *behavior model.*

The third step may involve building stub code as well as the actual code to properly call the service itself. This set of steps is the sunny-day, idealistic scenario for web service invocation, and, if each step goes without a hitch, would it be correct to say the service was *used* or *reused?* That is, the problem with the term *reuse* for SOA and web services is that it is wholly *pessimistic.* Clearly, there is no difference between *use* and *reuse* for web services. The normal case doesn't make the distinction between a service meant to be used or reused—the service simply exists *to be* used.

This means that *reuse* is part of what it means to be a service in an SOA; if this wasn't the case, the defining components of the service, including the *service metadata* wouldn't mean very much and every service invocation would mean a human-centric *a priori* meeting between the service provider and service consumer. To reiterate the point here, part of the nature of service oriented architecture is to collapse *use* and *reuse* together, so the proper question isn't the positive one, namely *how do I make my services reusable?* Instead, it makes more sense when framed in the negative form: *what practical factors prevent my services from actually being reused?* Note that the term *reused* here just means used widely, or used by more than a few consumers. Fundamentally, services are conceptually designed from the ground up to equate *use* and *reuse* as one and the same thing. The main purpose, then, of the next four sections is to outline the practical concepts that affect the reuse of services. The concepts are static binding, dynamic binding, opaque services, and data-driven services.

Static Binding

A popular comment regarding software reuse is that it is the Holy Grail for software engineering, and that it is rarely achieved. Our position here is that this argument must be qualified as it is easy to see examples of highly successful, widespread object reuse; one simply has to look at the enormous success of reusable object libraries such as Java or Microsoft .NET. To be sure, thousands of applications have been written against the Java class libraries from open source to commercial software products. Clearly, software reuse is not as elusive as once thought. So what drives this comment about reuse as an elusive target? One must distinguish between reuse in a static context and a dynamic context. That is, software reuse, whether it is object reuse or service reuse, is in fact achievable if we are talking about *statically bound* code, or software bound at *compile time*. The obvious disadvantage here is that if we are reusing software at compile or design time, this doesn't bode well for connecting back to business events, which ostensibly change much faster than one can re-factor software. You should also realize that static binding as referenced here is also related to the concept of *interface decoupling;* that is, if the method call is representing *in* the data itself, there is less dependence on static binding or compiled interfaces. Here we can use the term *effective reuse* which simply means that statically bound components have high reuse potential (as seen in the case of object reuse), but lower effective reuse, which refers to the type of reuse connected to overarching business events. We will use the term effective reuse as distinguished from *actual reuse* throughout this section to distinguish between reuse as it applies to changing business and reuse as it actually happens.

Dynamic Binding

It seems as if the comment about reuse being a Holy Grail is really referring to dynamically bound objects or services; that is, the ability to search for available services and bind to the interfaces in real time as the result of a decision reached within a specific business process. To be sure, this type of reuse is much harder to obtain in practice, but it is highly desirable for business.

Why is dynamic reuse an elusive goal for software and services in general? There are many positions to take on this, but the two main arguments in this area are the *search-and-distinguish problem* and what we will term the *clairvoyance argument*. The search and distinguish problem is the obvious problem of searching for a service in real time and dealing with multiple "hits" or results, specifically with deciding between services that promise to offer access to the same underlying capability. If we assume that we are to artificially constrain the list of hits and only return one, then the "search" mechanism isn't really what is being offered, but instead a return to static binding with a closed set of choices, which may as well be bound statically based on decision logic. The related problem here is ensuring that the *service metadata* is accurate and even consumable (processable) in real time, including the totality of the interface definitions, message exchange patterns and proper policies for correct service invocation. Because of the real-time nature of dynamic binding, there is no second chance if there is a mismatch between what the service advertises and what it actually provides, especially with regards to operational metrics, such as advertised response times and service-level agreements.

The second argument is the clairvoyance argument, which refers to the inability to predict the future with service interfaces and capabilities. That is, one cannot predict the future use of a service with perfect clarity, and for dynamic real-time binding, perfect clarity is required. This means that a given service with set interfaces is only guaranteed to be usable by those that can meet the interface requirements. If a new potential web service consumer comes about that has its input data in just a slightly different form, it will be unable to call the interface as it stands, and due to business constraints, it may not be cost-effective or feasible for that caller to match the interface contract.

These aspects give dynamically bound services the properties of *low actual reuse* and *high effective reuse*, which means that in practice service reuse in a dynamic matter doesn't really happen, but there would be great benefits if some of these fundamental problems could be overcome.

Opaque Services

An *opaque service* is one that is capable of some sort of generalized processing, divorced from the semantics of the data itself. That is, the service is agnostic to the payload and performs some useful function considering the payload itself arbitrary. Some examples of an opaque service might include a *digital signing service* or a *data transformation service*, where only certain assumptions must be met about the data itself and the capability provided is effectively semantically ignorant of the payload. Given that we are explaining service oriented architecture in the context of XML, many opaque services can be conceived of in XML-centric processing terms. Some examples of XML-based opaque services are described as follows:

- An XML transformation service, based perhaps on XSLT that could be used to mediate between different XML languages

- An XML security service, for digital signature and encryption

- XML routing services that make a decision to move a message to a destination based on preliminary outer routing headers

- A data validation service, such as XML Schema or equivalent

- A persistence or caching service for an opaque data payload

- A web services compliance checking service, for checking the fidelity of message structure

The previous list just contains a few examples of opaque services; many more could be mentioned. The one thing these all have in common is that they are generalized services that can potentially be used by a wide range web service consumers, but because of the general nature, there is less of a chance they will be useful. Therefore, these types of services are termed *high actual reuse* and *low effective reuse.*

Data Driven Services

The term *data-driven service* is used to describe services that encapsulate rich private business logic tightly coupled to a specific process. A concrete example of this would be a booking and billing web service specific to an airline reservation system. In this case, the service has to have very specific knowledge of the format and contents of the identity to be booked and billed, as well as access to the reservation and payment systems in very specific ways. Most data-driven services are conceived as private to an enterprise, in the form of internal web services used for application integration. Moreover, the service metadata for this type of service is expected to be highly specific to the business use case, and may use a number of subordinate child services. That is, data-driven services are often composite services tightly wound up in a business process.

The way that data-driven services are described here, they seem to have little potential for *actual reuse* because they are conceived of as specific; in some cases data-driven services involve wrappers over existing legacy systems such as mainframes. Cast in this light *data driven* services within an enterprise are usually instrumental for application integration. In terms of reusability, it would be highly desirable for a booking and billing web service to be reused for, say, a different airline (if the business owns a consortium of airlines), but clearly in practice this would be difficult for reasons just explained. Due to these aspects, we will term data driven services *low actual reuse* and *high effective reuse*. Figure 3.5 shows a visual summary of the four concepts around service reuse for XML based services within the context of an SOA.

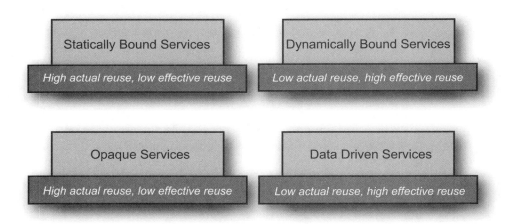

Actual Reuse: *When a service is used, or can be easily used by more than one consumer*

Effective Resuse: *When it matters that a service is used by more than one consumer*

Figure 3.5   Summary of Service Reuse Concepts

SOA: Myths and the Pragmatic Way Out

Service Oriented Architecture has become all things to all people. For people working on distributed computing for a while, it appears like old wine in a new bottle. For Enterprise Application Integration specialists, it (by equating SOA to "Web Services") appears to be the latest way for integrating applications. In order to address these myths, we are going to move from concepts to technologies. First we define *services* in a real-world IT environment, identify the differences vis-à-vis EAI and distributed computing technologies, technologies required to realize SOA, and follow through with an example of a manufacturing company. In Chapter 4, we define the technologies and the gaps that still exist in order to realize SOA in more detail along with the impact of SOA on the infrastructure.

What Exactly Are Services?

In Chapter 1, we provided a definition of *services* based on the OASIS SOA-RM specifications. Now, we will try to define services in a manner that is less conceptual.

The service must do one of the following, or it is not built or acquired as a service:

- It offers operations that can be usefully shared within more than one software solution or business process. Our position is that in order for a service to be shareable in such manner, the service has to be exposed as an XML-based service with the messaging semantics (see section on integration for definition and Chapter 4 ESB Section for details) in the message itself *defined in an interoperable manner and independent of the transport*. Note that this definition does specify SOAP as a wrapper. Further the messaging semantics requirements clearly separate it from the Enterprise Application Integration technologies that were based on MOM (messaging oriented middleware) or pub-sub technologies, with clearly separate channels for messaging semantics (usually tightly coupled with a particular MOM vendor software) and data. We will see the differences more starkly in our definition of the ESB technology and the gaps in the industry.

- It offers operations that can be usefully shared within several higher level services. Our position is that in order to fulfill this requirement the operations *must not* be RPC-style exchange and that the result of operation be in an XML or XML envelope based formats. This requirement separates it from some of the typical usages of older distributed computing technologies where RPC created a tight coupling between the end points.

■ It provides access to operations that can be embedded in variety of UI styles. In order to fulfill this requirement, the operations, in addition to the above requirements, must support event and request-response based models *at the content layer*. This refers back to "smart data" concept introduced in Chapter 1, where the products have to either directly, or after appropriate translation have to dynamically interpret the instruction in the data or its wrapper in order to make appropriate control flow decisions.

■ It brings together information from several sources providing a 360-degree view of a major business resource. This requirement, while it sounds general enough, targets the "coarseness" of a service. The concept of "coarseness" of service is not emphasized enough in discussions on SOA. A service by nature is fairly coarse, orders of magnitude coarser, than say, an object model. So trying to compare SOA to OOA/D is like comparing apples and oranges; both can coexist peacefully. There is a caveat to this statement, however. If by using the "coarseness" argument of an "enterprise service," a software product limits you in the messaging styles, reliability semantics and data format choices. We argue that it is no longer an "enterprise service" but a MOM-based EAI solution with a web services wrapper (which by the way, is a fine thing, just not SOA).

■ It does not require any physical resource (networking, server or storage) required by the service provider to be identified at compile time for the consumer. Any software component that requires any infrastructural element to be identified at consumer compile time, does not qualify to be a service. In fact, we will go as far as stating that any so-called Enterprise Service that disallows the use of an intermediary by creating artificial technology hurdles is not really part of an SOA. SOA should be aiming towards a service-infrastructure–agnostic consumer.

Assuming we have busted some of the myths around SOA, let's move toward a bigger picture.

In Chapter 2, we introduced the concept of types of services and business domains. To expand upon that concept, we can define services as one of four types:

■ Enterprise or Business Service—A widely understood service that identifies a major identifiable process step in the key business processes. For example, a patient health record is an enterprise service for a hospital. Enterprise services usually are accessible across business domains. Following our definitions of characteristics of services earlier in this chapter, in the real world, the business services are likely to be statically bound and slowly changing (or at least not have to be "discovered;" it should be a small enough number in an enterprise identifying key business services).

- Domain Service—A service that provides functionality that is relevant to enterprise services but is not necessarily used and understood uniformly will be classified as a domain service. Following up on an enterprise service example, in a manufacturing setting, forecast demand is a core business service that may have limited usage outside of its domain of supply chain. The rate of change of domain services will likely be higher than business services as they will evolve continuously based on business requirements. These services are likely to be dynamically bound.

- Infrastructure or Utility Service—A "translation" service in many domains. For example, translating data from non-XML to XML and vice-versa. This type of service is very close to an opaque service as discussed previously. The infrastructure services are a nice encapsulation of repeatedly requested stateless processing. The rate of change of domain services is likely going to be higher than business services although less than domain services, as they will not evolve necessarily for small changes in business operating processes. These services are likely to be statically bound for performance reasons.

- Wrapper Service—Wrapper services are services created in order to encapsulate past sins—by that we mean wrapping legacy systems that are too expensive to change. Based on our earlier definition of services, it is likely that wrapper services will not past muster as services of a true SOA. However, pragmatists that we are, we acknowledge that wrapper services will continue to be created. However, it is important that they be identified as such, so the gaps in the theory and realization of easily reusable IT assets can be identified and corrected over time. As we discuss in Chapter 4, given the choice between wrapper services and wrapper ESB, we will pick wrapper services as the lesser of two evils.

SOA Reality

Service Oriented Architecture is not about ripping out running software and replacing it with its new version that is "services-enabled." This is a difficult concept to grasp, and is something most software vendors depend upon for selling their latest versions of software. So we will reiterate that SOA cannot be had on a CD-ROM (or a 12-pack CD-ROM for that matter). Just because particular software provides a container to create and host web services, it does not follow that the IT environment is service-oriented. In fact, we will go as far as to say a Service Oriented Architecture can be layered upon the many different kinds of legacy environments as long as some infrastructural components are addressed (see Chapter 4) and certain changes made to the existing infrastructure.

Big Bus, Little Bus

Layering done just to provide a service interface to every application will result in disparate and non-interoperable "services-enabled" islands—an outcome not very different from today's complex mix of messaging and J2EE/.NET islands of applications. A real-world SOA should address this middleware heterogeneity through the right mix of layering and rip-and-replace. This is where the concept of *big bus, little bus* comes into play—we introduce this concept here and expand it in more detail in Chapter 4. As we explore SOA in vertical industry deployments, the big bus, little bus pattern emerges across industries.

The typical example used while discussing SOA from its very beginning is about a service consumer looking into a directory for a service the consumer desired and then dynamically invoking that service through its contract definition. However, in reality, there are some key technical issues with this simplistic view:

1. Semantic Context: There is no easy way to dynamically figure out the semantic context of a service. A SupplierService contract defined in a directory is only useful if the consumer can dynamically find out the real capabilities of the service.

2. Service versioning: Assuming that the semantic context is not important, the consumer has no way of finding out which version of a particular service it needs to bind to.

3. Service composition: A service is likely to be composed of other services. For example, an enterprise service may be composed of parts from several domain services. Or a domain service may be composed of several fine grained services. There is no easy way

to define dynamically which services a particular service is composed off.

4. Transport Binding: While HTTP binding is the most (if not the only) interoperable binding for a service contract, HTTP transport is unreliable. So unless all services reside in identical runtime containers, dynamic transport binding is nearly impossible. And if all services were residing in the same identical runtime container, what is the Enterprise need to move to SOA at all?

5. Data formats: An operation of a service typically will result in some data that needs to be passed to the consumer by value or by reference (for optimization reasons). This data set may be in any format (XML, binary large object, fixed or variable field non-XML, and so on). In order for this data to be processed in a business process runtime environment, you must be able to derive the schema of the data in order to act upon it.

The above are just a few issues as we begin to look at real-world SOA deployments. In order to address these and other issues, in addition to infrastructure solutions and service containers, an overarching IT architecture is needed. In Chapter 4, when we discuss ESB, we describe an IT environment with an architecture based on separation of domains and associated enterprise services, with local domain services orchestrated locally, and enterprise services orchestrated across domains, as illustrated in Figure 3.6. This concept of big bus, little bus, where big bus is designed with intermediaries and little bus is designed with either proxy-based ESB or service container based ESBs is a core building block to an Enterprise SOA environment.

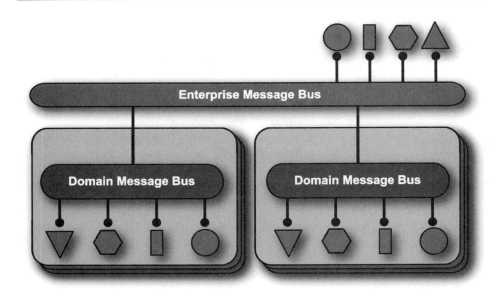

Figure 3.6   Big Bus, Little Bus

Messaging, EAI, and SOA

In the Enterprise IT environment, several usage models require support for different messaging patterns (request-response, publish-subscribe, brokered service, peer-to-peer and queuing), as illustrated in Figure 3.7.

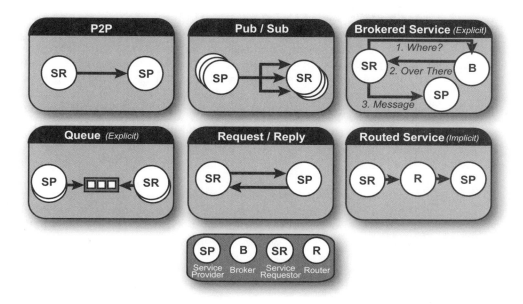

Figure 3.7   Messaging Patterns

Even within a single domain and definitely across domains, the need for multiple messaging patterns and message reliability enforcement is not the same for all services. However, all existing messaging solutions go against the grain of what SOA is expected to deliver for IT by one or more of the following sins of messaging:

1. Tightly coupled addressing: Most MOM (messaging oriented middleware) solutions have addressing tightly coupled in the messaging layer, making systems non-interoperable and not well suited for loosely coupled applications. ESB solutions built on top of legacy MOM solutions have not addressed this problem fully.

2. Lack of intermediary support: Most MOM solutions do not support intermediaries by default. While dealing with legacy applications, intermediary is the only practical possibility for interfacing between service-oriented and non–service-oriented computing. ESB solutions built on top of legacy MOM solutions have not addressed this problem fully. This problem leads to a middleware heterogeneity problem where you have non-compatible MOM implementations, essentially repeating the problem at a higher level.

3. Tightly coupled quality of service: The quality of service attributes (also called *delivery assurances*) such as once-and-only-once delivery, ordered delivery, guaranteed delivery or transactional integrity are today provided through the messaging runtime that enables the service request and response exchange (synchronous or asynchronously), and not as part of the message itself. This static runtime binding of quality of service again hinders usage of services in a reusable and interoperable manner.

4. Network dependency: Some messaging solutions built on UDP packet based networking environments are too tightly coupled to the underlying network capability to allow for any reusability of service outside of that network.

5. Client-code dependency: Most messaging solutions require client libraries to be deployed beforehand at every endpoint that intends to be part of the messaging environment. This makes dynamic consumer addition/modification impossible and does not allow for services exposed through this environment to be dynamically reused.

Messaging requirements are a major reason for inability to realize true SOA. The standards that are currently close to maturity such as OASIS WS-Reliable Messaging do not fully address all messaging directives and leave the implementation details for the vendors, driving features that tie the message to the messaging framework. In the big bus, little bus pattern in Chapter 4, the big bus uses the HTTP based universal tunnel with WS-Reliable Messaging capability that allows for loosely coupled addressing, and network and client-code independence. In this pattern the legacy messaging interoperability problem is diverted to the intra-domain little bus.

Security

To be sure, the topic of SOA security can easily encompass an entire book, and there is good reason to do so: SOA security is portrayed as a major impediment to broad SOA adoption. We treat SOA security in two places in this book: in this section, we give a brief sketch of SOA security at a conceptual level and in Chapter 4 we outline security in a more comprehensive manner. The reader should consider this section a short introduction to some of the deeper issues mentioned in Chapter 4. Our view of security for SOA is pragmatic—we look at security issues for SOA as end-to-end and not in isolation. What this means is that one *must* assume an SOA deployment is going to need to interact with and utilize existing security infrastructure in the data center.

Conceiving SOA security with this assumption highlights some of the main problems with practical SOA security—the need for SOA to fit into to the big bus, little bus concept and the need to interact with legacy systems, especially databases, directories, PKI systems, and other established security processes and policies that aren't SOA enabled (and likely won't ever be).

Our view is that practical SOA security must take into consideration the following seven core concepts: *usability and risk, trust, message level security, transport level security, identity management, security policy, and threats.* Each of these concepts is described briefly here and many are expanded upon further in Chapter 4. In this case, the concepts are phrased as important central questions to be asked of any SOA Security deployment.

1. *Usability and Risk:* This concept is absolutely key; the question here is how SOA security fits with existing assumptions about usability and risk? Usability and risk are connected for secure systems—the more secure a system becomes, the less usable it becomes. This is a fundamental security tenet. These two questions are the most difficult to ask and to get straight answers on: That is, what is the *purpose* of a SOA security technology—does risk decrease with a manageable decrease in usability? Simply put, what is the cost of deploying SOA security and does the new technology actually improve the overall security balance of the system at hand. One should never deploy security technology for the "coolness" factor or for its own sake, but always for some larger gain, or greater balance between risk and usability.

2. *Message Level Security:* SOA systems differ from traditional distributed computing architectures in that they tend to carry more information at the message level, in the messages themselves. This is a result of *decoupling* as described earlier in the chapter—data is getting smarter and clients are getting "dumber," so to speak. What sort of security considerations do the messages have as they traverse multi-hop paths across the big bus?

3. *Transport Level Security:* Given that data is in fact getting smarter, what sort of benefit can be gained from using transport level security (such as tunnel security, either with IPSec or SSL/TLS). When does transport level security break down in an SOA deployment?

4. *Identity Management:* In an SOA deployment, service and human identities tend to be carried along with messages. What sorts of considerations are needed to share these identities across the big-bus or within the little bus? Which standards or technologies can help and which vendors advance interoperable identities?

5. *Security Policy:* SOA security technology must be rationalized with existing security policies, especially with the big bus, little bus assumption where SOA is just a piece of a larger architecture. SOA Security standards permit an XML-based expression of security policies for SOA deployments, but how does this connect to *existing* security policy definitions and to what extent can the two be connected?

6. *Threats:* To what extent does SOA technology expose new attack surface areas? If previously closed systems are opened up with SOA interfaces, how can they be sufficiently protected against possible threats?

This is just a taste of some of the security questions and concepts that SOA brings forth. As we look in detail at the security issues in Chapter 4, keeping in view the big bus, little bus pattern, the transport and message level security is likely to be enforced at the big bus while the threat mitigation and fine grained access control is enforced in the little bus.

Performance

Now let us look at the myths and reality on SOA-based applications infrastructure performance.

This is a fairly complex issue that delves into SOA runtime capabilities and limitations. SOA performance could be impacted by several factors. Starting at the business process orchestration layer, a standard BPEL design that requires service invocation for all process steps can turn out to be a bottleneck. Depending upon the runtime execution engine, it can be extremely slow due to lack of distributed runtime support, blocking service calls, pass-by-value of operational attributes of services even amongst local processes, lack of scaleable multi-threaded support, similar treatment of local and remote services, and so on.

Taking it another level deeper, the performance issues may be due to extremely fine-grained services engineering by overeager developers leading to many layers of several service invocations for each enterprise and domain service. Performance issues at the service creation and composition layer could also be due to inefficient transport binding of services.

Further down the stack are XML technology issues such as parsing, transformation, validation, serialization, and marshalling. The assertions are made (all with some degree of truth) that text XML is too verbose, XML processing such as XSLT transformation (required to transform from XML to any other format using XML stylesheet language) is too slow, and the combination of XML serialization, parsing and marshalling is performance dog. XML processing performance has continued to improve by leaps and bounds over the last few years (open source implementation of Apache XSLTC has doubled in performance over last two years, and other pluggable libraries offer even higher performance) to a point where this is no longer a limiting issue except for the most performance-intensive deployments. The trend toward having thread-safe XML parsing, transformation, and schema validation libraries that work well on multi-core environments is likely going to address the remaining concerns.

To improve the odds of not running into performance woes:

1. Insist on demonstrably scalable (with threads), distributed, and performance oriented business process execution runtime environments.

2. Insist on demonstrably performance-optimized service containers (that, for example, automatically use parameter-by-reference for local services and by-value for remote services). Design coarse grained services—services are not objects!

3. Insist with vendors to provide thread-safe and multi-thread scaleable XML libraries to take the best advantages of additional cores on the servers and improve performance.

4. Selectively use solutions built for performance, especially in inter-domain ESBs (see big bus in Chapter 4) in order to have an infrastructure that can handle unexpected surges yet offer availability.

Quality of Service

Quality of service (QoS) for SOA addresses four functional and non-functional attributes of services such as performance (throughput, response time), reliability, availability, transactions and security. There are several issues in relation to quality of service that are only marginally solved by today's solutions.

1. How to define all aspects of quality of service in a standard manner.

2. How to ensure that the quality of service, once described, is interpreted in a services environment by service consumers and producers in exactly the same way.

3. How to ensure that the changes in the quality of service attributes of a service are propagated through the service consumers and producers that use the service.

4. How to ensure that the quality of service attributes take effect not only at the application layer, but at infrastructure, network, and storage layer so the QoS advertised by a service is actually is deliverable.

For these reasons, the reality of quality of service definition and enforcement in a SOA environment continues to rely heavily on the capability of the runtime environments such as Enterprise Service Bus and service containers. This is also where the risk is the highest of a vendor lock-in and of the architecture moving away from being truly loosely coupled and reusable.

We will discuss how these challenges are being addressed in different vertical markets in later chapters.

Summary

- SOA's use of XML as a technology foundation is fast becoming a universal communications standard, replacing port-based communications used in earlier distributed software methodologies. However, the port-based systems will continue to operate for some time as legacy protocols; any practical SOA deployment must consider the needs to integrate and provide for coexistence of this heterogeneous mix.

- SOA methodology leverages the concept of modular reuse to save time and reduce the complexity of systems by removing redundant components that are effectively "reused" by many systems. Data services provide some of the highest degree of service reusability.

- For any sizable SOA implementation, a "big bus, little bus" concept is a common architectural thread, and is cited in all the large vertical market SOAs that we surveyed. Important points include hierarchy of service busses with local domain semi-autonomy, and the distinction between external and internal services, which adds the proper mix of real-world concerns to an SOA architecture.

■ Traditional "non-functional requirements" like security, performance, and QoS are of prime importance for SOA, especially SOA conceived with XML as a backbone. XML by itself only defines a very high level standard; layers of functionality must be defined on top of it to make an SOA implementation successful.

SOA Technology Infrastructure

"Nothing worth having comes without some kind of fight."

—Bruce Cockburn

The last chapter provided an analysis of the definition and advantages of services, how SOA is similar to and differs from past experiences in IT architectures, and the technology issues that need to be addressed for an IT environment to enjoy the benefits of SOA. Chapter 4 explores specific product categories that help in addressing the technology issues discussed in Chapter 3. These essential plumbing products, if carefully picked to address the nature of business and existing state of the IT environment, can amplify the effectiveness of SOA with an agile and business-responsive infrastructure while providing scalability for growth and well-managed security.

Focus on Enabling the Message

At the infrastructure core of all SOA implementations is the transmission and reception of messages as stateless, self-contained entities. All essential SOA infrastructure is centered on this concept. The best SOA infrastructure implementations make message handling providers and consumers a transparent, almost trivial consideration. Operational simplicity combined with an uncompromising focus on security, manageability, and scale is the ultimate SOA infrastructure objective.

Figure 4.1 provides an illustration of the technical framework required to accomplish the realization of SOA based solutions.

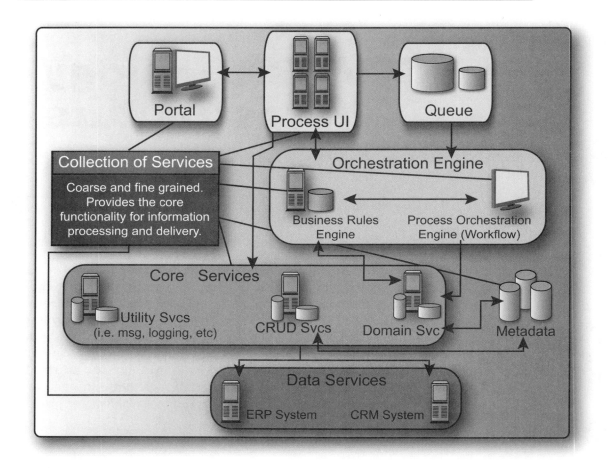

Figure 4.1   The Technical Framework to "Assemble" Services into Solutions

This framework provides a very high level view consisting of core and data services, tied together with standards based process orchestration mechanism that orchestrates the services based on the business rules. In the following sections, we will discuss some of the specifics details within this high-level framework, such as Service creation and composition environment (for creating core services), Enterprise Service

Bus (for composing and orchestrating services), Business Process Management, SOA Security and SOA Management and standards. We will also take a high level view of the implications of SOA adoption in data centers.

Service Creation and Composition

While considering the technology infrastructure for SOA, the first decision has to be the platform for creation of any kinds of services and composing of services in order to realize SOA. Despite the availability of several products in the market that offer to simplify the task of creating and composing services, abstracting the use of these services away from the underlying implementation of the service runtime continues to be a hard goal to achieve.

Most solutions provide a mechanism that can at best be used to create a web services façade to a .NET or J2EE container based applications. For the most part, application server environments available today have a variety of implementations to provide such functionality, but most implementations prove to be non-interoperable and require the user to delve into the J2EE or .NET layer in order to make meaningful services possible. Therefore, while this is an asset to existing J2EE or .NET container deployments that need to expose web services (not to be confused with SOA), we question whether the tightly coupled services environment really provides SOA at the service container level for these reasons.

There are two evolving technologies vying to be a standard means of service creation and composition for .NET and J2EE environments: WCF (Windows Communication Framework) and SCA (Service Component Architecture). Both aim to provide a design time and runtime environment to create services (singular or composite) while offering to manage transactions, state and security based on service contracts and service policies. SCA is still in definitional stages and mature implementations are further out with several technical gaps that have yet to be filled.

Even if careful attention is paid to ensure interoperability while creating and composing services today, given the limited and varying support of WS* standards in various application server stacks, it is unlikely that anything but the simplest of services can be orchestrated in a mixed application server environment. Some precautions in implementations now, however, can provide beneficial over the long run:

■ Always create WSDLs for service contracts. Do not use solutions that cannot read and use WSDLs.

■ Always use WS-Policy and WS-SecurityPolicy implementations even if the final standardization is yet complete.

■ Insist on conformance to WS-I interoperability where possible.

■ Resist working bottom-up on SOA (for example, try and avoid using existing session beans as the directive to help define service contracts. Chapter 2 describes the process to follow to design services from a business perspective).

Strive to use a standard transport binding to services where possible (such as HTTP), and if required to use proprietary binding use proprietary extensions sparingly of each, if at all. For example, most JMS implementations extend the JMS specification, and if extensions are used then the environment is no longer "loosely coupled." The eventual goal is to get to a uniform wire protocol for asynchronous messaging, just like HTTP is there for synchronous request-response.

Please note that in relation to service composition and service orchestration, another three-letter acronym seeks attention: JBI (Java Business Integration). In our view JBI should not be confused with providing a service creation and composition framework or for that matter, an Enterprise Service bus technology (more on this later). JBI is really intended to provide the ability to integrate Java-based components with non-Java environments. Furthermore, in most implementations JBI requires a J2EE Server itself, so its implementation is really going to create a "container of containers."

Enterprise Service Bus

While some sort of a messaging environment with ability to offer standards based integration across heterogeneous applications and networks is critical to realization to SOA, exactly what does and does not constitute an Enterprise Service Bus (ESB) is a contentious issue between the EAI solutions and "ground-up" ESB solution. We are not going to attempt to come up with a standard definition as we do not believe there is one. At this point, let us consider the characteristics of the "plumbing" infrastructure required in order to realize the "universal tunnel" nature of SOA (as described in Chapter 3).

Let us first look at the common features expected from some sort of SOA plumbing, and what the SOA plumbing should provide:

■ Data interoperability: In the definition of Services in Chapter 3, we defined services to be exposed as an XML-based service. So in today's IT environment, with several generations of software in place, data transformation is required from any legacy or XML format to the normalized XML format used by the services environment and vice versa.

■ Messaging interoperability: Continuing from our definition of services in Chapter 3, the XML-based services need to have the messaging semantics in the message itself *defined in an interoperable manner and independent of the transport.* Further, the messaging patterns (request-response, publish-subscribe, brokered service, peer-to-peer, queue) described in Chapter 3 need to be supported. However, legacy applications may not have messaging capability to the extent required, or more likely, have tightly-coupled messaging semantics to the messaging system, such as one vendor's implementation of JMS (and thus non-interoperable with other JMS or other messaging implementations). If you are looking to deploy a product that refers to itself as an ESB, it is essential that it can decouple both the message pattern information and the quality of service information from the specific messaging system the product supports and have it as a part of the message itself. This should be enabled in a real ESB, even if today, due to lack of standardization, it may not be possible to actually move away from a proprietary messaging system embedded in or used by the ESB. Standardized, inexpensive, and ubiquitous messaging is not here today, but if the past is any indication, this is likely to happen sooner rather than later. You may want to design your environment today so that it does not become obsolete in two years.

■ Transport interoperability: The legacy applications in an IT environment are likely to use diverse transport methods such as plain-old TCP/IP sockets, ftp, HTTP, IIOP, SMTP, POP3/IMAP, and so on. The adoption of SOA is unlikely to "rip and replace" what has been working for a long time. Therefore, the SOA plumbing has to support many different transports, mediate between different transports, and be extensible to support the ones it does not support natively.

- Content-based routing: The loosely coupled SOA environment needs a mechanism to be able to change content routing in a runtime environment through configuration changes. Furthermore, the binding of an asynchronous service request or a response to a content route needs to be dynamic and not static. This is only possible, if the content route is not statically bound in all of the messaging patterns except simple synchronous request-response.

- Scalability: The SOA environment needs to be scaleable horizontally and vertically. If more requestors request the same services, the SOA plumbing should be able to support that in a cost-effective manner. If more services need to be made available, the SOA plumbing should be able to provide that effectively as well. The section of this chapter on Service Oriented Infrastructure (SOI) explores the latter and how it relates to the underlying hardware and operating system (the infrastructure under SOA).

- Quality of Service: (reliability, performance, availability, and so on): Enterprise class services, in many cases, demand dependable and predictable Quality of Service (QoS). The QoS level of any given service should be enforceable by the SOA enabling technology. This contract should be in an interoperable, preferably XML-based representation that can be used by a runtime environment while allowing dynamic updates. WS-Policy related standards efforts have made meaningful progress in coming up with a standard representation but in all likelihood products will have to extend the basic quality of service semantics in the standard to be fully useful in an enterprise environment.

- Manageability: Enterprise class services will have to be managed throughout their lifecycle. In some cases, this requirement may be driven by a mix of billing, monitoring, regulatory, and possibly other requirements. This also implies that service contracts and QoS contracts associated with the service need to be managed from design-time to runtime to upgrade and eventual decommissioning.

- Security: A service oriented IT environment within a domain needs to provide access to services and operations with differing security characteristics such as privilege levels for access, authentication, authorization, auditing confidentially, and non-repudiation. If a service is exposed outside a domain, it requires additional protection. Furthermore, if a service is exposed to an external customer (or the World Wide Web in case of some REST-based services available today), it will require added security.

- Core Enterprise Capabilities: Security, logging, caching and monitoring at multiple levels of granularity become critical in an SOA-based IT environment due to business or legal requirements. These capabilities too are part of common SOA plumbing requirements.

So far, we have skirted the issues that divide those who seek to define an ESB. Let us take a closer look now at this issue. Essentially there are three schools of thought on ESB.

The first school of thought states that ESB is nothing but a set of software patterns that need to be supported. So any software that supports those software patterns can be considered an ESB. Typically, this represents the views of the enterprise application integration product vendors who support many if not all of the ESB-like functionality in their hub-and-spoke solutions, although several end users also support this same position.

The second school of thought states that the core of ESB is the messaging bus environment, as opposed to hub-and-spoke, and that this messaging bus environment is the most important (but not the sole) requirement for software to be called an ESB product. This category typically has separate web services management products that collect management events to populate out-of-band management consoles.

The third school of thought maintains that ESB is the "container" for services, and is being a "container" itself is a requirement for software to be called an ESB product. This requirement separates this school of thought from the second, whose products are proxy-based adapters and not service containers. Typically, this category eschews messaging bus as the core requirement, is more closely tied to J2EE, and considers service orchestration as a core requirement of an ESB.

Table 4.1 compares and contrasts these three definitions of an ESB.

Table 4.1   ESB: Differing Definitions

	ESB = Software Patterns++	ESB = Messaging++	ESB = Service Container++
Core components	Hub-and-spoke integration servers	Proxies based adapters, optional brokers and management consoles	Distributed service containers
Platform	.NET or J2EE (usually one) container	Independent	J2EE container
Messaging	Available	Available	External
Transformation	Hub	Proxy	Container
Transport	Hub	Proxy	External
Content-based Routing	Hub	Broker	External
Scalability	Additional hubs		Distributed containers
Quality of Service	Hub	Proxy	Container
Manageability	Management console integrated with hub	Stand-alone management console	Management console integrated with containers
Security	Usually external other than access control	Proxy or broker	Service container
Interoperability	Poor	Poor	External

Containers and Adapters

Containers and adapters adapt software to be used in SOA message-passing environments. Volumes have been written about the attributes and distinction of various frameworks, containers, and adapters. While we won't cover these in detail, it's worthwhile to discuss container and adapter attributes that can either help or hinder an SOA implementation.

Most enterprise SOA implementations strive to provide for interoperability between capabilities from many vendors, and for the integration of custom-developed capabilities as well.

While SOA interoperability is a common goal, it's not endemic to all SOA implementations. Frameworks from many vendors have their roots in Enterprise Application Integration (EAI) technologies that were very popular in the 1990s. In fact, the most robust libraries of adapters that can quickly retrofit an off-the-shelf application to message-based environments were developed by companies that specialized in EAI. Care must be taken to implement SOA infrastructure that enables integration of cross-vendor and locally developed services.

Now that we have discussed the differing views of ESB from the vendor's perspective, let's take a closer look at it based on the organizational and technical issues we have discussed in prior chapters.

Big Bus, Little Bus

We will now assess high level objectives that need to be addressed while architecting an SOA environment using any ESB technology. In Chapter 3, we talked about business domains that need to be identified for services. Figure 4.2 is an example of business domains in a manufacturing focused organization. As identified in Chapter 3, the objective is to create Enterprise Services that have visibility across domains, Domain Services that are relevant to a specific domain and Utility Services that are created to support the Domain and Enterprise services.

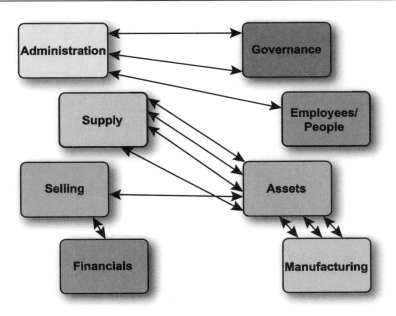

Figure 4.2   Business Domains in a manufacturing focused organization

The domain bus or "little bus" should expose, compose, and orchestrate Domain Services while using Infrastructure and Utility services. The domain bus is likely to engage data-driven services, services that require static binding, and have a set of known service consumers, as shown in Figure 4.3. The domain bus is targeted to address integration issues.

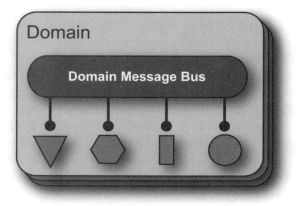

Figure 4.3   Domain Bus or Little Bus

An example of a domain bus or a little bus is shown in Figure 4.4. This is the supply chain management domain in an enterprise.

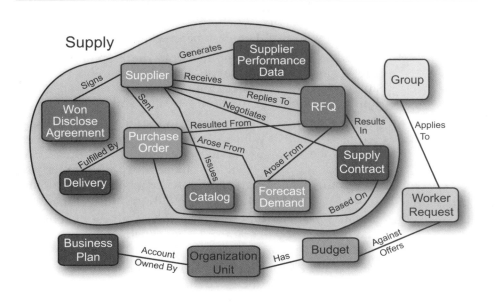

Figure 4.4   Intra-domain SOA

The key characteristics of an intra-domain SOA are:

1. *A range of complexity:* A small intra-domain IT environment could be as simple as having a few .NET servers and exposing tightly bound service instances that can be composed to address domain-level concerns. The other side of this spectrum is a mixed environment over legacy J2EE and .NET servers with multiple messaging patterns and a legacy EAI hub-and-spoke–based messaging environment. Based on complexity of the environment, a suitable solution for intra-domain bus needs to be selected from any of the three options mentioned earlier, based on how much time, effort, and cost are justifiable for a domain-level SOA. The more dynamic the business, the more the investment is justified for rip-and-replace SOA, as the changes can be made in an agile fashion.

2. *Finer-grained services leading to limited loose coupling:* While loose coupling is the goal for intra-domain SOA environments, this benefit is going to have a tradeoff against finer grained services required at the domain level. The fact remains that services exposed at the domain level are going to be more tightly coupled to the underlying legacy environment. This is going to be the situation regardless of what kind of ESB solution is chosen.

However, the domain ESB should be chosen to provide loosely coupled service composition, process orchestration, transformation, and content-based routing.

3. *Limited security requirements:* As the intra-domain service bus, the requirements for security are likely going to be limited to authentication, authorization, access control, and auditing with limited requirement for confidentiality and non-repudiation.

4. *Static binding:* Any major changes in the business processes required within a domain are going to in turn require changes at the service level (as services are going to be finer-grained), and therefore in turn require changes to the underlying legacy environment. So there may not be enough return in terms of reuse for investing in directory solutions at the intra-domain level.

5. *State awareness:* Within a domain bus, the service message state may have to be recognized and capabilities such as two-phase commit provided.

6. *Complex composition and orchestration:* The service composition and process orchestration can be fairly complex and have significant business logic coupled in the composition and orchestration.

7. *The bridging of disparate technologies:* The intra-domain ESB, regardless of how it is realized, should be able to easily bridge disparate systems based on any programming language, supporting any transport, and with disparate messaging mechanisms.

8. *Known messaging patterns:* The messaging patterns at the domain level are well-defined and the changes are likely to be planned in advance. An ESB solution for a particular domain, therefore, needs to support the messaging patterns required, and be extensible to support additional patterns as needed.

As opposed to the domain bus, the enterprise bus, or "big bus," bridges domains (Figure 4.5) and has some specialized requirements that different from the little bus.

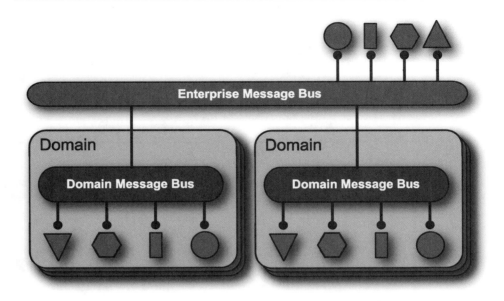

Figure 4.5   Enterprise Bus or Big Bus

The primary requirements from the big bus environment are:

- Orchestrates enterprise services that are coarse grained and useful across domains; for example, from the supply chain domain depicted in Figure 4.4, the enterprise services for purchase order, supplier, RFQ, contract, requisition, and demand forecasting, shown in Figure 4.6.

- Acts as a message router

- Is loosely-coupled (ambivalent to business document schema)

- Only interrogates message header/properties

- Should not implement any business (domain) logic

- Has stateless messages

- Is able to integrate enterprise class capabilities (service virtualization, logging, caching, security, monitoring, and so on)

- Bridges domains

- Has transport/protocol switching

- Scales horizontally and vertically to meet changing demand

- Is ambivalent to business document (message body), adding value to messages regardless of content

- Maintains contract driven communication between service and consumer

- Has a flexible architecture that can expand and contract without breaking a contract

- Supports the dynamic addition of consumers

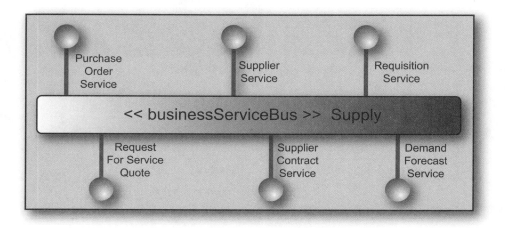

Figure 4.6   Big Bus Orchestrates Enterprise Services[1].

The big bus and the little bus environments work together to deliver enterprise scale Service Oriented Architecture, shown in Figure 4.7, where the "tight-coupling" if any, to infrastructure or legacy applications are limited to little bus. The benefits of such an architecture are that it reflects both the reality of IT evolution and organizational structures.

---

[1] Based on the CBDI SOA Maturity Model and Adoption Roadmap methodology

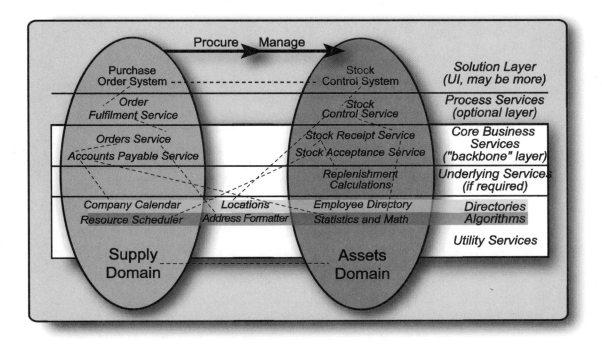

Figure 4.7   Big Bus in Relation to Little Bus.[2]

SOA and Business Process Management

The tangible output of a service oriented IT organization is the automation of business processes by "wiring" each task in a business process to a service that can meet the data and processing needs of that task. The emergence of standards and SOAP XML Web Services architectures creates the opportunity to rapidly implement, monitor, and continually update business processes. These processes often span multiple systems and constituents across the value chain, integrating a corporation's suppliers, customers, and trading partners.

---

[2] Based on the CBDI SOA Maturity Model and Adoption Roadmap methodology

To more concretely describe this association between business processes and SOA services, let's take a simple example, illustrated in Figure 4.8.

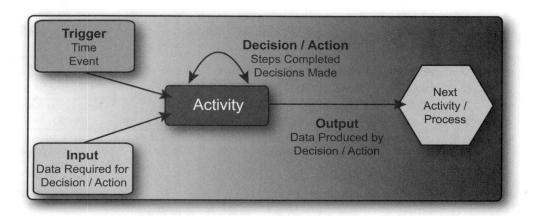

Figure 4.8   Association between Business Process and SOA Service

As Figure 4.8 shows, each activity (or task) in a business process has a trigger, set of input, a decision or action, and an output that can be fed to another activity step or to an entirely new business process.

A specific example of a simple manager approval business process (for things like employee vacations, travel, procurement, awards, and so on) can be found in Figure 4.9.

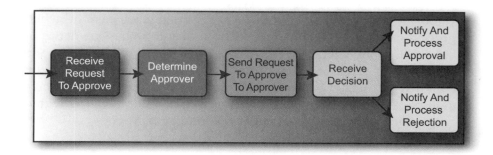

Figure 4.9   A Business Process

In this example, four linear activities branch into one of two sub-processes (approval or rejection).

When implementing this business process with a service oriented architecture, you would acquire services to implement each activity in this business process and then model the triggers, inputs, actions, and outputs in a system workflow that ties the services participating in the business process together. Figure 4.10 describes this modeling activity at a high-level.

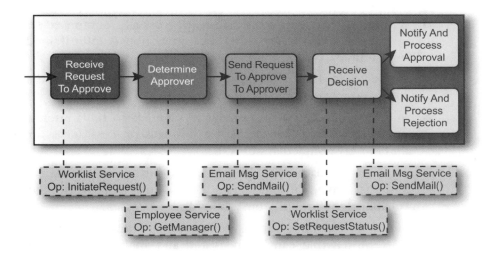

Figure 4.10 A Business Process Using SOA

Business Process Management (BPM) systems provide a suite of tools for the solution assembly organization (as discussed in Chapter 2) to rapidly capture business process requirements at a the process activity level rather than at a systems function level (similar to the diagrams above). BPM makes it easier for business analysts to participate in the development process, ensuring that new applications support business requirements that affect an organization's key performance indicators.

Some key features to look for when selecting a BPM tool set for your enterprise SOA architecture:

■ Supports highly collaborative internal and external business processes capture multidimensional problems to globally connect people, systems, and external events across the value chain.

■ Uses leading standards, like standardized forms of XML, that allow you to model and execute transactions and collaborations between applications and people both within and outside of your enterprise.

■ Manages all aspects of the execution of parallel business processes from beginning to end.

■ Supports the integration of complex, long-running business processes that execute over the course of days, weeks, and months.

■ Supports structuring the business process as a composed set of a sequence of activities using an interactive graphical modeling environment (such as BPEL or UML).

■ Implements data structures using business documents that are managed in a centralized administration repository.

■ Supports effective management of changes to both internal and external systems that support a business process across diverse and loosely coupled systems.

■ Captures all data, including external partner data, that existing systems have difficulty handling. This helps maintain the reliability and integrity of systems and processes.

■ Stores transactional data as documents in a granular, content-rich XML format that can be measured and analyzed in a document state and tested against key performance indicators.

■ Supports an auditing mechanism provides significant "business intelligence" about how to optimize processes over time.

Many BPM systems consist of the following sub-components:

■ *Business Process Modeling/Mapping:* Tools for graphically depicting the activities and flows for AS-IS and TO-BE business processes.

■ *Workflow automation:* Tools for mapping process activities into service interfaces. Also provides the means for notifying end-users of incoming work queues and handles the dispatching of data, tasks, transactions and documents across systems, services, and users.

■ *Business Rules Engine (BRE):* Tools for describing policies (if-then-else/case statements) that drive the decision/action behavior of activities within the business process and/or handle routing or other transaction processing decisions within a business process and associated workflows. BREs provide the means to centralize and catalog rules in a concrete and explicit way for easier change management.

■ *Business Activity Management (BAM):* Tools for monitoring the runtime state of any business process including historical trends on key performance indicators for the process. This allows the continuous improvement of business process to identify things like bottlenecks, unexpected redundant processing, open-loop control scenarios, and so on.

BPM systems can be procured from many different sources. Pure-play integration and ESB vendors provide BPM toolsets as do the major enterprise application vendors like the major ERP suppliers. Whether you go with a best-of-breed, pure-play BPM solution or one that is integrated with the remainder of enterprise application capabilities is the key decision you need to make regarding BPM. As to whether you should invest in BPM when implementing an SOA and when to make that investment, those are much easier questions to answer if you have already made the decision to pursue SOA.

BPM will be the primary toolset for implementing applications by your solution assembly organization (as described in Chapter 2), so it will be one of the very first infrastructure investments that will need to be made once the first set of services in the portfolio is established. As to the question of selecting the best of breed versus integrated application BPM, that will be a decision you make on a case-by-case basis, analyzing the capabilities the vendor offers, their pricing, and terms relative to your requirements and expectations.

SOA Security

The problem of SOA security is cited as one of the great barriers to widespread SOA adoption. This general statement gives the impression that solving security for SOA is contingent upon certain standards and technology, and once these mature we will all begin to reap the benefits of SOA. This makes it seem like the SOA security problem is a lingering pebble in your shoe, and if we could just remove it, SOA would rule the technology world. It would do us well, however, to recognize that *security* is not a small pebble, but a huge rock, and that solving security for SOA is not a binary event, but a complex web of technology and process tradeoffs that cross every level of the technology stack. In this section we will argue that it is more beneficial to think of SOA not as a new technology stack with security vulnerabilities that just need to be patched, but instead in contrary terms: The SOA model and technology stacks highlight and bring forth existing security deficiencies at *all* levels, not just traditional technology areas. In other words, security is not an attribute of SOA as much as it is an attribute of the complete *end-to-end business process* that SOA enables.

The next three sections provide an overview of SOA Security. The first section is a primer on making security practical, especially for SOA. The second section describes SOA trust concepts. The final section is a brief summary of SOA threat concepts. All three sections cover security from a practical standpoint for SOA with the hope that you will have a greater understanding of what security means for your particular usage model.

How Secure Is Secure?

This question is surely a philosophical one. What is the correct way to measure the security of a complex interconnected network with multiple stakeholders, business partners, and possible insider threats? How does one measure and deploy security policy uniformly? Does it boil down to technology choices such as *everyone must use two-factor authentication*, *all web services must be authenticated with digital certificates*, or *all passwords must be rotated every three months?* In truth, no technology choice amounts to increased security without an understanding of the weakest link in the entire system. Further, in some cases, adding additional security layers increases the attack surface area, opening the possibility for new threat vectors that were not before possible. This statement is true for any type of complex system that needs to be secured, whether it is a traditional IT network, a complex SOA deployment, a home alarm system, or locking up your car when you go shopping at the mall. For example, suppose you decide that a certain computer contains sensitive information that you wish to protect, and further, that this computer needs to be protected with *perfect* security. What would be your course of action? You could disconnect the system from any network, and store it in a locked room with an 8-inch' steel door and give the key to the systems administrator. This security model still has two possible attack vectors: (a) the attacker can attack the *key* by picking the lock or attempting to steal the key (and duplicate it) from the administrator, or (b) the attacker can try to break through one of the walls, the floor, or the ceiling. This example illustrates two points about the security of systems in general. The first is the aforementioned *weakest link property*. That is, the attacker only needs to attack the weakest link in the system to get to the computer, and further the *weakest link* is somewhat relative. For instance, if the attacker is an expert locksmith, picking the lock would be easier than breaking down the door, or, if the attacker was an expert at building security, she might be able to determine that the thickness of the walls was less than the 8-inch door and attack the system from this angle. The second point is the relation between usability and security. In general, the more security added to a system, the less usable it becomes. If we look at the example of the computer locked in the room, one way to make it more secure is to remove the door completely and encase the computer in a steel room with no doors. All else being equal, this system is more secure than the similar system *with* the 8-inch steel door because there are less attack vectors (there is no longer a key) but it is surely less usable. In this case, one can argue that the usability of this particular system is near zero. You may be wondering what this contrived thought experiment has to do with SOA security. From a practical standpoint we must be sure not to get carried away with flashy technology-centric security solutions because the weakest link property will *always* trump a specific technology choice.

Usability and Risk

The previous example serves as a reminder that one must consider the breadth of the entire system and then choose an *appropriate* technology to achieve the right amount of required security. Inherent in any security policy choice is the notion of *risk;* what is the risk, or cost of a security breach versus the usability of the system? For example, you may impose a security policy that says that all SOA partner interactions (messages) must be signed and encrypted with a 2048-bit RSA digital signature and 256-bit AES key, with signing keys rotated monthly. If you find, however, that the total value involved in these specific interactions is *smaller* than the cost of implementing and maintaining the policy, then you have entered into a losing proposition and it makes sense to scale back the security to maintain the balance of usability and risk. To be sure, however, some risk is too great to be measured—such as a breach that shows up on the front page of the newspaper—and in these cases the extra security *may* increase the overall value. Strangely enough, however, most security policy is not implemented to fine-tune the overall balance of usability and risk. This is because risk is sometimes very hard to measure, and in many cases it is easier to impose the greater usability burden than to carefully analyze the weakest link in system and go through the trouble of comprehensively balancing risk, usability, and security in a holistic manner. What happens in the practical case is often very different, and security is generally implemented for two reasons that have very little to do with the *actual* security of the network, whether it involves SOA or otherwise. The authors will term these *practical security heuristics.* They are called heuristics for two reasons: (a) because they sometimes increase the security of the system as a whole (but often may not), and (b) because they tend to ignore whether the system is really secure or not.

Standards-based Security Heuristic: This heuristic makes an appeal to a specific technology standard in an attempt to derive security properties from it. For example, a policy that says *all web services must use SSL v3.0, all secure email must use S/MIME, or all SOAP message must use OASIS WS-Security v1.0.* For each of these statements, it is a general appeal to a standard or specification that implies it is secure, but this heuristic ignores the weakest link property. For instance, simply saying that SSL v3.0 must be used may not be secure enough because SSL doesn't scale over multi-hop paths, or saying that SOAP messages must use WS-Security doesn't necessarily mean increased security because WS-Security can be used without encryption or digital signatures. In general, the appeal to a standard or specification is a fallacy if the intent is to increase security, although it may, albeit accidentally, increase the security of a system in general.

Interoperability-based Security Heuristic: This heuristic is similar to the standards based security heuristic, but instead it is based on an external partner communication. This heuristic occurs when one partner decides to impose a particular standard for security, and then this particular standard must be used by all who wish to communicate with that particular entity. To this end, the security standard exists *not* to increase security, but to provide interoperability. One way to test and see if your organization uses the interoperability-based security heuristic is to reflect on security technology choices and ask yourself if any of these exist simply because they were a requirement to interact with a given partner. One contrived example of this would be: *We have to use OASIS WS-Security because if we don't, we can't perform business interactions with partner X.* Here the security standard *may* increase security, but the reason it is chosen is not to increase security, but for the sake of interoperability.

For SOA security it is best not to think in terms of specific technology standards, but instead focus on how the SOA technology stack changes traditional security paradigms. The next two sections focus on how SOA changes two key aspects of distributed computing: trust and threat.

SOA Trust Concepts and Technologies

SOA trust means know how you *trust* a particular SOA interaction. It is about allowing an interaction to take place. The word interaction here could mean a specific message, or a session of messages. In general, trusting a particular message or sessions of messages ties directly back to the identity of the sender and further, how this identity ties to the message itself. This concept of *message-level security* is a pillar in SOA trust and distinguishes SOA security from "web security" where there is a larger separation between the identity of the sender and the interactions themselves.

One way to think about SOA trust concepts is to compare how identities propagate in a traditional *web* exchange versus a SOA or *web services* exchange. In a web exchange, there are two ways in which identities are shared between a client and a server. In the case of server side SSL, the identity of the server is carried in a digital certificate and the identity of the client is generally represented as a user name and password as some part of the HTTP protocol header, either using HTTP basic authentication or overloaded within the query parameters themselves. This is the most basic type of authentication used on the web when logging into secure web mail, or online shopping. In some rare cases, SSL with *mutual authentication* is used, where the client also presents an X.509 certificate (instead of a user name and password), but this is a rare use case as it involves cumbersome certificate management on the client side. This use case is seen within the financial industry for certain high-value interactions.

Message-level Security

We will be using a very specific definition of *message-level security* in this chapter. Message-level security is *data privacy* or *authentication* properties tightly coupled to an atomic web service message, either sent alone or as part of a session. The key property is the tightly coupled nature; a security *statement* is tied to a specific message rather than the session or transport. Without mentioning a particular *standard*, such as

OASIS WS-Security, we can say quite definitively that message level security is not new or revolutionary. There are many different standards or ways in which a given message, whether part of a SOA exchange or not, can be given message level security properties. Examples include signing a PDF document or using a file encryption tool or cryptography toolkit (such as OpenSSL) to encrypt documents or messages before sending them or storing them. So what makes message level security important for SOA? In order to understand further, we examine the history of message level security as it applies to XML, which falls under the topic of XML Security.

XML Security

If you recall Chapter 1, one key technology assumption for SOA is the XML assumption. Consequently, if you wish to understand message-level security for SOA you need to examine two relevant XML Security Standards: XML Signature and XML Encryption. Both of these W3C standards bring together XML and cryptography in a new way; previous to XML Security, digital signatures or encryption was thought of as an all or nothing proposition. That is, documents could be signed or encrypted, but it was best for the operation to be thought of as occurring all at once. What this means is that there is no easy way to sign or encrypt *just* parts or pieces of a document. With XML, however, you can now address just a portion of an XML document as defined by a document subset, or sub-tree. This means that you can have very complex security properties applied to a document, such as partial encryption (some nodes), partial digital signature, or an arbitrary overlap of the two. Another point to be made about XML Encryption is that if you just use a traditional encryption tool (such as OpenSSL) to encrypt the XML document, you will end up with something that is non-XML, a binary octet stream, when the operation is complete. This highlights another important property of XML Security, namely that it is *XML preserving*—the result is still XML, even if the entire document is encrypted.

For digital signatures, XML Signature works in a similar way but has some important differences. First, an XML Signature can also be used selectively; that is, one can sign portions of an XML document and leave others untouched, but the real difference between XML signature and XML Encryption is the *canonicalization* requirement. In short, XML Signature has a required *canonicalization* step that removes syntax differences from XML (such as attribute reordering or line ending changes) that may be introduced inadvertently when XML is nondestructively processed. The business impact of the canonicalization step is that it is very performance-intensive, and on large XML documents, canonicalization may be the most expensive operation overall. In some vertical applications, the cost of canonicalization alone drives the need for purpose-built XML acceleration technology because off-the-shelf or open source software typically performs poorly.

SOAP and OASIS WS-Security

Building from our initial assumptions about XML as a foundational technology for SOA, we are immediately presented with a problem regarding XML Security. That is, the flexibility inherent in these two standards requires more constraints on how they are applied, and further, highlights the need for a security *token* framework. The word token here is a representation of an identity, such as a user name, X.509 certificate, Kerberos ticket, or e-mail address. Why is a *token framework* also required? The reason is because XML Security really just specifies data privacy and message authentication mechanisms with no extensible way of associating identities with keys. This is the basis for WS-Security— it offers a standard way to apply XML Security to web service messages as well as an extensible token framework. For the purposes of this discussion, this is in the context of SOAP (Simple Object Access Protocol), which is a thin XML structure and the main protocol used in XML-based Web Services. Figure 4.11 shows a conceptual view of WS-Security and how it fits within the SOAP protocol, specifically the SOAP *header*.

OASIS WS-Security Example

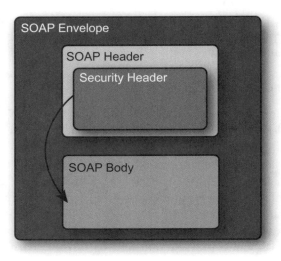

Figure 4.11   OASIS WS-Security Concept Model

In Figure 4.11, you can see that the outermost structure is the SOAP Envelope that contains a header and then a body. Within the header is the *security header* and for OASIS WS-Security, the <Security> element. Within this element is the standard place to put information generally of three types: (a) a representation of the identity coupled with this message (usually the sender)—in the case of SOA, *multiple* identities could be associated with a message, (b) encrypted keys that can be used to decrypt any optionally encrypted portions of the *body* or *header*—in the general case the body is usually encrypted, and (c) Signature blocks that describe which portions of the document are covered by an XML Signature. In this case, the <Security> element would *contain* multiple <Signature> elements, or XML Signature blocks. Finally, OASIS WS-Security allows for any of these items to be optional as well, for example, a SOAP message may carry only an identity, or it may contain only a signature; the exact operations required are contingent upon the security policy for the SOA exchange in question.

So to summarize thus far, we have described *how* messages can be signed and encrypted in a standard way through the use of WS-Security, which ultimately relies on XML Signature and XML Encryption. Further, we have introduced the concept of the identity token bound to the message in the Security header, but we haven't said more about identities just yet. Identity management is a perennial problem in security, especially across disparate domains. In the next section we will introduce the core problem and then reflect on how identities are understood in the context of SOA.

SOA Identity Roles

There are two logical identities in the SOA model: The *service identity* and the *consumer identity*. This mapping holds true for real-world services as well, such as the dry-cleaners, and even partially for the online bookstore. The bookstore knows who you are and you know who the bookstore is. How does the problem of identity relate to SOA when we begin to mix it with message-level security and add in scenarios where messages cross multi-hop paths and interact with different trust domains that may cross identity boundaries?

First you have to realize that our notion of identity is not as clear as we'd like, and most current security technologies that are in place only partially approximate our identities. In the case of the online bookstore, the online bookstore only categorically knows it is talking to someone with a certain user name and password (or possibly, X.509 certificate, in the case of mutual SSL), it doesn't know it's really *you*. This may seem like a trivial distinction, but the problem grows on itself when you move to the SOA model where the service consumer is not a human, but another computer system, and further, there may be multiple such *consumers* within a given domain. To further complicate the problem, you may have delegated identities, or a person that kicks off a string of web services message exchanges. To outline all of the possibilities, we will use a visual identity model that represents three distinct entities on either side of an SOA interaction.

In Figure 4.12, three entities are represented on the service consumer side: the actual consumer (human) triggering the web service call, the system (computer, software) sending the request, and the message itself. Similarly, on the *service provider* side you have the identity in the message, the identity tied to the system, and the identity of the *specific service*. You can think of the identity of the service as one of possibly many services offered by one system or piece of software. You should also note that we've fit the consumer-provider interaction into client-server terms here to simplify the model, although SOA deployments may have each entity playing a dual role.

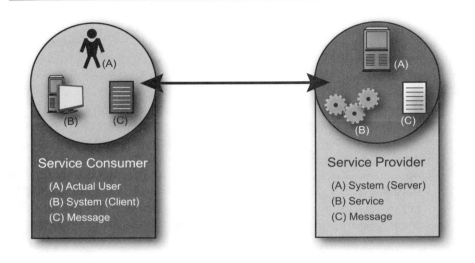

Figure 4.12   Identity Roles in SOA

Given these possibilities, only a few are practical. We will identify four common cases as follows: simple point-to-point, point-to-point with message-level security, simple multi-hop, and multi-hop with message level security.

Simple point-to-point: This model collapses the identities of the many of the entities. A simple point-to-point model recognizes the identity of the system as identical with the identity in the message as well as the human involved, or more precisely, has no need for other identities but the system. In the simple case, a *specific* identity may not be important. For example, consider a business-to-business web service that provides where a supplier provides general pricing information. In this case, all the supplier needs to know is that the request comes from a certain trusted company or partner, the actual *person* making the request is may not be relevant (although we might conceive of a web service that does recognize identities more carefully). This implies the message itself need not carry an identity and further, the fact that it was John Doe or Mary Jane initiating the request is not important either. The *simple point-to-point* model is usually achieved through the use of trusted IP address checks or transport-level security.

Point-to-point with message-level security: This model may have a need to protect information within the message itself or provide audit mechanisms. In this case, some message-level security properties may be required, such as signing outgoing requests, or encrypting sensitive portions of the message. The implication here is that the message, once it reaches its destination, may be stored for some long term purpose. It is extremely important to keep in mind, however, that messages can't be encrypted or signed without a key, and the *identity* tied to the key is what makes the task more difficult. In this model, the signer may still be a private key associated with the *system*, and not a human. Similarly, the encryption key used may belong to the recipient system (in the case of public key encryption), not a *single identity*. This case uses the same identity model of system-to-system interaction, but adds in message level security and authentication operations.

Simple multi-hop: This model generally involves a live human user who kicks off a SOA interaction. Here, the identity of the human may need to be propagated to the service itself; this case is multi-hop because the human interface for a SOA interaction is generally *not* a web service client, but a web browser. One example of *simple multi-hop* may be a Web portal that drives an SOA request through to a back-end web service. This case generally requires the human identity be propagated into the message, but message-level security may not be required for audit or encryption. The simple multi-hop case is similar to the simple point-to-point, but with the addition of the human identity tacked on to the message. There is another type of multi-hop case that is less prevalent, but worth mentioning and that is the case that involves multiple systems (cross enterprise or intra-enterprise) rather than a human to kick-start the process. In this case it is generally useful to identify each service (as well as the domain or computer) using message-level identity tokens as well.

Multi-hop with message-level security: This is the most complex case of them all and is generally seen in multi-hop SOA deployments that require message-level encryption and digital signatures *along with* human (requestor) identities coupled to each message. It is best to think of this case as permissive. That is, with OASIS WS-Security and XML Security, it is possible to achieve multi-hop deployments with message-level security, but generally the design of such systems in a secure way is difficult due to the numerous key management issues that exist across these disparate systems.

You should recognize that within each of these cases, the way the identity is represented, or the *token type,* can vary. Common token types for SOA messages include user-name/password tokens, X.509 certificates, and SAML (Security Assertion Markup Language) assertions. Other token types are available but they are out of scope for our purposes. User name tokens are common with POC or initial SOA deployments because user name and password authentication mechanisms are still by far the most common authentication scheme. Some SOA deployments will use X.509 certificates, especially for cases where documents and messages must be digitally signed, but the drawback here is the key and trust infrastructure required to use X.509 tokens. Many enterprises can use X.509 tokens within the enterprise, but the cross-domain trust problem has prevented X.509 from dominated inter-enterprise message exchange. A newer token type, SAML, is a standard XML structure for identity, attribute, and authorization information. SAML-based technology has been touted as the next major identity paradigm because it ostensibly allows enterprises to share identities in a seamless manner. The critical drawback with SAML, however, is the fact that it doesn't really solve identity mapping; it merely provides a standard structure and protocol for identity information. SAML standardizes a structure, not the identities themselves. This means that a SAML assertion representing John Doe in Enterprise A may actually contain wholly different information than a SAML assertion representing John Doe in Enterprise B. What SAML is used for is identity normalization. That is, identities may enter the edge of an SOA and become *mapped* to a SAML structure for easier handling and possible federation or sharing at a later time. You can think of a logical credential mapping operation that takes a user name, password, X.509 certificate, or custom security token and generates a SAML assertion in some canonical way such that there is a single representation of the identity tied to an SOA message.

As you can see in this short sketch of SOA trust topics, identity management is central to SOA trust concepts, and SOA technologies that introduce message-level security only bring existing identity problems to the forefront.

SOA Trust-related Myths

Because security is a hot topic for SOA, some identity and trust related myths about SOA have evolved due to misunderstanding or marketing "FUD." We will conclude the section with some trust-related SOA myths:

■ *The SSL Myth:* The basic question is whether or not SSL/TLS (RFC 2246) is 'good enough' for SOA security. This is of course a trick question because SOA security, like any sort of security in general, is *relative* to the specific policies and risks within an enterprise. The short answer is that SSL *is* good enough for SOA security if you are (a) dealing only in point-to-point web services, (b) have no need for message-level security for audit or privacy, and (c) have no need for identities tightly coupled to each SOA message. The drawback of SSL is that it is transient, which implies it only provides transport-level data privacy and authentication. When an SSL connection terminates, audit is very difficult, and SSL has a hard time scaling over multi-hop paths.

- *The Myth of WS-Security:* The basic question is whether or not conforming to WS-Security makes an SOA interaction secure. Again, another trick question related to the *relative* nature of security. The answer is to look at what WS-Security provides, and make sure that all of the options WS-Security provides are actually used. WS-Security should be used when you require (a) message-level digital signing on SOAP messages, (b) message level encryption on SOAP messages, or (c) a standard place to put identity information in a SOAP message. You should realize that if you use WS-Security for (c) only, you have no guarantee that you get the other security benefits unless these are explicitly used.

- *The Myth of SAML:*_There is a prevailing myth that if SOA deployments "just used SAML," identity would be seamlessly shareable across disparate applications and enterprises. The reality of SAML is that it is much like an empty name tag. It defines the *structure* of the identity, not the *content*. For example, one could define "John Doe" in a SAML assertion by use of an e-mail address. Another equally valid way of representing with John Doe in SAML would be with a distinguished name (DN), or by defining John Doe with a set of attributes, such as a specific SSN, date of birth, and home city. The basic problem is that not all enterprises use the same attributes for their identities. Identities are conceived of and stored differently across enterprises, and SAML does not guarantee identities will be interoperable, just that they are all carried in the same XML wrapper.

The next section is a brief overview of SOA threat concepts, which are more closely related to network security concerns.

SOA Threats

Chapter 3 introduced a paradigm shift called the *universal tunnel*. With this model of SOA, you can see applications converging towards communication over a single network port using a common basic dialect (XML). One common statement regarding this shift is in relation to the purpose of traditional network firewalls, usually it is something like "with SOA, firewalls are meaningless" or some similar alarmist claim. The reason given for this claim is the observation that port 80 is the new universal port, and there is a trend for network applications to tunnel through port 80. If you take this trend and shine a negative light on it, you may also say that attackers will look for ways *through* port 80, as many other ports are now blocked by a traditional firewall. From a security architect standpoint, this is a great example of the weakest link property at work; attackers necessarily move to the path of least resistance, and from a threat perspective, SOA appears to provide this opportunity.

If you step back and take a historical view, you can see how initial protocols have slowly evolved into what we will term *secure replacements*. Figure 4.13 shows a mapping between various network- and application-level protocols circa 1995 and then shows the secure versions that have replaced them in the modern datacenter.

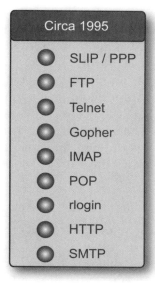 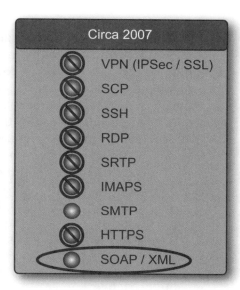

Figure 4.13   The Universal Tunnel Revisited

You should realize that SOA implementations are powerful enough to effectively re-implement many of these currently "forbidden" protocols over port 80. For example, FTP is a forbidden protocol in many data centers, yet the same file interaction can be exposed via a web service that calls an FTP service internally, effectively undoing all of the work done to move data centers away from FTP. This is the meaning of the statement, "with SOA, firewalls are ineffective"—SOA is a very effective *super tunnel* for almost any distributing computing interaction. From an IT security point of view, then, it is imperative to keep a close watch on what sorts of web services get exposed, as they may just be reopening old threats in new ways.

SOA Lifecycle Management

When implementing SOA, the fundamental paradigm of how change is viewed and managed is altered. With traditional application development, change is a discrete event that is tightly managed between established release cycles. In SOA, change is constant. At any one point in time a new service can be composed from one or many existing services. An existing service can be customized or its implementation or interface versioned.

Managing this level of change within an SOA environment while preserving enterprise stability requires new tools and new ways of thinking about governance, change control, testing, and release management. SOA lifecycle tools provide an organization with the means to manage their SOA investment in a properly controlled manner while still achieving the agility benefits that SOA offers.

What is key in managing your SOA investment is to have a reliable repository of available services, which is the first fundamental capability of a lifecycle management tool. It provides the storage repository, metadata definitions, and workflow tasks to ensure that any services recorded in the repository have a completed and validated service interface, metadata tags, quality of service terms, and that the service is approved for use within the enterprise. Also, these lifecycle management systems ensure that the appropriate policies are followed when versioning an existing service in order to hit the established balance of backward compatibility while minimizing redundant capability in the services inventory.

Managing this repository of available services is one of the key tools for your service procurement organization. As services are built, bought, or otherwise acquired, the service procurement organization will ensure the service is properly registered in the repository and that it follows all of the policies established by the enterprise architecture organization.

Next is the consumption of services from the repository by the solution assembly organization. In this aspect of the lifecycle services will be discovered and marked for consumption in application-specific composite services and/or business process tasks. This is an extremely important aspect of the SOA lifecycle for the operations team so that regression analysis can be done to determine what other downstream impacts need to be mitigated when an individual service has failed. It also helps the service procurement and enterprise architecture organizations understand which services are actually being used and which ones are not in order to make further refinements or investment decisions.

It is critical to get the SOA lifecycle management tool in place as you begin to move from the early learning phase of your SOA roadmap to ramp (that is as you move from crawling to walking). Your ability to successfully scale, meet agility goals, and at the same time have a stable, reliable enterprise is dependent on making this investment successfully. In the market at the time of this writing, there are a handful of strong, established vendors with proven implementations and ROI.

SOA Management

As we have seen, SOA with XML as its foundation is such a general concept that it continues to pervade all aspects of enterprise computing, *management* being no different. But what does *SOA management* really mean? Is it simply a set of standards, a view into business process execution, or a homogenous method and framework for managing devices of all types within the data center? As expected, different stakeholders are involved when the term *SOA management* is uttered, and each of these stakeholders views it from a unique perspective. Approaching the topic from the traditional divide of *business* and *technology* camps, we can outline the general viewpoints in four general categories: (a) business process monitoring and governance, (b) competitive threat, (c) management *using* a SOA, and (d) management *of* an SOA. As it stands, these four viewpoints proceed from general to specific when considered in business and technology terms.

Business Process Monitoring and Governance

From a business stakeholder perspective, assuming SOA is a means towards *business agility*, SOA management can really mean only one thing: how well is my SOA supporting my business goals? That is, for the business stakeholder, SOA management is simply a means to monitor and ensure SOAs are performing to "optimum agility," so to speak. With SOA, application availability, performance, capacity, and metrics are closely aligned with the business, so rather than thinking of SOA monitoring or management in terms of technology, it is conceived in business terms; with SOA, the services themselves *are* the business, so the distinction becomes collapsed.

Further, the business stakeholder takes the traditional *monitoring* concept a step further. If the job of SOA management is to provide a cohesive view of the business process, then it should also allow for *state changes*, or central control as well. This means other than simply reporting on the health of services, SOA management should offer a means to raise and lower service level agreements (SLAs), author, apply, and change service policies in response to changing market conditions, as well as new service provisioning and teardown. In other words, business needs are driving the underlying SOA management functionality. These governance concepts are considered "pie-in-the sky" from a bottom-up viewpoint as the realities of integrating a large number of disparate technologies into one holistic view remain a real challenge.

Moreover, existing management systems vendors will tend to see this type of integrated view as a *competitive threat*. Fully integrated management dashboards tend to marginalize existing footholds in proprietary management protocols and technology.

Competitive Threat

As alluded to in the previous section, the term *SOA management* can be construed as a *competitive threat* to existing management systems vendors. You can frame the argument by describing the core problem *SOA management* purports to solve: First consider a data center or enterprise full of heterogeneous IT resources, all from different vendors, all with *different* (or mostly different) systems management technologies. IT management would of course enjoy cost savings if one could integrate these and provide a cohesive view. The market created by this problem is fulfilled by *management software providers* who aim to reduce the complexity by providing a single point of control, which generally only has meaning within a specific subset or domain of the enterprise. Essentially, we now have *management software provider* heterogeneity and the problem repeats itself at a higher level.

SOA management, then, promises to provide a global SOA-based standard or framework that unites all manageable resources using SOA. There is little doubt that should such a framework come to fruition, it would remove the importance of *management software providers*, as the resources to be managed would be accessible directly via standard SOA mechanisms (such as web services) rather than through *agent technology*. This, then, is the competitive challenge that a fully integrated SOA management framework would present to existing management software providers. Of course, existing vendors could meet this challenge by adopting the global SOA framework, but this again becomes a time-to-market race between vendors and standards support, moving their products away from specific features and towards "standards as features," which makes vendor positioning around SOA management standards another bitterly fought battleground (see the next section on SOA standards).

In the next section we will outline some of the concepts around SOA management and present the distinction between management using SOA technologies and concepts, which is a wider discussion, and management *of* an SOA.

Management Using SOA

Management *using* SOA considers any device, service, or piece of software a proper candidate for management. That is, the discussion is not restricted to how one should manage an SOA, but how can SOA be used to manage any device. To be sure, the term *any* here means just that—a plasma TV, printer, DVD player, server, IP telephone, or even MP3 player. The stakeholder with this view of SOA management sees SOA as instrumental for any type of resource or device management.

One may ask how SOA management rationalizes itself with traditional management architectures. That is, the traditional model for managing devices is to include a small piece of code, usually called an *agent* that speaks to the device to be managed and provides information to the central management software, which queries and receives events from all such agents. Even this simple model has three variables with two possibilities for each: (a) agents can be tightly or loosely coupled to the managed resource, (b) agents can support proprietary or standardized communication protocols for central manager communication, and (c) agents can support proprietary or standard communication protocols for talking with the managed resource itself.

This complexity is a boon to systems management companies, who generally have proprietary systems that include all (or more) of these possibilities. SOA management, on the other hand, tries to normalize this agent model by building *agent bridges, adaptors,* or adding *native WS stacks.* An *agent bridge* is a wrapper around an existing agent that provides web services interfaces, an *adaptor* wraps a native API in a managed resource with a web services API, and a *native WS stack* is the addition of a complete web services stack that sits co-located with the managed resource. In this sense, SOA interfaces represent a *universal agent* of sorts. Once managed resources become enabled with universal agents conforming to a particular management standard (such as WSDM or WS-Management) the management of resources using SOA can begin. At this point the reader may be asking the most specific question, how does management *of* web services work with SOA?

Management of an SOA

As mentioned at the beginning of this section, management *of* a services oriented architecture is the most specific of our four questions. The first thing to realize is that service oriented architecture doesn't necessarily *have to* be managed by an SOA-based technology. In fact, the *agent model* as described in the previous section *can* work just fine for SOA management, especially if the environment or architecture contains purpose-built devices for SOA acceleration or security that need to report lower level events for performance reasons. In this case, it may make more sense for a tightly integrated native type of agent to report performance, service, service operation, and SLA information back to a central manager.

Management of SOA can also be achieved by lighter-weight agents sitting closer to the services themselves. This type of integration generally relies on the extension capabilities of the specific web services infrastructure. Here, the agent passes service-level information such as specific service called and operation metrics to the central manager. A looser version of this integration is also possible where the SOA infrastructure makes explicit calls to provide information to an agent, which then reports it back to the central manager. Finally, SOA infrastructure that already supports a web services management standard, such as WSDM or WS-Management, essentially comes pre-loaded with a *universal agent*.

Web Services Management Integration Types

Figure 4.14 outlines the four web services management integration approaches.

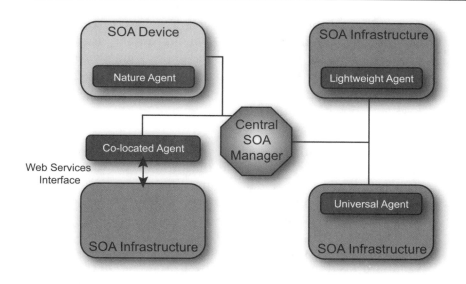

Figure 4.14 Integration Possibilities for the Management of Web Services

In Figure 4.14, a central SOA manager is shown managing three different SOA infrastructures as well as an SOA device. The manager itself represents a vendor product or product concept that aggregates and governs the SOA and provides a unified dashboard type of view. The SOA *device* represents a device such as an XML security gateway or accelerator that carries an embedded agent for reporting service level events and metrics. The SOA infrastructure is a generic concept that refers to any one of the leading vendor or open source web services enabled application servers.

The *device* case is the most tightly integrated as the native agent is probably compiled for the target operating system of the device itself. The remaining three cases represent integration at a higher level, with the co-located agent being the loosest of the three as it essentially sits next to the device and receives *some* events (but perhaps not all) and is likely in a read-only type of mode. The *universal agent* represents SOA infrastructure that is pre-enabled to support a specific web services management standard that must also be supported by the SOA manager as well. This example shows that SOA management, at least in the case of management *of* an SOA carries with it no implicit requirement that SOA must also be the instrument of management, though it may provide benefits in the future by avoiding agent integration. The true test of an SOA manager should be how well it achieves the management and governance functionality requirements rather than which specific protocols are used to implement the underlying management framework itself.

SOA Standards

SOA standards are a double-edged sword; on one hand they are absolutely necessary to achieve the promise of SOA, but on the other hand standards have a dampening affect to technological innovation. After all, if every product supports all of the same standards, and there is a standard for every feature, product and vendor differentiation becomes increasingly hard. More and more, vendor products cite standards support as features, leaving potential customers questioning the true value proposition for SOA. If the best products simply support the latest standards, then time to market seems to be essential, and those companies who are closest to the latest and most accepted standards will always be ahead of the pack. Due to this fact, SOA standards often represent bitterly divided battlegrounds for both business and technology stakeholders.

The aim of this section isn't to compound the problem further by pitting SOA standards against each other in an exhaustive comparison, but instead aims to give the reader the necessary tools to decide for themselves amongst the ever-increasing ocean of SOA standards out there. This section focuses on the business aspects of standards for SOA rather than technical comparisons. It gives an overview of real-world considerations for SOA standards, including topics like *vendor positioning, the standards hype cycle,* and *standards backlash*. It is difficult to predict the relevancy of an SOA standard without some measure of clairvoyance. To this date our opinion is that the most *fundamental* SOA standards are those that will be the longest lived, such as XML, XPath, XML Schema, and XSLT. Even standards such as SOAP are already being challenged as too heavyweight for some applications.

SOA Standards and Vendor Positioning

The first question one must always ask of a new or proposed SOA standard is *who* is proposing this standard and what *specific problem* does it attempt to solve? We use the term *vendor positioning* to describe

SOA standards created outside the scope of a standards body with a future goal of official standardization. This tactic has proved to be highly effective for certain SOA standards such as WS-Security and WS-ReliableMessaging. With this tactic, a vendor specification is made between a few large players in the market and over time it becomes adopted as a *de facto* standard by some portion of the SOA market. This tends to happen through targeted technology evangelism efforts. Once the vendor specification has reached some accepted maturity level, it is typically "shopped" to one of the major standards bodies including the World Wide Web Consortium (W3C), Organization for the Advancement of Structured Information Standards (OASIS), International Organization for Standardization (ISO), or Distributed Management Task Force (DMTF). This tactic is particularly effective when the vendor specification becomes adopted as an official standard; the originator of the vendor specification is typically many man-months ahead in the development cycle and can go to market in a much quicker manner.

This *vendor positioning* phenomenon is part of what drives the extensive proliferation of SOA standards. In some cases, vendors oppose new emerging standards because of some existing technology investment to the detriment of SOA adoption at large. One example of this concerns SOA attachments, where there are multiple ways of adding opaque binary attachments to SOAP messages. One method, which uses MIME, is called SOAP with Attachments (SwA) and defines a simple extension to SOAP and MIME to add additional MIME parts. This mechanism is opposed by Microsoft, which has its own method of attachment handling, called DIME. Because of the large market share of SOA infrastructure held by Microsoft, SwA represents a threat, but in the end the consumer is the real loser as there is no way to provide true interoperability for attachments across disparate (Microsoft and non-Microsoft) environments, which further impedes the adoption of SOA. As we will argue later in this section, *vendor positioning* is one of the contributors to standards backlash in SOA.

Standards Hype Cycle

SOA standards tend to follow a typical cycle, which we will call the *hype cycle*. The hype cycle is what happens to every SOA standard once it is announced in a standards organization such as OASIS or W3C. The first phase of the cycle involves public announcement or support of the new standard (if it doesn't conflict with existing *vendor positioning*). At this point, each vendor wants to have a positive association with the new

SOA standards effort and may send representatives to participate in the standards process itself. After each vendor is sufficiently on record as an active participant, attendance begins to dwindle, often leaving a core standards team that is much smaller than the initial number of participants. It is in this stage that the standard is put to the critical test; if the standardization effort is completed, it generally ends with less glamour than when it was announced. Paradoxically, once a standard is completed it has less hype and generally less buzz than when it was conceived. This is what we call the *burial phase* of the standard, where the standard isn't necessarily ignored, but it is buried in the background as a new standard has taken the spotlight. This curious phenomenon tends to happen when the *next* version of a standard usurps the original, adding a suspect amount of new real-world capability, leaving the market in a constant state of wanting the latest and greatest standard. In our experience, the SOA standard, if it solves a genuine problem, begins to reach real adoption at the end of this hype cycle in a quiet, anti-climactic manner. Part of the reason for this is the fact the standards are anathema to product differentiators, adding little value over competitor products other than time to market considerations. Figure 4.15 shows a pictorial representation of the hype cycle.

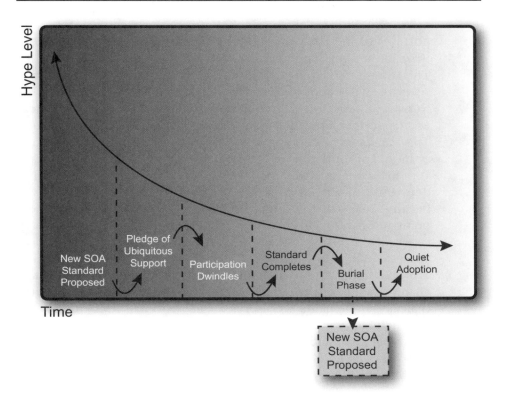

Figure 4.15 The SOA Standards Hype Cycle

In Figure 4.15, it should be noted that it is usually during the burial phase that the *new* version of the SOA standard comes to the forefront, overshadowing the old and casting doubt on the original standard's level of adoption in light of the new and ostensibly *better* version. It is at this point where the cycle repeats itself and the hype continues.

Standards Backlash: WS-Heavy and REST

At this point we must ask the question *why are there so many SOA and Web Services standards?* Part of the answer lies in the fact that SOA is a new and emerging area, but we believe the genesis of this problem lies with XML itself. That is, XML is such a *simple* syntax on its own that it needs layers upon layers of standards to constrain it to achieve a simple scenario. For example, defining a payload-agnostic request-response message paradigm that does some basic message processing involves about five different standards: XML for the wire format, XPath to address portions of the payload, SOAP to define the request envelope, WSDL to describe the service interfaces, and HTTP to handle the actual transport. This doesn't even begin to consider additional functionality such as security (WS-Security), discovery (UDDI), or business process (BPEL), just to name a few. In reality one could come up with a sophisticated SOA exchange that literally involves a standards count in the double digits. This standards-laden approach to SOA is sometimes referred to as "WS-*" or more appropriately as "WS-Heavy."

One can argue that the addition of so many layers of extra standards does little to aid interoperability and support business agility. Further, because many of the initial SOA deployments begin as simple point-to-point integration projects, WS-* is simply too heavy for some projects, especially prototyping efforts. The alternative to WS-Heavy is an architectural style called REST, which stands for *Representational State Transfer* and refers to a general computing paradigm of client side state change being driven by URL-based resources. This architectural style typically implements web service calls with just XML, XML schema, and well defined unique URI resources. The advantage to this style is that it is lightweight, arguably more readable, and doesn't require a heavy stack of web services standards. One can view REST as the pragmatic response to the bitter fighting over which vendor will own which SOA standard.

Application of SOA to Infrastructure: SOI

The principles and methods of SOA can be applied at any layer in the stack. When applied to infrastructure, the resulting managed assembly is referred to as Service Oriented Infrastructure, or SOI.

SOI can be thought of as the bottom layer of a services oriented stack in the enterprise (with upper layers focused on data, applications and business process), and enabling a dynamic resource provisioning capability to the enterprise. The unique aspect of SOI is the controlling of hardware-based infrastructure using software services, with the objective being to provide a fully managed, zero-touch basis to control data center IT resources with reduced cost of operations and increased availability of systems.

SOI Benefits Linked to Utility Computing

To understand SOI, it's good to first consider the benefits of the more general concept of utility computing (and variants of it such as grid computing), with which SOI can play a key role. Utility computing enforces loose coupling between the software applications and services and the hardware infrastructure they run on. Utility computing "pools" compute resources to create easily provisioned capacity, on demand. The pools flex to adapt to dynamic capacity demand, using software services (SOI) for management command and control. Figure 4.16 shows this transformation of IT capacity.

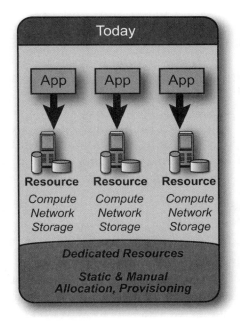 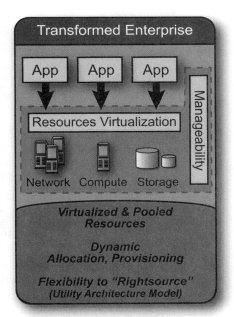

Figure 4.16   Transformation SOI Virtualized Pools of IT Capacity

Utility computing can be described as instantiating managed services on a shared infrastructure. This can be accomplished in several ways, involving techniques such as abstraction, virtualization, grid computing, automation, and web services. Alternatively, utility computing can be described as a concept that uses several means to deliver a variable cost model through providing capacity as needed and billing by usage.

When properly executed, a utility computing infrastructure base provides a transparent, virtualized set of infrastructure services, freeing applications and services from the specific server, storage, or network topology they run on. The aspect of virtualization is critical; computing resources must become nameless, faceless commodity entities for utility computing to successfully abstract them and leverage them in a dynamic environment. Once that is accomplished, manipulation through automation methods can extend capabilities of the infrastructure in ways that were not previously possible.

The term utility is apt to describe this, as it is functionally similar to on-demand provisioning that utilities organizations (such as electric and gas companies) provide. The actual source of the utility's capacity is not of interest to the consumer (a toaster or gas stove, for example)—only the end product and ability to deliver needed capacity need be anticipated. A comparison of an electrical utility and utility computing is provided in Table 4.2.

One may ask, what is the value in providing abstracted, virtualized interfaces to utility infrastructure? The most prominent reason is that virtualization can abstract and stabilizes infrastructure elements that IT processes utilize, and this can dramatically increase the return on investment for IT business process transformation. To achieve this value, orchestrated provisioning of compute, network, and storage together is needed. Without this, the IT silos of technical experts in server, network, storage, and security may not be effectively integrated.

Application of utility infrastructure is in early stages of maturity. Innovative commercial products, touted as "virtual infrastructure management" or "data center automation" capabilities, offer the means to manage limited pools (dozens to hundreds of servers and pools of SAN and NAS storage) of resources in an abstracted fashion and employing rules- and policy-based management techniques. Little standardization or operability between these capabilities exist today. However standards will naturally be adopted as the market evolves. Yet there can be significant operational benefit gained today through increased efficiency these products provide.

Table 4.2   Comparing Electric Power Utility to Utility Computing

Electric Power Utility	IT Utility Computing
Additional power (with limits) is always available and can be used on demand. We don't need to submit an application, or requisition a new power plant. We just expect the power to be there when we need it.	Applications get the resources (compute, storage and network) they need to scale-up to meet demand.
We have a "pay as you go" model— we only pay for what we use.	Consumers (projects, programs) are "charged" for the compute, storage, and network resources they actually consume. Additional standby capacity ("headroom") is provided by the "utility." We may still have some excess capacity, but a single pool could be shared by all applications.
There are many sources of power—oil, coal, wind, hydroelectric, solar, and so on. The electricity from these sources all gets mixed together and we don't necessarily know or care where they come from.	Capacity is provided by many different networks, storage systems and heterogeneous compute systems, but would present the same general interface.
When there is just not enough power to go around, the power company can prioritize and direct power to critical needs such as hospitals.	During the end of the month, available capacity can be directed to ensure that the warehouse solutions have the capacity they need to pick, pack, and ship. During close, we can ensure finance applications have the capacity they need, even if that means de-allocating computing resources from lower priority applications.
We get extremely high availability and generally take it for granted. Often the system routes power around failed sources or transformers so we don't even notice the glitch.	We get extremely high availability and take it for granted. When a server fails, the solutions continue to run with minimal impact.

Utility Computing Facilitates Scale-out of Services

Utility computing provides a dynamic environment that can assign resources as needed. As we increasingly move to a services oriented environment, the infrastructure must be able to adjust to changing loads by creating additional service instances as needed (as well as extinguishing them as appropriate).

Since most services should be stateless, this means that we will largely have the freedom to add additional instances as necessary to handle load, or to reduce latency, or to guard against equipment or facility failure (for business continuity of disaster recovery).

This freedom means that we can scale out services by adding computing resources where they are needed and of the size needed. To continue the power utility comparison, this is a situation similar to *microgeneration,* where power can be generated close to the load being served, by smaller than usual power plants—an alternative method of scaling.

New instances created to handle load might be created alongside existing ones, such as on an additional core in the same multi-core processor, for example. This would have several advantages (it might ease routing, for instance); but there are reasons why additional instances might be placed elsewhere.

Modeling the Environment

A cornerstone of effective management of an IT environment is representation of the environment in a database or a model. Physical assets are identified and captured into a model used to manage inventory and to control property movement. Traditionally, there has been a relatively static mapping of network, servers, storage, clients, and applications, together with their relationships, and so the relationship between these items could be maintained manually. But the introduction of service-oriented application architecture in conjunction with utility computing changes everything.

As monolithic applications are decomposed into their component services and we identify common elements to become shared, reusable services, there are advantages to executing these services in a dynamic environment. But this means that the way that mapping is accomplished also has to change, and must be better suited to a dynamic environment—the kind of environment where instances can be created and extinguished as loads and other requirements change in response to changing business conditions.

To accomplish this, rather than binding a specific application instance to a specific server, service components must be related to classes of servers that host services. The abstracted mapping of specific instances of service to server is best accomplished in the infrastructure, with only an indirect reference exposed to the application layer.

Use of a Model Enables the Infrastructure

In the deployment of abstracted services infrastructure, a stateful model of the as-built infrastructure becomes a common integration point for all tools and processes that touch the lifecycle state of a running infrastructure (and its supply chain, and so on). The IT Information Library CMDB concept loosely addresses this, through specifying a common storehouse of configuration information. A single repository is needed, because if a data type has multiple "authoritative" definitions, attempts to automate business processes will unravel quickly.

When the properties, state, and status of managed elements that make up a service offering can be abstracted and stabilized, the return on investment for end-to-end management changes:

- The relevance of created automation broadens to more than one solution stack

- The economic life of the automation stretches out to more than one refresh/upgrade cycle

After successful infrastructure virtualization, the ROI for automation investment starts to accrue (instead of rip/redo/replace in every refresh/upgrade cycle as before). The "TCO breakthrough" can only be achieved when virtualization is implemented in a technology independent way. Just as APIs like that of a PCI bus enable an ecosystem of interchangeable moving parts while preserving implementation differentiation (and ROI for product innovation), we can also benefit from a defined virtual infrastructure interface.

Utility computing enables the relationships to be fully dynamic and self-regulating. Any "snapshot" of which service components run on which infrastructure component may be valid only for a brief time, until the self-regulating nature of the utility system reconfigures for a new, optimal state. Continuous service monitoring is required to respond to changing demands on the services.

This has other advantages as well, such as the ability to deploy new "builds" to classes of servers rather than to individual servers, which should ease the task of change and release management, and should provide a more uniform execution environment.

This effectively changes the meaning of deployment, since for most purposes this is accomplished for software components when they are stored in the DSL with the appropriate metadata available in the CMDB.

In addition, the ability to deploy to a logical representation of a computing resource makes it possible to re-factor the infrastructure, giving additional flexibility to the implementers of the infrastructure, while providing stability through virtualization.

The use of a model of the environment provides an abstraction that is useful for reducing today's tight coupling between an "application build" and the server on which it is installed. Instead, an application can be largely assembled from already-deployed service objects, and can effectively be deployed to the model. The actual mapping of software components to the execution environment can be performed dynamically when needed. In addition, this abstraction gives additional freedom to infrastructure implementers (including OEMs) to re-factor the infrastructure to provide the best benefits (in cost or features) without causing upheaval in the logical design.

SOI as a Key Enabler of Utility Computing

Utility computing, in conjunction with service-oriented architecture, provides the ability to scale out services to allow for flexibility in responding to demand, as SOI enables utility computing by providing the software interface underpinning enabling programmatic manipulation of infrastructure. With SOI infrastructure abstraction, there is no longer a need for static binding between software and named hosts (such as DNS names) or IP addresses for the software systems to function. Pools of resource are allocated based on the demand conveyed by management services in response to SOA system capacity requirements.

In the multi-layer services oriented enterprise stack, as shown in Figure 4.17, SOI is a foundation on top of which SOA utility and business services run. SOI-enabled hardware—with standard interfaces able to respond to standardized, programmatic instructions from management and automation systems—provide the most elemental underpinnings of the SOI layer.

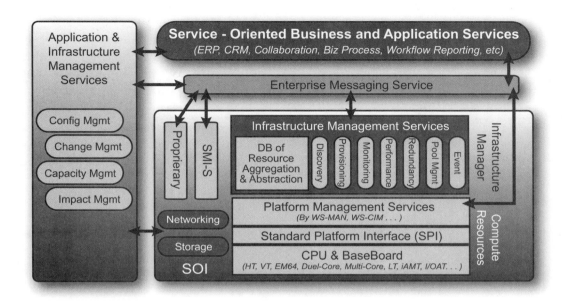

Figure 4.17   SOI Function in the Services Oriented Enterprise Stack

In this multi-layer stack, SOI should provide many, if not all, of these functions:

- *Orchestration*: Managing hardware as a set of distributed and, to some extent, fungible resources, shifting from a static, "one-application-per-box" paradigm to dynamic provisioning based on real-time workloads and activities. This provides the ability to realign compute, network, and storage resources as needed.

- *Asset discovery and management*: Maintaining an automatic inventory of all connected devices, always accurate and updated on a timely basis.

- *Provisioning*: Enabling "bare metal" provisioning, coordinating the configuration between server, network, and storage in a synchronous manner; making sure software gets loaded on the right physical machines; taking platforms in and out of service as required for testing, maintenance, repair or capacity expansion; remote booting a system from another system; and managing the licenses associated with software deployment.

■ *Virtualization*: Making it possible to run multiple applications sharing one physical machine or storage device to increase utilization rates, or to allocate multiple machines and storage devices to one application to increase performance. In other words, one-to-one dependencies between applications and platforms are removed. This capability provides unprecedented flexibility in meeting SLAs.

■ *Load balancing*: Dynamically reassigning physical devices to applications to ensure adherence to specified service (performance) levels and optimal utilization of all resources as workloads change.

■ *Capacity planning*: Measuring and tracking the consumption of virtual resources to be able to plan when to reserve resources for certain workloads or when new equipment needs to be brought on line.

■ *Utilization metering*: Tracking the use of particular resources as designated by management policy and SLA. The metering service could be used for charge back and billing by higher-level software.

■ *Monitoring and problem diagnosis*: Verifying that virtual platforms are operational, detecting error conditions and network attacks, and responding by running diagnostics, de-provisioning platforms and re-provisioning affected services, or isolating network segments to prevent the spread of malware.

■ *Security enforcement*: Enforcing automatic device and software load authentication; tracing identity, access, and trust mechanisms within and across corporate boundaries to provide secure services across firewalls.

■ *Logical isolation and privacy enforcement*: Ensuring that a fault in a virtual platform does not propagate to another platform in the same physical machine, and that there are no data leaks across virtual platforms that could belong to different accounts.

■ *IT operations processes*: Setting up generic micro IT operations as building blocks to standardize IT processes and enabling interoperability across heterogeneous system management products.

The programmatic management of SOI enabled infrastructure is performed through a Standard Platform Interface (SPI), which should be based on open standards, such as WS-Management. This helps to ensure interoperability between the SOI enabled infrastructure and management systems.

Leveraging SOI for Operations Agility

Once an infrastructure base is SOI enabled and managed, automation of systems can exploit the synergy between SOA and SOI. This can be best illustrated through some examples.

Suppose the puzzle-piece objects A, B, and C in Figure 4.18 represent three SOA business services. Let A be a service that creates month-end employment reports, B, a service that response to requests to read employee master data, and C, a service that distributes the reports to subscribers (through printing, e-mailing, and so on).

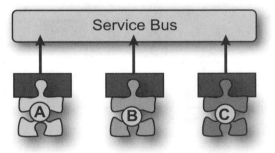

Figure 4.18   Three Enterprise Services

One thing may be immediately obvious: the data service B is required by the execution of services A and C. And, in an enterprise, B would likely be demanded by many more services as well, as employee master data would be a highly used, key information resource.

Network, storage and computing resources are provisioned to provide these services: the provisioning of resources is controlled by SOI management of network, storage, and server shared resources pools. That is, because the SOI enabled equipment is virtualized and abstracted, the resources can be arbitrarily assigned to meet the capacity needs of the SOA business services. In Figure 4.19, a grouping of resources X are assigned to A; Z is assigned to C and both Y1 and Y2 are assigned to B.

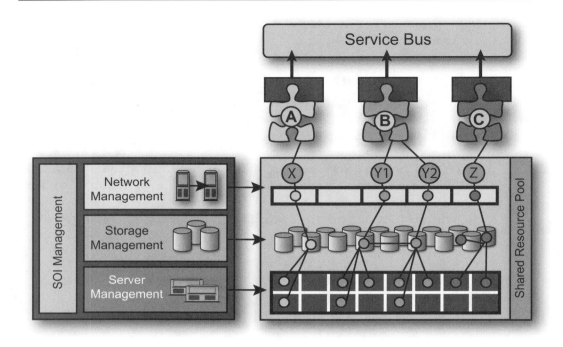

Figure 4.19 Three Enterprise Services Using SOI

In this scheme, there is an implied exchange of information between the SOI management capability and the SOA service directory. When the SOI management system executes an action making service A available through infrastructure X, that information must be shared with the SOA service directory, so that future requests for A are directed to and served by X. This abstraction of service location is one of the most significant benefits of SOA: consumers can use A, B, or C through the abstraction provided by the service directory and/or message routing with no need to care where the service is located, infrastructure-wise.

In the diagram in Figure 4.19, why have two sets of resources (Y1 and Y2) assigned to B? Because, as previously discussed, B represents a highly shared, scaled data resource (employee master data), making it a service that must be continuously available. By providing redundant, independent instances of service B (SOI infrastructure groupings Y1 and Y2), the service can be maximally available, even if one of the two Y instances are not available (note the line linking the storage resources of

Y1 and Y2 implying that the data is kept in sync, possibly through active mirroring or other duplication). Such redundancy can be applied to any business-critical service that has a service level requirement mandating continuous availability.

Also implied in the diagram is that Y1, Y2 and Z have multiple server resources assigned to each service instance, implying a load balancing capability that is under the covers of the SOI managed capability (load balancing happens virtually and is abstracted with no realization needed by the services using it). Such load balancing has been available for many years as it has effectively served the needs for scalable web services infrastructure; that mechanism becomes a valued intrinsic capability in the SOI management capability.

Explicit versus Implicit Demand Triggers

The SOI Management capability orchestrated the provisioning of X, Y1, Y2 and Z, in response to SOA service demands. These demands can be triggered in two ways;

- *explicitly* – where an operator may initiate a manual action, responding to business requirements the trigger" initiating a provisioning action and resulting capacity change, or

- *implicitly* – where automation rules dictate (imply) the actions SOI should take to respond to dynamic environmental conditions, creating an automated operations environment that self-adjusts to changing situations.

The term *autonomic* can be used to describe the implicit demand triggered action that keeps the SOI capacity balanced with changing conditions.

This is potentially a very powerful concept with respect to operations automation. Shifting business conditions can include anything from capacity demand swings due to regular business fluctuation (end of quarter close or manufacturing shift change), or capacity changes due to equipment outages, whether a server, disk, switch, or even an entire data center may go off-line.

Illustration of Orchestrated Scripting

We will use a pseudo-code script example to illustrate how the SOI managed infrastructure rules can be used to provide autonomic response to changing conditions. Let "service response" be a numeric, monitored indication of how responsive a service is to service requests—such service monitoring is a fundamental utility function of SOI. In this case, if a threshold of 0.2 seconds is exceeded in overall service response to requests, the service is considered to be operating under its intended capacity. A rule could be stated like this:

```
If (B service response > 0.2 seconds) then
    Provision additional service set Yx
End if
```

It may also be a parameter of normal service that each individual instance of Yx services should always respond to requests in less than 0.5 seconds, otherwise that instance is considered to be unhealthy or defective; an additional rule could account for this:

```
For all (Yx instances) in (service set B)
    IF (Yx service response) exceeds 0.5 seconds then
        Remove Yx from service set
        De-provision instance Yx
        Flag Yx infrastructure for HW health check
    End if
End
```

A follow-on action to the execution of de-provisioning in this rule would be to inspect the infrastructure of the malfunctioning service set for possible problems.

Finally, if the number of instances of Y had been increased to deal with a surge in demand, later on, it would be desired to scale back Y service instance as demand diminished (to no less than two instances, which ensure availability). We can again

```
If (B service response < 0.1 seconds) and (# of Y instances > 2) then
    Remove last Yx from service set
    De-provision last instance Yx
End if
```

In summary, the result of these three scripted sequences would be to:

- Dial up infrastructure capacity to deal with demand during peak periods
- Dial down capacity during quiescent periods of inactivity
- Remove infrastructure from service that may be defective

In practice, more detailed and extensive rules would be developed to deal with the many error conditions and possible variations of the operations environment. Additionally, other factors such as desired geographic diversity of services (operating services in locations far apart from one another), shown in Figure 4.20, could account for business conditions such as global service response and business continuity and disaster recoverability.

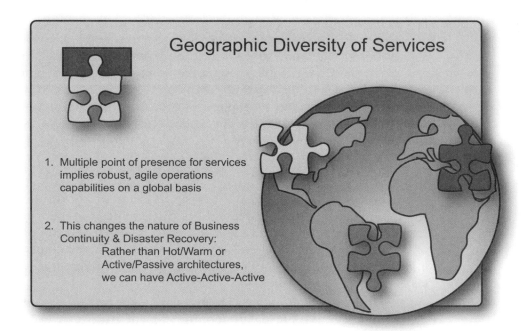

Figure 4.20   Geographic Diversity of Services

As automatic processes match demand to resources, reconfigure the environment as needed, and reroute work around failing components, the human focus can change to assuring that services and business processes are functional. The availability of any particular server, disk, or network component will be nearly irrelevant.

The infrastructure will be designed such that equipment failures will result in minimal downtime. When imminent failures are detected, the goal would be to have no downtime at all through proactively moving the service to other equipment.

Stateless Service Operation and SOI

The agility described in the above illustrations depends in part on the business services maintaining a stateless mode of service-to-service communication. If stateless, single-message-payload communications are the norm, then a service instances can be stopped abruptly with no long-lasting impact to the higher level use of the services.

However, if consumers of services have stateful and long-lasting session-based communications with the services where several messages are exchanged to complete a transaction, it would be much more complex for SOI to dial up and down service capacity, since state of all sessions would need to be figured into each of the SOI actions. Hung stateful sessions could delay SOI actions for unacceptable periods of time.

Changing Nature of IT Roles

As the utility computing and SOI infrastructure rolls out over time, and as we achieve the kinds of advantages that we hope to obtain, we would expect for there to be changes in the skills required and the proportion of IT professionals working in various roles. Today there are many people involved in application implementation, server configuration, and other tasks. Over time, this will change as we see impact from:

- Tools that will map the required services and other components to a logical representation of the infrastructure;

- An autonomous, physical infrastructure (the computing utility) that can dynamically map the logical representation onto physical components; and

- Infrastructure features that can keep services running through self-correction capabilities that can reroute around problems, automatic allocation of additional resources as needed, migration of workload from failing components, and so on.

It should follow that these kinds of benefits would free up resources, and allow them to be brought to bear on business process design and implementation. When the desired state is reached, activity can focus on this and on mapping business process requirements to services and logical infrastructure.

Since the computing utility will be capable of automatically mapping the logical representation to physical components, infrastructure design and implementation will be less resource-intensive, and should largely be accomplished outside of the context of a given project or program. Lastly, the benefits of features such as self-configuration and self-correction will ease the routine operation and maintenance of the infrastructure. This should be manifest in the enterprises reduced need to audit, track, and maintain records of infrastructure configuration, and eliminate any need for tracking organizational infrastructure ownership. It will be as though the burden of planning and operating one's own electric utility were lifted in favor of a "pay for what you use" model with relatively simple consumption planning and usage billing.

Thus over time, we would expect to have less overhead and therefore less operations personnel focused on infrastructure operations, and over time a larger proportion of IT personnel working on business process design and implementation, and mapping to logical components; the proportion spent on infrastructure design, configuration, and maintenance would be reduced.

Summary

- The concepts of enterprise bus and domain bus (big bus, little bus) serve to slice SOA into two distinct forms: intra-enterprise and inter-enterprise. The distinction and abstraction between these domains allows scalable SOA in a practical architectural approach. The little bus is characterized by the following considerations: range of complexity, limited security requirements, static binding, tighter coupling, state awareness, known message patterns, orchestration and technology bridging. Alternatively, the big bus is often characterized by coarser services, message routing, loosely coupled services, statelessness, scalability, contracts, increased security requirements, and dynamism for new participants.

- Business Process Management (BPM) systems provide the connection between the technology and business stakeholders when implementing a SOA, and allow the capture of requirements and processes at a business level rather than a technical level. To this end it is important that BPM systems are targeted at the right user audience. However, the underlying model for the business process should use an XML-based modeling language (such as WS-BPEL) to help insure a level of interoperability and future-proofing.

- Security can be a key impediment to a trusted SOA implementation, and care must be taken when defining the security architecture. The focus on messaging brings with it new problems such as message level security and message-level identity management and normalization. However, in many cases the problem of security within the context of SOA is often the fault of pre-existing security holes that are brought to light. That is, SOA has a tendency to reveal existing security problems rather than create new ones.

- The relevance of SOA standards and their applicability to actual implementations is something that should be closely watched. Often times burgeoning SOA standards act as bandwagons that offer strategic or political gains rather than real technology advantages. Furthermore, beware of falling into the false dilemma of standard A "versus" standard B when in most cases practical considerations require *both* to be supported in the end.

- SOI (Service Oriented Infrastructure) can be considered a key enabler that brings SOA into the realm of utility computing. SOI enables hardware to be virtualized and abstracted such that the resources can be arbitrarily assigned to meet capacity needs. This concept is not new, however, and has been pushed under the guise of grid computing with little success from the academic or enterprise communities. While SOI is not yet mainstream, enabling standards such as WS-Manage are allowing a much more rapid maturation. Ensuring that a single authoritative database structure is used to capture and maintain the infrastructure model is a key to SOI success.

Chapter 5

SOA in Government

An elephant: A mouse built to government specifications.

-Lazarus Long, from Robert Heinlein's *Time Enough for Love*

Government institutions across the world, at the national, regional, and local level, are a large consumer of technology. For these governmental institutions, engaged in providing services to the citizens and corporations in the areas of defense and national security, health, taxation, law enforcement, judiciary, environment, energy, social services, disaster management, land use management, technology plays an important role in getting information from and to the "users," that is, citizens and businesses, and sharing information between agencies.

However, as in large corporations, information technology in government institutions has been built in silos with interoperability and exchangeability of information only considered as an afterthought to the architecture. For example, government agencies tend to consider their information silos in terms of their specific agency objective, leaving service-orientation concerns by the wayside. This leaves an integration problem down the road when agencies begin to communicate with each other or between their users. Here we can draw a parallel between the big bus and little bus, where communication with other local, regional, and national agencies fall into the big bus category and communication with citizens and businesses fall into the little bus category. Admittedly, integrating the information silos of various governmental institutions is a tall order for reasons that have little to do with technology.

There are some encouraging signs that this is changing. In the United States, for example, the Office of Management and Budget's (OMB), Office of E-Government (E-Gov) and Information Technology (IT) have established the Federal Enterprise Architecture (FEA) Program, which provides FEA reference models. These reference models are set of tools that equip the government institutions with frameworks and tools to enhance collaboration and analyze investments to reduce redundancies, improve performance, service quality, and encourage reuse.

Let us take a closer look at the Federal Enterprise Architecture (FEA) models to see if they bring us closer to the vision of Service Oriented Architecture as laid out in Chapter 1, and discussed from a technology perspective in Chapters 3 and 4.

From the e-gov portal that defines the FEA[1]:

> The FEA is being constructed through a collection of interrelated "reference models" designed to facilitate cross-agency analysis and the identification of duplicative investments, gaps, and opportunities for collaboration within and across Federal Agencies.

Figure 5.1 shows five FEA reference models. The next two sections give a closer look at two of the reference models from the FEA, the SRM (Service Component Reference Model) and DRM (Data Reference Model). These two models are important to highlight because, first, the SRM reflects that the services need to be derived from business objectives (as discussed in Chapter 2), and second, the DRM deals with the issue of canonical data representation, context and exchange, one of the most important problems in realizing SOA in government.

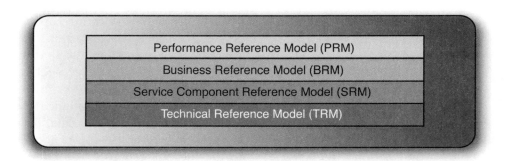

Figure 5.1   Federal Enterprise Architecture

---

[1] http://www.whitehouse.gov/omb/egov/a-2-EAModelsNEW2.html

Service Component Reference Model (SRM)

The FEA Reference Model defines SRM as follows:

> The SRM is a business-driven, functional framework classifying Service Components according to how they support business and performance objectives. It serves to identify and classify horizontal and vertical Service Components supporting federal agencies and their IT investments and assets. The model aids in recommending service capabilities to support the reuse of business components and services across the federal government. The SRM is organized across horizontal service areas, independent of the business functions, providing a leverage-able foundation for reuse of applications, application capabilities, components, and business services.

The Service Component Reference Model's objectives appear to be in-line with the Business Architecture defined in Chapter 2. Recalling from Chapter 2, Business Architecture provides the main linkage to map business process requirements to SOA capability, and so can be thought of as the blueprint that decomposes and translates business requirements into pieces that can be assembled. In this way, SOA "leads" with Business Architecture, and delivers its implementation through a combination of data, application, and technology. The Service Component Reference Model (SRM) is providing a business driven framework that leads to reusable set of ready-to-assemble services.

By performing complete assessments of the current and future state, you can clarify what functions of the applications and IT infrastructure can and/should be decomposed into reusable services. You can also clarify where standardization of functionality is required and customization is really needed.

By using the Service Portfolio Planning process described in Chapter 2 iteratively, the OMG and FEA can evolve the Service Component Reference Model to specific reusable services. You will see a few examples of such usage in government later in this chapter. By following this process, it is possible to protect against further technology silos being created for a short-term objective. In the United Kingdom, for example, a major e-government initiative launched early in this decade has pushed to make all government services available online. However, the initial direction of focusing on "online" delivery models, rather than a set of underlying services, has meant an explosion of "portal" type offerings that are not as well adopted (except for cases where regulation mandates adoption).

Let us now take a look at the FEA's data reference model. In a government environment, where most agency systems have evolved in silos, data, its representation, its context and the methodology of exchange, become critical foundations for SOA. The Data Reference Model attempts to provide guidance on how to achieve these goals.

Data Reference Model (DRM)

The Data Reference Model (DRM) is described as follows:

> It is the FEA mechanism for identifying what data the federal government has and how that data can be shared in response to business/mission requirements. The DRM provides a frame of reference to:
> • Facilitate Communities of Interest (which may be aligned with the LoBs (Lines of businesses) delineated in the FEA Business Reference Model) in establishing common language.
> • Enable needed conversations to reach credible cross-agency agreements around: governance, data architecture and an information sharing architecture. The DRM provides guidance to enterprise architects and data architects for implementing repeatable processes to enable data sharing....[2]

The Data Reference Model goes on to define three key concepts that require standardization by the specific government community of interest (COI); data context, data description and data sharing.

The *data context,* to be agreed on by a government community of interest (COI), is the purpose for which the data assets are being defined; what subject area should the data address, who needs it, who maintains it, how it is accessed, stored and secured (left for later versions of DRM) and how it ties into the FEA Business Reference Model (BRM).

The *data description* is the specific structure and semantics of data required based on the data context.

---

[2] http://www.whitehouse.gov/omb/egov/documents/DRM_2_0_Final.pdf

The *data sharing* is defined as the set of services that are standardized for data sharing for the data context area with the specific data description.

While data context, data description and data sharing are abstract terms, in most if not all instances of realization of the DRM, the data description is provided in XML schema, the data context is defined by XML namespaces, and the data sharing is defined using XML-based request-response exchange patterns that can be used within a Web Services framework.

In our SOA law enforcement use case, we will discuss how concepts outlined in the DRM and SRM reference models come together to address a real world problem using SOA.

SOA in Law Enforcement

A good example of usage of Service Oriented Architecture for efficient and effective information availability at the point where it is needed is among the government agencies focused on preventing crime and providing internal security.

In the United States, many federal, state, and local agencies are engaged in crime prevention and internal security. Starting at the federal level, it includes the Department of Transportation and the Department of Homeland Security (within which can be found the US Immigration and Customs Enforcement and US Customs and Border Protection branches). Extending it to states and local agencies, it includes, state departments of corrections, local and state law enforcement agencies, courts, and any number of related agencies.

In most law enforcement agencies, in order to search for information on suspects, the personnel use different networks and systems, each with their own authentication, search mechanism and result data formats. Searching through these independent information silos creates inefficiency, missed linkages across information silos, and ultimately, poorer law enforcement. For example, if an Illinois State Police officer requested a criminal history record from Iowa, the search might have to be done through specific terminals that accept field-value pair-based queries, while the results coming back may be in Iowa law enforcement data format that may be quite different from that of Illinois. In this example the system used to provide the message switching capability is the National Law Enforcement Telecommunications System, or NLETS. NLETS provides a message switching system linking together state, local, and federal law enforcement and justice agencies for the purpose of information exchange. This service, which does not host any information itself, is based on frame relay. It is used widely by all of the states and all federal agencies related to justice. The data exchanged include driver records, state criminal records, license information, immigration records, AMBER alerts (an alert system designed to help locate and protect children), hazardous material (Hazmat) warnings, weather bulletins, terrorist alerts, and so on. NLETS records over 40 million transactions every month.

The information flow for someone from a state law enforcement agency performing a query similar to one described above that uses the NLETS service, the National Crime Information Center database (NCIC) service, state department of motor vehicle records, and so on, is illustrated in Figure 5.2.

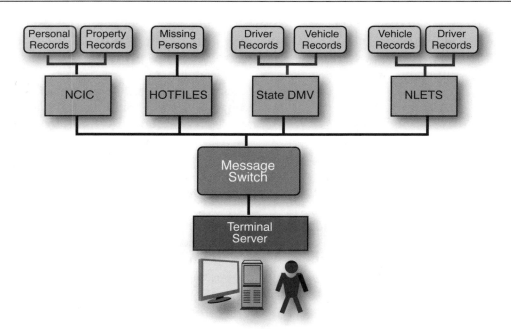

Figure 5.2   State Justice Environment for Accessing Law Enforcement Information

Authorized law enforcement personnel use the state law enforcement portal interface to request information based on a driver's license. The server (terminal server) receiving the request then forwards it to the state message switch over TCP/IP. The message switch acknowledges the message, and then, based on the query parameters, sends it to the state systems such as the state department of motor vehicles, NLETS, NCIC (with access to gang and violent activity records, stolen gun, license plate, and boat records, and so on), and state hot files (for missing people). The responses from these systems are then sent back to the terminal server, which then converts the data into a normalized format to the extent possible for the law enforcement agent on the terminal.

However, in order to provide a uniform interface for search and results for the state law enforcement personnel in the above example, point-to-point mapping at the terminal server was the only viable option available.

In order to create a canonical data format that the state departments of justice could use, thereby reducing the n times (n-1) mapping problem to 2n, as shown in Figure 5.3, the U.S. Department of Justice's Office of Justice Programs (OJP) and the Global Justice Information Sharing Initiative (Global) came up with the Global Justice XML Data Model[3] (GJXDM). The GJXDM includes a data model, a data dictionary, and an XML schema.

---

[3] http://www.it.ojp.gov/topic.jsp?topic_id=43

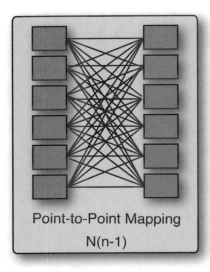
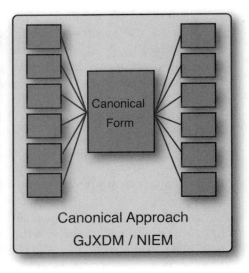

Point-to-Point Mapping
N(n-1)

Canonical
Form

Canonical Approach
GJXDM / NIEM

Figure 5.3   Point-to-Point versus Canonical Approach for Justice Data Exchange

With NLETS adopting GJXDM and offering a Web Service based interface for querying for justice information across states and other states adopting the GJXDM model, the point-to-point data mapping problem is reduced to a canonical data exchange.

The criminal justice information captured through this model includes rap sheets, court case records and juvenile files.

With GJXDM as the canonical XML data format, the data flow can be simplified in that the terminal server just converts to and from GJXDM. The one negative point to be noted here is that GJXDM is a fairly complex set of XML Schemas, and processing actual workflows based on GJXDM can be fairly computationally intensive unless XML processing is accelerated in some manner.

However, we do not have any reusable service at this point. For example, if an authorized homeland defense application needed access to the state justice information, from a strict "Service" definition, no *service visibility* or *interaction model* is available as defined in Chapter 1. Conforming to such a service visibility or interaction model would allow more direct access to the state department of motor vehicles data. Using GJXDM, the homeland defense agency must have a terminal server deployed. This translates into costs both in terms of time and real investments

Several other systems are also available that have complementary and overlapping purposes. A few examples include:

- HSIN (Homeland Security Information Network), which makes real-time threat information available to law enforcement and first-responders through a web based system.

- The Regional Information Sharing System (RISS), which links law enforcement agencies throughout the nation for multi-jurisdictional crime fighting and anti-terrorism. RISS is a shared intranet service.

- FBI's Law Enforcement Online (LEO), another secure intranet service, provides web-based access to law enforcement related information.

All of these are examples of systems with the same core problem: they are conceived in terms of a single agency purpose in the form of a silo. Each of these systems was built independently, with different authentication schemes and usage models. If we think in terms of the ultimate aim of justice information sharing, they are really trying to solve similar problems and could benefit from a service-oriented, canonical form style approach. Left as they are, these types of silos will suffer from security lapses due to disparate authentication schemes, duplicate data entry, maintenance problems, and general inefficiency from the user's perspective.

The use of the message switch is limited to the application that conforms to the strict specifications imposed by the message switch and terminal server for data exchange. For example, if a different usage model emerged that required the use of different components from the state department of justice systems information model, it is likely that a new custom interface similar to the message switch and terminal server will have to be built.

In order to provide more actionable information at the point where it is useful, several architectural issues need to be addressed that bring this environment closer to SOA concepts. One criticism of these suggestions might be that most of them are not implemented due to organizational boundary issues rather than technology. However, through careful technology choices, the architecture could be started at any service end-point and expanded based on acceptance by others therefore avoiding the "everything or nothing" pitfall often associated with technology.

Common Vocabulary: Data Standards

Extending data interoperability for the public safety throughout government bodies is a pressing need: while GJXDM is a commendable effort from the Department of Justice community, the need of wider data interoperability across public safety related government agencies is immediate. The National Information Exchange Model (NIEM) is a partnership of the U.S. Department of Justice and the Department of Homeland Security, and is designed to develop, disseminate, and support enterprise-wide information exchange standards and processes that can enable jurisdictions to effectively share critical information in emergency situations, as well as support the day-to-day operations of agencies throughout the nation. In the NIEM specifications, GJXDM is one of multiple data contexts, each one of which has their own namespace, with common data description and data sharing guidelines. A NIEM based data exchange will allow for services across Department of Justice, public safety, health and Homeland Security to exchange data in canonical form.

Common Service Interaction Profiles

However, as described in Chapter 3, SOA as the universal communication tunnel based on acceptable set of protocols and standards requires more than an interoperable data format. At a state agency level, this might translate into agreeing into either a common transport (such as HTTP, HTTP(S), or IBM MQ Series), or deploying systems that can interoperate between different transports and different interaction models (publish-subscribe, request-response, notification-only, and so on). It is critical, therefore, to look at the patterns supported by the Enterprise Service bus deployed in these environments. These patterns should also be supported by the service composition and business process execution environments.

Services: SOAP and (not or) REST

As U.S. Department of Justice related information, such as Amber Alerts, need to be shared widely with public, the service concept does not need to be tied down to a specific technology artifact, that is to say, that a service can be made available as a REST or a SOAP service based on requirement and the infrastructure components such as ESB platforms for integrating within a state agency, or across state agencies, should not be restrictive on how the services are made available. It is quite likely that portions of Department of Justice related applications will become service oriented from the ground up, while others will start off as service facades. For example, the FBI's LEO Service could be made available as RSS feeds based on XML without reengineering the entire application, and could then integrate into the service bus at a state department of justice. The service bus should be able to provide interoperability between the SOAP and REST based services.

Security on the Network

The provincial and national governments are cautious adopters of technology in public safety for obvious reasons. Security is bound to be a top concern while considering services based architecture in order to better share information with other state and federal agencies for public safety. To ensure at least a minimal level of network security, the public safety environments are on encrypted private networks.

The good news is that in order to get started with SOA within state agency IT environments, the SOA security requirements, while stringent, are addressable with technology available today.

- SSL Authentication: To verify the domain associated with the specific agency by parsing and validating the session-level (SSL) certificate.

- Canonical data validation: Enforce the GJXDM/NIEM specific content model, with the ability to support multiple schemas for variations on data models across agencies.

- XML Content Attack Prevention: Protects against XML Context attacks, including semantic threats, Denial of Service threats and parser exploits.

- Authentication and Authorization: Authorize the requesting person (not the system) for the specific operations using the credential presented. This is usually done by matching the user and group information in an LDAP-accessible X.500 directory and ensures that attributes match for a specific operation.

- Security conformance: Verify the WS-I Basic Security Profile conformant WS-Security header on the SOAP message containing the OTA payload.

Moving towards Evolutionary SOA Adoption in Law Enforcement

As we discussed in Chapter 2, the Enterprise Architecture needs to lead the SOA adoption effort and define a stepwise plan towards it. The Enterprise Architecture's primary charter is therefore to define the service portfolio, define a service oriented roadmap, and establish a service governance process.

Service Taxonomy

An example of how tightly coupled information can be exposed as services in law enforcement is illustrated in Figure 5.4, which is one representation of types of business services in a state department of justice. These and other similar services have a broader usage in state government agencies and can be orchestrated as part of a services workflow in a big bus environment.

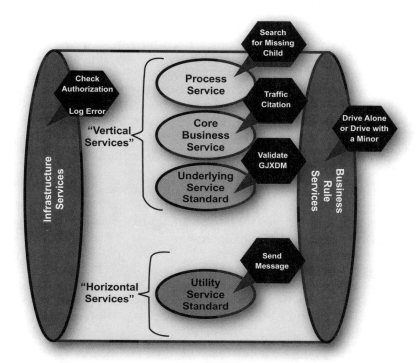

Example of Core Law Enforcement Business Services

        Citing Officer - organization & affiliation, relationships, plus roles/groups

        Subject (Driver) – summary or full person record, Driver License information

        Appearance – court case details

        Citation – issued to records, issued from records

        Incident – road conditions, intoxication, speed, charge, etc.

        Vehicle – identification, registration

        Document – pictures

        Location

Figure 5.4   Example Service Taxonomy for Law Enforcement

As we have seen in other verticals, in order to create a set of reusable services that can be composed at a business process layer, the IT environment has to build a stack of services. The lowest part of the stack performs horizontal, reusable technical functions such as content routing, messaging, and security.

The key elements of the law enforcement service taxonomy are the core business services. These services are coarse-grained and provide highly shared data relevant to most law enforcement and public safety related business processes. This includes data lists of law enforcement officers, subjects, agencies, vehicles, as well as key transaction data types such as citations, incidents, appearance, and so on.

With these (and other) business services, applications can be composed to deliver key services such as searching for missing person, or searching for a match on a stolen vehicle in a manner that is easily changeable and extendable.

Further, as these services need to be exposed external to the state justice agencies, they can be composed to conform to data exchange patterns required to interoperate with external agencies using GJXDM or NIEM based canonical data exchange.

Service Infrastructure

The set of infrastructure components required for SOA deployment were discussed in Chapter 4. Based on the law enforcement use case, it includes:

- Service Containers: In law enforcement agencies, the IT adoption by necessity is cautious in nature. This means that a tremendous amount of data is in legacy formats. In order to be able to create a flexible service oriented environment without massive reengineering, the service container solutions need to be able to provide a service façade to legacy systems.

- Enterprise Service Bus: Once the core business services are defined and can be made available by using appropriate service containers, a service bus environment is required in order to create composite services and business process workflows associated with the composite services that are based on business use cases. Reliability and auditing are key requirements in law enforcement to execute business process workflows. So utility services such as messaging (reliability, ability to have intermediaries, multiple service interaction profile support for messaging patterns such as fire and forget, request-response, publish-subscribe), and security (addressing validation, authentication, authorization, access control, and auditing), need to be carefully architected in a reusable manner.

It is critical, however, that the features of Enterprise Service Bus be looked at for their applicability to the law enforcement, and in general, in government.

> The ESB must have high-performance standards based local and remote services composition and orchestration environment.

> The ESB should be able to work with XML workflows, SOAP or REST.

> The ESB should offer core utility services such as transformation, sophisticated content validation, security, content routing, web services firewall, and non-XML adaptation.

> The ESB should not be tied down to a vendor-specific messaging implementation.

> The ESB should be vertically and horizontally scaleable and to the extent possible manageable from a single console.

For rest of the chapter and in other sections of the book, to differentiate an ESB with the above features with a name, we will refer to it as Hyper-ESB.

Figure 5.5 illustrates an SOA implementation in law enforcement. Comparing Figures 5.2 and 5.5, the law enforcement personnel's requests are now serviced by a service bus that invokes a relevant business process that then composes underlying business services in order to execute the process workflow. The business services use the underlying horizontal utility services such as messaging and security that are available transparently in the Enterprise Service bus. There are today still barriers to full SOA realization in the law enforcement environments that require reliability in message delivery with the flexibility of SOA. The point-to-point named queue based proprietary messaging mechanisms do not allow for intermediaries that could dynamically bind to arbitrary queues based on request and response content. And the SOAP based reliable messaging (OASIS WS-RM) protocols are not yet mature enough to offer interoperable capability. So the pragmatic solution is to encapsulate messaging service in a manner that when better solutions are available, the underlying queuing mechanisms can be replaced without big impact to system availability.

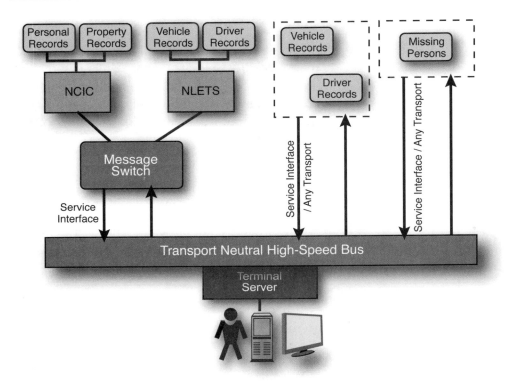

Figure 5.5   SOA Environment in State Justice

■ External Gateway: With a service bus environment with service containers, with agency SOA environment is realizable. However, as we discussed earlier in the law enforcement use case, the business environment has changed—better information access is needed to and from the state law enforcement agencies, closer interoperability is needed with other public safety agencies such as public health, and ability to disseminate information to public is needed for emergency purposes. With these expanded requirements, creating point-to-point interfaces to each segment of external user base is not viable. What is needed is a secure reliable means to exchange information with the external agencies, that allows for network based isolation and security and SOA security with content awareness to secure, and then send/receive messages to appropriate responding services (or consumers). The exchange patterns with external agencies are going to be based on canonical data (GJXDM/NIEM). However, as different agencies are at varying stages of XML adoption for data interchange (this is before they begin to consider SOA), some of the key authentication and request information is embedded as part of payload itself and not in the SOAP wrapper. So the gateways have to be able to execute process flows that include what we identified earlier as security requirements, with the additional requirements to be able to take action based on the specifics in the payload.

■ In case a Hyper-ESB type solution is adopted, ESB and External Gateway can be collapsed onto one solution thereby reducing total cost of moving to Service oriented environment.

The Service-Oriented Adoption Roadmap

The various state law enforcement agencies within the United States are at all stages of SOA adoption. The mistake to avoid really would be to just address data exchange with external agencies as required by them and by the Department of Homeland Security, as a piecemeal application, rather than building SOA environment within the state law enforcement agencies, extending it to other public safety agencies at state level using Enterprise Service Bus and service containers and then extending it to other external agencies using an external gateway.

Summary

While the cautious nature of technology adoption by governments may indicate a slower adoption of SOA, our experience has been that government agencies in the United States and across the world that have taken the lead with SOA have seen immediate benefits in reusability and reduction of redundancy in software and hardware. We also discussed how in the United States, the federal government is creating reference models in order to encourage reuse and cut costs across agencies, and that these reference models reflect closely the SOA principles and objectives.

In this chapter we covered how related to public safety are facing new challenges can be transformed through SOA, especially when used closely in conjunction with public safety data vocabularies. Usage of the vocabularies is becoming a requirement for vendors offering solutions to the U.S. Department of Homeland Security, justice and public safety agencies. Despite adoption of vocabularies, however, it is apparent that legacy data in non-XML formats will continue to be quite prevalent in government agencies due to wide variation of new technology adoption.

In addition to vocabularies, security and privacy are critical key to adoption of SOA in government agencies especially the ones that focus on law enforcement, homeland security, and other public safety functions. The basic set of SOA security standards are mature, and provide the security capability needed to ensure privacy and integrity of data. Additional capabilities for content-based attack prevention and canonical data validation can be added by using external gateways or XML Firewall solutions.

Chapter 6

SOA in Financial Services

Finance is the art of passing money from hand to hand until it finally disappears.

—Robert W. Sarnoff

Financial services is a very broad category that covers businesses engaged in capital markets, insurance, mortgage, retail banking, and so on. The financial services industry has been a fairly consistent lead adopter of technology and its requirements have led to evolution of information technology in general. Primarily involved in trading of information goods, the ability to manage and effectively utilize information technology has provided the competitive edge to companies offering financial services. Therefore it comes as no surprise that service oriented architecture has been influenced by requirements of the financial services industry and is finding increasing adoption in segments of this industry. For the purpose of this book we will limit the discussion on the use of service oriented architecture to use cases in capital markets and retail banking IT environments.

Figure 6.1 describes the interlocked nature of financial services businesses. While we will focus on intersection of information technology and SOA in capital markets, the underlying drivers for adoption of SOA are relevant to others as well.

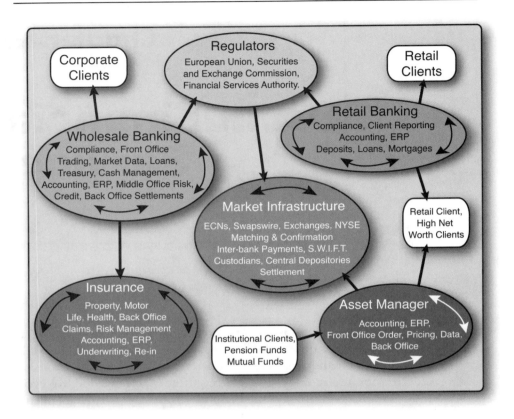

Figure 6.1   Financial Services Industry

Within capital markets, three types of entities are involved. First are the exchanges, where the transactions of stocks, bonds, and other investment vehicles such as derivatives are conducted. Second are the buy-side firms or the companies that primarily raise capital for the purpose of managing investments, such as mutual funds, hedge funds, pension funds, and so on. And finally, the sell-side firm provides several services, including the ability for the buy-side firms to make large trades on the exchanges. For the rest of this section, we focus on the sell-side architecture. The reason for doing so is that sell-side information technology architecture is facing significant challenges going forward because of their unique requirements driven by the performance, the impact of the changing nature of buy-side companies, and the changing regulatory environment.

Let us take a look at a simplified business process in trading. For this example, we examine a fixed income asset class such as stocks and bonds. As shown in Figure 6.2, for fixed income instruments (such as bonds and equities), the buy-side (portfolio managers and investors) makes the decision to buy or sell, and gives the order to a broker-dealer organization. The trader from the broker-dealer organization looks for prices on one or several exchanges where the security is listed, and makes the trade. Once the trade is made, a confirmation of the transaction detail with the order needs to be performed to check the correct execution. When the transaction matches, the portfolios are updated and then the settlement is initiated. The securities are exchanged (usually through a global custodian) along with the payments. Once settlement completes, the payments and holdings at the investment manager's end are reconciled.

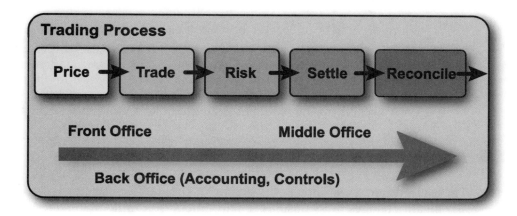

Figure 6.2   A Business Process in Trading

The sell-side information technology architecture has typically worked in three rather independent silos, in many cases, for each class of investment vehicle, such as bonds, stocks, and derivatives:

1. The front-office tier usually consists of trader workstations that connect with the exchanges and electronic communication networks (ECNs). Front office tier is used by the sales and trading professionals for executing trades. The trading workstation

usually has software that either polls or subscribes to information from multiple sources, including exchanges, deployed to provide meaningful information in a timely fashion in order to make the best trading decision possible. This tier interacts with exchanges and ECNs for receiving the latest market data and executing trades. The latency demands on the front-office tier including the workstations, the network and the connectivity to exchanges and ECNs are intense due to the time-sensitive nature of trading. The key requirements for the front-office are near zero-latency trade and quote execution.

2. The middle-office tier provides trade risk management, pricing, credit, insurance, and other pre-settlement services after the trade is executed in the front office. The level of integration between the front office and middle office depends a lot on the instrument traded and the specific financial institution. While the front office is focused on performance, the middle office has to ensure that risk management and regulatory issues associated with trades are addressed. The middle office requires complex computations (such as Monte Carlo simulation) that require large compute server farms. As we will discuss later, it is this tier where adoption of SOA offers the most business value.

3. The back-office tier typically provides the post-trade settlement services, such as accounting, data warehousing, and settlement. The volume of actual messages is low but the value of the messages can run into billions of dollars. Performance is not as critical as it is in the front-office and middle-office tiers.

Technology Drivers for SOA

The sell-side financial industry segment in the capital markets is seeing significant changes in its business environment. A sample of changes that are relevant to unique requirements and nature of SOA deployments in this segment are:

Multi-asset trading: Investors (buy-side) are no longer looking at just one specific product, but instead are evaluating a collection of asset classes, such as derivatives, equities, foreign exchange, and swaps. The asset management side of the business is therefore pushing for more standardization and automation across asset classes. While the predominant standard used in most exchanges in developed countries to represent equities and fixed income products is FIX (Financial Information eXchange)[1], and FIXML (Financial Information eXchange Markup Language); the derivatives have also seen the significant standardization and automation. However, multi-asset trading today is not automated, because the asset classes have a vertically integrated infrastructure, as shown in Figure 6.3.

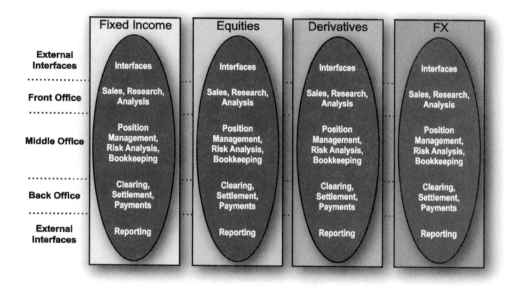

Figure 6.3   Technology Silos Based On Financial Products

Algorithmic trading: The global financial markets have seen tremendous growth in the hedge fund and asset management segments. This has meant that the number of financial transactions has increased greatly over the past few years as has the level of complexity of these transactions. Algorithmic trading has been made increasingly common by hedge funds. It is defined as a collection of financial instruments (equities or derivatives) traded as a block based on algorithms. A single trade therefore needs to be routed through several internal systems for pre- and post-settlement services. Quotes on all equities (traded on any of

---

[1] http://www.fixprotocol.org/what-is-fix.shtml

the worldwide exchanges) need to be received and the algorithm driving the basket needs to be processed. The trade needs to be executed rapidly by getting best possible execution—minimizing latency of quote and trade from the exchanges to the front-office trader's desk and back, even by hundredths of seconds, translates of significant competitive advantage in this environment.

Changing global regulatory environment: Financial institutions engaged in capital markets do business in a highly regulated environment. Several regulations such as MiFID[2] in the European Union and Reg NMS[3] in the United States have had and continue to have significant impact on the IT architecture of financial industries. (For example, the T+1 regulation earlier, which was an expensive effort on part of the financial community for trade settlement within one day of trade, led to migration from a manual process of passing trade information from front office to middle office to deployment of application servers and EAI solutions in the middle office.) The MiFID directive essentially directs the capital market participants to provide the best execution in terms of price, liquidity, order size, costs, and so on.

Changing nature of exchanges: Exchanges are becoming increasingly electronic the world over, and while the revenue the exchanges generate from certain asset classes such as fixed income is declining, derivatives have become a key area. These factors, among others, are leading to significant consolidation among exchanges.

Use Case of SOA Deployment in Middle-office

It would be tempting to consider for a minute the possibility of moving the entire sell-side architecture to a more services-oriented one. What would such an environment look like? There are already XML-based standards in different stages of maturity available for the major financial instruments, such as FIXML for fixed income assets and FpML (Financial Products Markup Language) for derivatives. An overlay publish-subscribe architecture that can operate across networks and can be deployed in a

---

[2] "Markets in Financial Instruments Directive", http://europa.eu.int/eur-lex/pri/en/oj/dat/2004/l_145/l_14520040430en00010044.pdf

[3] "Regulation NMS", http://www.sec.gov/rules/final/34-51808.pdf

distributed manner in front offices and exchanges, where stock quotes and trades are routed in XML-based standards. In such an environment, any endpoint can dynamically subscribe to relevant information by using XPath[4] or XQuery[5] based subscriptions. The subscriptions can then be locally and dynamically bound to real network addresses through the use of a distributed addressing table. In such an environment any financial environment can be traded on any exchange with minimal of tight coupling due to data formats and exchange data interface APIs except for the dependence on the network interoperability to the extent the pub-sub environment cannot operate seamlessly over different networks. Quote and execution over such a pub-sub environment based on XML then interacts with the middle-office services such as risk analysis using an ESB orchestration environment.

A conceptual view of this scenario is illustrated in Figure 6.4. At the bottom of the stack are utility and underlying services. The coarse-grained business services provide highly shared data such as order management, position management, risk analysis, market data, and so on.

---

[4] Language for addressing part of a XML document, http://www.w3.org/TR/xpath

[5] Query language that can be used to query any XML data sources, http://www.w3.org/TR/xquery/ - 830k

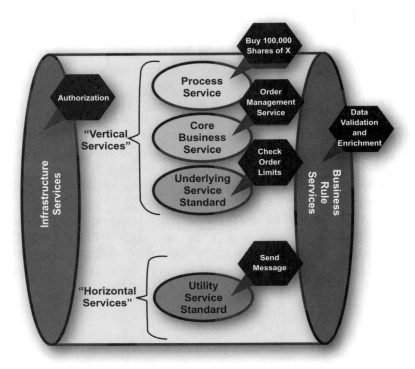

Example of Core Trading Business Services

        Market Data – From exchanges

        Order Management – Order splitting, order routing, interest rate derivatives, foreign exchange, bonds and equities

        Position Management – Position keeping, equity analytics

        Pricing Calculations

        Risk Analysis – Credit, risk analytics, scenarios

        Trade Fulfillment

        Payments – SWIFT, Fedwire, etc.

        Billing

        Accounting – FSI GL

        Confirmations

Figure 6.4   Example Service Taxonomy for Trading

Now let us take a less conceptual and more practical view on this architecture. Significant technical limitations make such an approach unlikely in the short run. The application architecture specific limitations are:

1. The performance-intensive nature of the front-office tier makes it unlikely that the environment described above will be realized until aspects of XML processing such as XML parsing and XPath execution become as fast and lean in memory and CPU utilization as (or better than) native mechanisms deployed today. This limits the scalability of the data distribution architecture based on the quotes and orders in XML.

2. Even if XML processing was not an issue, network latency has driven the sell-side environment to use proprietary messaging for publish-subscribe networks. Any advantages of a flexible trading environment that emerge from loosely coupling the data are likely to be minimized by tighter coupling of the network.

Please note that so far we have not talked about web services per se—that is, trades and price quotes wrapped in a SOAP envelope. Given the widely documented performance overheads just in XML processing, it appeared to us a moot point to discuss another layer of processing to be incurred due to XML-based envelopes. Over the middle to long term, however, we believe that widely available hardware acceleration for the processing elements discussed above, combined with interoperable messaging, will enable massive transformation of the front-office environments, possibly even changing the underlying business models for sell-side enterprises.

With that background, let us take a look at more effective and near term use cases for Service Oriented Architecture in the middle office of financial institutions that can address the emerging business trends highlighted earlier.

The end-to-end business process is still locked up in tightly coupled asset-class based applications. These applications are controlled by a broker-based EAI environment tied together with underlying named-queue based reliable messaging architectures. Let us consider the inherent tight-coupling in this environment.

1. The messaging mechanisms are based on named-queues, implying tight coupling of the messaging clients with the messaging servers.

2. In this environment, all rules for routing data between applications responsible for pricing, risk analysis, insurance, and

other pre-settlement activities are centrally managed and deployed.

It is important to realize that even if these end applications were exposed as web services, the nature of the implementations is such that order routing is tightly coupled to the applications and messaging. With the changing regulatory environment, changing mix (multi-asset trading), scale, and automated trading, the pre- and post-sale settlement processes have to be overhauled.

Program Trading Use Case: Identifying the Gaps

The desired goal in these environments is likely to be an end-to-end program trading driven entirely by algorithms where order data is automatically routed to the service and the entire execution can be performed reliably with performance guarantees. Furthermore, the architecture should be able to respond to regulatory and industry changes rapidly.

Program trading may involve fixed income instruments, derivatives, or other financial asset classes. In order to provide a program trading environment across asset classes using service oriented architecture, three types of issues must be addressed. First, the information in a program trade request must be conveyed and understood in an interoperable form. This information may relate to a single asset class or multiple asset classes. Second, there must be an enterprise services orchestration layer that can orchestrate, execute, track, and log the business process involving various subsystems required in execution of a program trade request. And finally, it must be possible to send and receive this request in an interoperable yet reliable manner.

Let us consider each of these issues one by one. On the data format issue, we will use examples of fixed income and derivatives. Now in its fifth version, the Fixed Income eXchange (FIX) standard has been used primarily for fixed income securities; it provides a mechanism to encode both the session and application layers, independent of the underlying network protocol. FIXML provides for XML encoding of the application layer. The Session layer is kept separate, because the financial institution may have other messaging environments such as JMS (Java messaging service) implementations that ensure reliable, ordered, and once-and-only-once delivery required in trading environments; or that it can be replace with a SOAP layer.

Derivatives, on the other hand, have only recently begun moving towards a standardized format. Derivatives such as credit swaps, interest rate swaps, and foreign exchange swaps are by nature customized products. The business process thus far has been based on a term sheet agreed upon by the buyer and seller. Increasingly, however, the derivatives are defined using the FpML standard. A certain degree of automation has been achieved in derivative trading by defining the product in FpML format, as shown in the example in Figure 6.5, and performing the trade, such as a credit swap, and then confirming it once using shared platforms such as Depository Trust and Clearing Corporation (DTCC). This process removes the manual matching of the two confirmations, as was done until recently. However, in order to have full end-to-end automated business process for inter-bank derivative trade execution, much more needs to be done.

```
<?xml version="1.0" encoding="utf-8">
<!--== Copyright © 2002-2005. All rights reserved.

    == Financial Products Markup Language is subject

    == to the FpML public license.

    == A copy of this license is available at

    == http://www.fpml.org/documents/license

  -->

<FpML xsi:type="RequestValuationReport" version="4-2"

  xmlns="http://www.fpml.org/2005/FpML-4-2"

  xmlns:dsig="http://www.w3.org/2000/09/xmldsig#"

  xmlns:xsi="http://www.w3.org/2001/XMLSchema-instance"

  xsi:schemaLocation="http://www.vpml.org/2005/FpML-4-2../fpml-main-4-2.xsd">

  <header>

    <messageId messageIdScheme="http://www.fpml.org/message-id">VAL001</mes:

    <sentBy>ABC123</sentBy>

    <sendTo>DEF456</sendTo>

    <creationTimestamp>2004-05-21T17:29:04-00:00</creationTimestamp>
```

```
    </header>
<party id="party1">

    <partyId>ABCDEF</partyId>

</party>

<market>

  <yieldCurve id="USD-LIBOR">

    <name>3M-LIBOR</name>

    <currency>USD</currency>

  </yieldCurve>

  <!—Yield Curve Valuation for USD-LIBOR-vals  -->

  <yieldCurveValuation id="USD-LIBOR-vals">

    <objectReference href="USD-LIBOR" />

    <baseDate>2003-10-29</baseDate>

    <buildDateTime>2004-05-31T12:13:59-00:00</buildDateTime>

    <inputs>

      <instrumentSet>

        <deposit id="USD-LIBOR-input-1">

        <instrumentId instrumentIdScheme=http://fpml.org/instruments-pr-exam">

        <term>

.  .  ..
```

Figure 6.5   FpML for Derivative Trading
Reprinted from FpML® 4.2 Recommendation - May 14, 2007 with
permission of International Swaps and Derivatives Association, Inc.
© 2007 International Swaps and Derivatives Association, Inc.

For example, even when a contract is defined using FpML, there is
really no reference data to validate the context, no session or messaging
constructs defined, and no overall business process defined. These
elements are outside the current scope of FpML. However, these
contracts are important looking into the future, with derivative trading
on the rise along with program or algorithmic trading. In order to be able
to offer complete program trading environment using service oriented
architecture for derivatives, the FpML must have constructs similar to the
FIX Session layer encoded in a wrapper layer. With the ability to provide

reference data and session level information in an encoded form, the ability to create an automated program trading environment covering multiple asset classes is significantly enhanced.

Let us now look at the second issue limiting the ability to deploy SOA for program trading. As we discussed before, in the near to mid-term, it is likely that the front office will continue to trade based on performance-oriented but tightly coupled systems in asset class silos. To be able to create a flexible middle-office tier as shown in fig 6.6, where instead of asset class silos of applications, a set of horizontal services can be orchestrated to address the emerging business requirements, the ability to convert the front-office trade data into XML-based standards as discussed above is necessary but not a sufficient condition. A high-performance business process orchestration environment with interoperable yet reliable messaging is needed (sort of a *hyper-ESB*) that is not tied to either the network or the software deployed on any of the end-points. Unfortunately, many technological gaps must be filled before this requirement is met. In the trading environment, the need for high performance and scalability can hinder the adoption of a service oriented approach—this continues to be a gap as most ESB or ESB-like solutions do not address this high-performance segment very well.

Also, interoperable web services based reliable messaging continues to be an unresolved issue that the Web Services Interoperability (WS-I) organization is attempting to address. Alternatives coming from the financial industry itself, such as Advanced Message Queuing Protocol (AMQP), are attempting a major change in how messaging is done (we will discuss this in more detail in the next section).

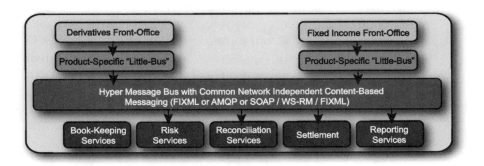

Figure 6.6 SOA Architecture for an Automated Trading Environment

Finally, we come to the issue of interoperable messaging. Services need to be loosely coupled while delivering the same quality of service as is provided by point-to-point message-oriented middleware solutions. Current efforts in the WS* stack towards reliable messaging suffer from several drawbacks:

The mechanism to get the source and destinations to agree on the quality of service such as once-and-only-once delivery, timing transactions, security, persistence to protect against various failure conditions, message exchange patterns, and so on are not part of the OASIS WS-RX standard. That leads to situations where, for example, vendors have differing proprietary implementations that enhance the message or the associated WS-Reliable messaging policy with delivery assurance requirements of the source and destination, thereby reducing the interoperability benefit of conforming to the standard. The WS-I organization has an ongoing effort to develop an interoperability profile dealing with secure, reliable messaging capabilities for Web services.

There are several scenarios in financial industry where REST-based message routing provides the best of both worlds—loosely coupled services as well as performance. However, specifications such as WS-RX provide only SOAP bindings limiting the ability to use a key infrastructure element such as messaging, for non-SOAP XML-based environments.

Considering these and other limitations some major users of messaging in the financial industry have come up with their own specification. As shown in Figure 6.7, AMQP, a recent non-XML wire specification coming out of Morgan Stanley and a few vendors, covers some of the gaps highlighted earlier. AMQP is a very simple specification that uses concepts similar to Simple Mail Transfer Protocol (SMTP) to support point-to-point, publish-subscribe as well as content-based routing, and has some open-source implementations available. It allows for intermediaries, does not bind to SOAP only, and provides for message exchange patterns and quality of service constructs missing in the current WS-RX specification. The big drawback to AMQP is lack of support from some of the major WS* stack software vendors. However, it offers some compelling concepts that should be used to enhance WS-RX specification.

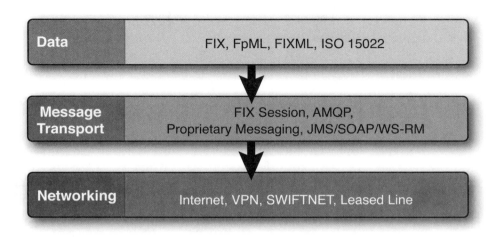

Figure 6.7   FSI Middle-office Infrastructure

Let us now shift focus to take a look at the use of SOA concepts to reduce the costs of back-office operations in retail banking. The purpose of this section is to describe a real-world use case for SOA in the financial services industry. Due to the practical nature of this type of description, we will include both business and technical aspects. Further, it should be noted that even though this use case is called an SOA style scenario, it is far from pure as it includes heterogeneous standards and technologies that don't fit under any definition of SOA. Some readers may stop here and argue that it isn't really an SOA deployment but a hodgepodge of technologies with some XML and web services style technologies mixed in. To this argument we would answer that most of the practical deployments of SOA use cases end up this way simply because of the complexity of private-industry technology deployments. Very rarely does a practical deployment of SOA include a full rip-and-replace with a brand new, pure SOA style architecture. In fact, we would argue that to date such types of deployments are few and far between. Second, in this particular use case, SOA was used as an internal moniker for pushing ahead technology change that receives *some* of the benefits of a pure SOA architecture. That is, SOA need not be implemented in its pure form to provide value to businesses so long as it is used as a label to refer to valuable technology artifacts such as interoperable standards, processes and workflows. As mentioned before, this example comes from an existing, deployed solution in the financial industry; as expected, we will give enough details to communicate the core SOA concepts involved but at the same time we must leave out certain details that might offer competitive advantage.

Business Drivers

The background of this use case is set in the banking industry and concerns the move to paperless banking and more specifically, electronic check processing. This follows the general trend of cost savings in the financial industry that began with the move to Automated Teller Machines (ATMs), then Internet-based (Web-based) baking and now to paperless banking. Electronic check processing includes both transaction processing of the check itself as well as archival and audit capabilities. As a cost-savings measure, banks increasingly rely on an outsourced service as this avoids investment in processing technology. Savings come in many areas including operations and maintenance of in-house processing software, avoiding penalties on tight SLAs (Service-Level Agreements) for check processing transactions, and the cost of supporting banking regulations. For this case, the entity offering the service is an outsourcing company with expertise in check processing, archival, and retrieval. Figure 6.8 shows this basic concept in terms of the general SOA model described in Chapter 1.

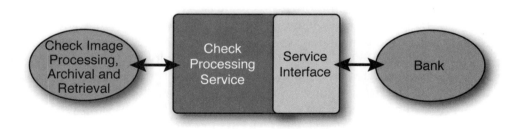

Figure 6.8   Check Processing SOA Concept Model

Figure 6.8 is a simple concept model. It shows the underlying capability being exposed as a service with a well-defined service interface. Further, the outsourcing company is allowing the possibility (and in fact hoping) that of one of n banks will sign up to use this service. In this case, each bank pays a fee to use the service and in response, is guaranteed a certain service response time. However, we must be clear about what is actually occurring: there are input and output aspects to this service. The input data flow is the image processing of a check; that is, banks send checks to be archived, and the output flow would consist in *queries* for specific check images and associated data, or even batch queries consisting in hundreds or thousands of checks in a single response bundle. For this use case then, we have four business level operations:

1. *Load Check:* Banks send physical checks to the outsourcing company

2. *Search Archive:* A bank wishes to search for a check based on query data

3. *Retrieve Check:* A bank wishes to retrieve a specific check

4. *Retrieve Checks (Batch):* A bank wishes to retrieve a set of checks

You should note that the first use case is a physical process and will not be represented as a service call. The second, third, and fourth cases all represent specific functions to be exposed by the service. The next section describes the technology-level issues that surround these cases.

Technology Drivers

How would the three functions previously mentioned be exposed as a service call? More importantly, what core technology issues are at stake? It is tempting to first apply a generic *pure* SOA or web services (WS-*) lens to the problem, but as we will see, certain pragmatic considerations get in the way. If we were to outline the technology considerations that surround this type of Business to Business (B2B) interaction, we might consider a number of issues such as *interface definitions, message exchange pattern(s), data, security,* and *performance* considerations. Notice that we aren't applying the breadth of technology issues such as *service monitoring, service management, service orchestration* and *choreography* because they don't apply for this business case. We have a bounded problem where the end goal is for banks to query for specific check data and obtain these results within an acceptable SLA. Let's look at some of the details of each of the issues we've just described:

■ *Interface Definitions:* How should the service interface be structured? What level of interface decoupling will be used? That is, how much information about the function call itself will be embedded into the message itself and where is it placed?

- *Message Exchange Pattern:* What sort of message pattern will be used? Will a simple request/response pattern suffice or is a more complex pattern required? Note that in this case the *future* version of this moves beyond a request/response pattern to a publish/subscribe pattern for performance reasons.

- *Data*: The data itself is a check, but has two logical parts, the image and associated metadata. Must we consider any special handling for this opaque image data?

- *Security*: What sort of security considerations will suffice here? Do we need message-level security or will transport-level encryption suffice?

- *Performance*: What sort of performance issues will come into play? How quickly is the service expected to respond to queries?

The next section tackles each of these technology drivers, but rather than being *prescriptive* we are being *descriptive*. That is, we wish to show first what was done in solving this real-world problem, recognizing that there may be a more elegant ways of structuring the solution. To this end, our description is practical and not theoretical; we aim to get at those aspects of the technology that were truly supportive of the business case.

Solution Description

The treatment of the solution description in this section will roughly follow the order of the technology drivers noted in the last section. The interface definitions as described by WSDL consist of operations for invoking a SearchRequest(), CheckRequest(), and BatchRequest(), as well as their appropriate synchronous response pairs. The transfer envelope used in this case was SOAP, but it was mainly used as a lightweight envelope. The SOAP message itself utilized a *document style* encoding, but was extremely liberal about including most of the information in the SOAP body itself, including credential and identifier information. That is, the SOAP header wasn't utilized in this case; instead, domain specific elements were invented to capture specific data type and parameter information for the function calls, rather than relying on SOAP types. As far as the binding style, it was a completely static style binding, where each participant bank had to know *a priori* the nature of the interface and the structure of the message. That is, the concepts of dynamic binding didn't come into play in this case. Example 6.1 shows an example SearchRequest message that remains conceptually faithful to the actual request sent in the use case without divulging specific competitive information. You should note that this example is annotated with specific comments (denoted with //) to call out some of the specific features just discussed.

Example 6.1: SearchRequest Message Example

```
<Envelope>
  <Header/> // empty header
  <Body>
  <sr:SearchRequest xmlns:sr="http://xyz.com/sr.xsd">

  // namespace qualified function representation

  <clientID>XYZ</clientID>

  // identity is in the SOAP body rather than header

  <timeStamp>123456</timeStamp>

  // custom timestamp element

  <searchCriteria>

  // search parameters are expressed as custom <criteria>
  // elements




  <criteria>
    <indexName>StartDate</indexName>
  <values>
    <value>20060203</value>
  </values>
  </criteria>

  <criteria>
    <indexName>EndDate</indexName>
    <values>
      <value>20060203</value>
    </values>
  </criteria>
  <criteria>
    <indexName>Account</indexName>
    <values>
      <value>123456</value>
```

```
      </values>
    </criteria>

// The search criteria shown here are start date, end
// date, and account number

    </sr:SearchRequest>
  </Body>
</Envelope>
```

What are we to make of this example? SOA purists would certainly balk at it and perhaps even cite it as a degenerate web services case that doesn't achieve the true vision of WS-* or SOA. The reasons to cite would be the use of SOAP as a lightweight envelope, lack of reliance on standards for "properly" expressing identities and timestamps, as well as the custom nature of the internals of the document. However, this viewpoint ignores some of the pragmatic considerations involved, such as the business drivers: little is gained by using a few standard elements from WS-Security unless there is a clear need, all it would do at this point is put extra requirements on each end of the interaction. Further, the security model for this use case is a *point-to-point* request-response model and doesn't mandate message level security. Instead, the real-world version of this use case relied on SSL/TLS for the authentication of each endpoint involved in the service interaction. We might imagine a more complex multi-hop scenario across multiple intermediaries that had a stake in processing the check. Should this occur, then a message-level solution like WS-Security would be more appropriate.

What of the check data itself? As we mentioned before, the check comes into the outsourcing company as a paper check that then undergoes image processing. This part of the service is considered separate from the *get* and *search* style operations applied to the check archive. Once banks begin making requests, the checks themselves are coming back as XML. However, in the case of batch operations (requests for many hundreds or thousands of checks), a publish/subscribe style of interaction may be a better option to achieve higher performance (response time) as individual banks can effectively subscribe to an "output bucket" based on a filter. In this scenario, rather than banks requesting a batch of checks that meet search criteria, each bank would have a set of subscriptions that they manage and could ostensibly receive the processed check images as they are processed. This would imply that some amount of *nom-XML* processing would become part of the service workflow. More specifically, rather than a *check archive* constantly being loaded with check data for batch processing, the service could be proactive in sending its responses to banks that subscribe to a search filter, but in doing so would likely end up transforming check image data into XML style responses "on-the-fly." Figure 6.9 shows a bird's eye view of the current application and Figure 6.10 shows the future (proposed) solution that responds to the batch requirement in a more elegant manner.

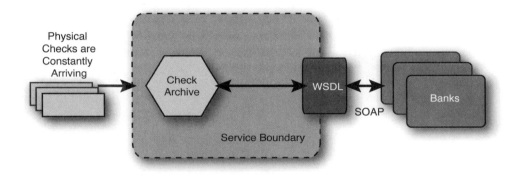

Figure 6.9   Current Check Processing Architecture

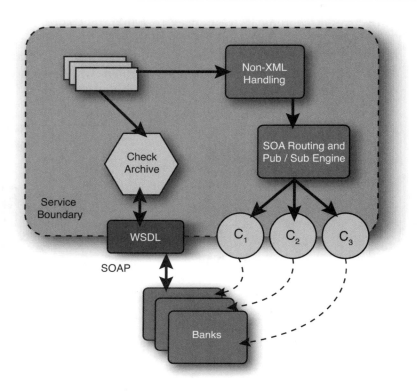

Figure 6.10 The Future Application Could Use Pub/sub to Meet SLAs

Figure 6.10 warrants some further explanation. What is happening here is we are expanding our notion of SOA in a new direction that includes performance oriented aspects by adding a new possible data flow: publish/subscribe. The bubbles C_1, C_2, and C_3 all represent "output buckets" or one-way messaging from the service to the banks. They represent subscriptions for some batch of checks that the bank is interested in. This sort of data flow adds more value than simply going back to retrofit the SOAP messages to be more standards-compliant, or more theoretically correct. The future application might adopt some version of web services events or notification standard to communicate between the service edge and the banks, but notice that there will always be *legacy* requirements, or custom data requirements that crop up. In this example the legacy requirement is non-XML data handling, where check image data and metadata must be parsed and repacked into an

XML-friendly response before it is routed to the proper subscription bucket. We have introduced a logical component here that is doing this SOA style routing, which is really a combination of high performance XML processing, non-XML data handling and publish/subscribe data flow support. You should also note that the expanded architecture doesn't necessarily replace the existing statically bound query mechanism. The reason why is because not *all* banks will have this type of SLA or batch processing requirement.

Summary

While there are several challenges for successful SOA deployments in financial services, we have admittedly addressed only the more basic of the issues. The benefit of such an approach is that the issues we have brought up are relevant regardless of the current state of IT in any of the financial services organizations. The unaddressed issues, such as those of management, governance, and a common information model, have a huge degree of variability based on the IT organization's point of view and legacy mechanisms to offer such capabilities.

Having said that, we will reiterate the common set of challenges across financial services:

- Financial services SOA implementations face many challenges beyond those that are technical in nature; issues of management, governance and common information model can impose a large degree of variability based on the IT organization's point of view and legacy mechanisms to offer such capabilities. SOA can be leveraged to neutralize many of these factors by providing a layer of abstraction between the financial services and the business processes that execute them.

- Most financial services transactional usage models have stringent performance requirements. The SOA-based business processes in today's Financial Services are largely limited to post-trade settlement steps, where performance is not so critical (such as processes to exchange trade capture reports, which are used post execution to report confirmed trades).

- In the middle-office, implementing SOA will require addressing performance concerns of XML processing (such as SOAP Parsing, SOAP/XML Validation, XSLT, XPath processing), non-XML adaptation services and service orchestration. Service scaling and

XML acceleration technologies can be key factors in accomplishing this.

■ The financial industry has its own set of standards such as FIX and SWIFT; some of these standards have evolved into XML based versions such as FIXML and FpML. The move to SOA will involve ensuring that these and other standards for exchanging the datasets in these formats encoded in proprietary systems are transformed into SOA based business processes.

■ The financial services sector has critical business services tied into legacy application platforms. The ability to easily create interoperable services from these legacy systems remains a key hurdle and requires a move to service-oriented middle-tier. WS-I profiles provide a good starting point for interoperability, however, for the many legacy applications that are unlikely to be revised ESB platforms may be needed to ensure services-oriented interoperability.

■ Messaging continues to be a key challenge in the financial Services multi-vendor environment. While standardization activity from end-customers and vendors continue, there is still significant maturation process that we need to go through in order to deliver vendor independent interoperable messaging.

Chapter 7

SOA in Healthcare

If you trust Google more than your doctor then maybe it's time to switch doctors.

—Jadelr and Cristina Cordova

Healthcare organizations today are challenged to manage a growing portfolio of systems. The cost of acquiring, integrating, and maintaining these systems are rising, while the demands of system users are increasing. Organizations must address evolving clinical requirements as well as support revenue cycle and administration business functions. In addition, demands are increasing for interoperability with other organizations to regionally support care delivery. Service oriented architecture (SOA) offers system design and management principles that support reuse and sharing of system resources across the healthcare organization. SOA does not require the reengineering of existing systems. With SOA, existing processing can be combined with new capabilities to build a library of services that are used as a part of solutions. Using shared services that are aligned with business processes, SOA strengthens interoperability while reducing the need to synchronize data between isolated systems. Services may be made available, no matter their location, to create solutions that reach beyond the desktop, the department, and the healthcare organization.

Introduction to the Use of SOA in Health Information Technology

A healthcare organization that depends upon a single system across the entire enterprise to support various departmental and care delivery needs often already has a solution that shares and reuses system resources. More typical is an organization that depends upon one or more enterprise-wide systems, supports department-specific needs with additional systems, has facilities that use their own instances of systems, and interoperates using a complex network of data interfaces. The organization that has a large portfolio of systems will more readily see the benefits of SOA. An SOA environment enables system assets to be accessed across the organization, providing opportunities for sharing system capabilities that are currently isolated. For example, SOA can help meet unfulfilled processing requirements without purchasing additional systems and can provide opportunities to standardize processing and data management. This means existing system capabilities increase in value as they are packaged and shared as services. Figure 7.1 presents examples of healthcare system functions and related applications. Though this figure does not contain a complete list of functions or systems, it shows the redundancy of system functions in a typical healthcare environment.

Function	PM / ADT	EMR	ED	Lab	RIS	PACS	Pharmacy	Dictation	Patient Accounting	Practice Management
Register Patient	X	X	X	X	X	X	X	X	X	X
Admit, Discharge, & Transfer Patient	X	X	X	X	X	X	X			
Manage Visit		X			X	X				X
Document Problem & Diagnosis	X	X	X	X	X		X		X	X
Order Lab Test		X	X	X						X
Order Medication		X	X				X			X
Order Exam & Service	X	X	X		X	X				X
Aquire Images						X				
Capture & Document Charges	X	X	X	X	X		X	X	X	X
Create Clinical Note		X	X		X	X		X		X
Confirm Eligibility	X						X		X	X
Create Bill & Claim	X			X	X		X		X	X

Key
PM / ADT - Patient Management & Admission, Discharge, & Transfer
EMR - Electronic Medical Record
ED - Emergency Department
RIS - Radiology Information System
PACS - Picture Archive & Communication System

Figure 7.1   Healthcare Systems and Functions

SOA defines a service as an independent unit of work that is self-contained and has well-defined, understood capabilities. A unit of work may be an entire process, a function supporting a process, or a step of a business process. With SOA, services directly support business processes as they are "discovered" and orchestrated as a system solution. The greatest opportunities for applying SOA to increase reuse and standardization are provided by those functions that are used across systems, departments, and organizations. If system functions are redundant across systems, then the corresponding business processes are likely related and may indicate the need for process sharing as services. In Figure 7.1, functions with substantial redundancy are:

- Register patient
- Admit, discharge, and transfer patient
- Document problem and diagnosis
- Capture and document charges
- Create clinical note

Each system function may be separated into tasks to further increase reuse opportunities for services. For example, the function "register patient" may be separated into the tasks "find and view patient record," "create and update patient record," "verify insurance eligibility," "document history" (new or update), and other business activities completed during the registration process. This granularity allows other services and applications to use parts of the "register patient" function. The task "find and view patient record" may be used by most of the organization, whereas the task "create and update patient record" may be used only by the admission and front desk staff. In some cases, the capabilities provided on another system may be superior to the capabilities currently being used in a process. For example, another system may use a "verify insurance eligibility" function that provides more capabilities than the corresponding item residing in the system on which the "register patient" function is processed. SOA provides an environment in which functions can be standardized and used across systems and processes.

Figure 7.2 presents a conceptual view of the "register patient" services function:

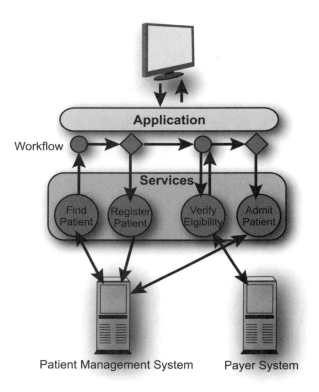

Figure 7.2 "Register Patient" System Function

As SOA is further adopted by the healthcare industry, collections of services as well as specific services will be available for adoption and use by a healthcare organizations Service Procurement organizational function (as described in Chapter 2). Since the location of a system providing services is transparent, these acquired services may be hosted outside the organization. For example, a Diagnostic Related Group (DRG) or other similar controlled medical vocabulary coding services may be available for integration into an organization's solution. The service may be located on an outside agency's system and used by a variety of healthcare organizations. An additional advantage enabled by SOA is that a single DRG code set can be easily kept up-to-date for the entire organization as well as for all healthcare organizations using the service. Figure 7.3 illustrates an example of service taxonomy for healthcare.

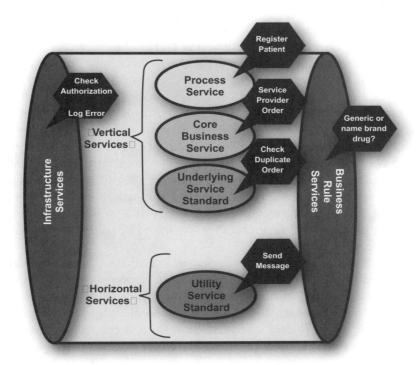

Example of Core Healthcare Business Services

- Service Provider – organization & affiliation relationships, plus roles & groups.
- Patient – including MPI
- Scheduling and Appointments
- Service Provider Order – labs, treatment, pharmaceuticals
- Encounter – including clinical results and recommendations
- Health Record – summary or full history
- Insurance – claims and referrals
- Accounting – hospital GL
- Document – scanned paper or DICOM image
- Location
- Material
- Event
- ACL – security access control list

Figure 7.3   Example Service Taxonomy for Healthcare

Addressing Healthcare Data Integration with SOA

In most healthcare organizations, a nurse uses multiple systems and devices while providing patient care. The nurse may switch from a patient management application for checking demographics and admission information to one or more electronic medical record (EMR) applications for viewing clinical notes on prior and current problems, to a charge collection application for ensuring correct billing, and to multiple ancillary systems for requesting an order. If the nurse does not have access to a system that supports contacting a patient's physician or reviewing another organization's clinical records, the nurse may need to complete these functions by phone or fax. These systems and activities support functions required to complete the overall care delivery process. In this example, however, nurses—not the system—orchestrate the various systems to support their work. The nurse is providing the interoperability.

Traditionally, healthcare organizations have supported interoperability by synchronizing data between various systems—as many as a hundred or more in some organizations. Patient information is managed in almost all of these systems. System databases are synchronized using data interfaces and, for less critical systems, duplicate data entry. Initially, data interfaces between systems were point-to-point, with each system having its own message format. As the number of systems increased, standard interface formats, such as Health Level 7 (HL7), and central data interface engines have been adopted by larger healthcare organizations. In addition, Internet-based communication has allowed organizations to exchange data with external organizations, such as payers. Figure 7.4 presents a common healthcare data integration architecture. This environment includes various types of servers, older point-to-point interfaces, and many interfaces processed through a data interface engine.

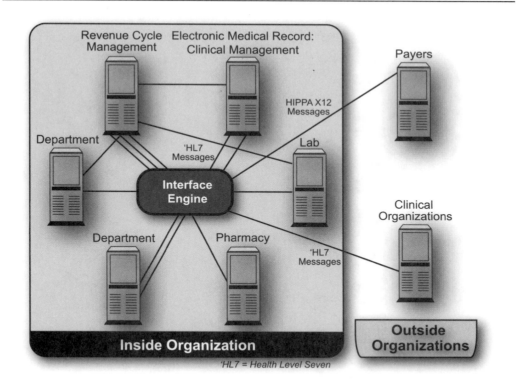

Figure 7.4 Common Legacy Healthcare Data Integration Architecture

Though data is synchronized between systems and system databases within and outside the organization, this data interface approach falls short of supporting data interoperability. Data processing and communication between processes involves multiple systems and redundant processing. To support the overall workflow, users must switch between several applications to complete a process. Systems must also be cleared of redundant data. With SOA, services are developed using existing system capabilities, as shown in Figure 7.5.

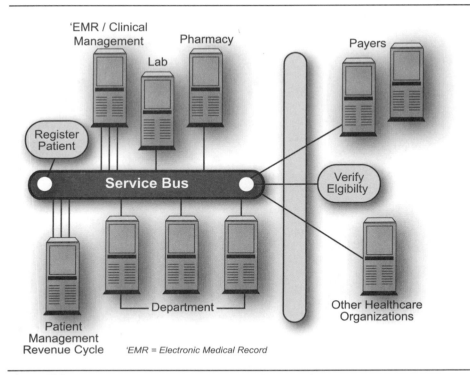

Figure 7.5   SOA Integration Architecture for Healthcare

With SOA, system processing is organized and represented as a set of services. Each service is made available to the entire organization through a standard interface. All departments that maintain or access the same information use the same service, making any data and processing redundancies transparent to users. Applications supporting a specific workflow reference one or more services, and each service communicates with the systems to which it is related. Users no longer need to switch between systems to complete a workflow and data is naturally synchronized across processes and supporting systems. Orchestrated services aligned with user workflows enable true interoperability among the healthcare organization's processes and people. To support compliance with the Health Insurance Portability and Accountability Act (HIPAA), organizations are increasing standard data communication with payers. In addition, integration with other healthcare organizations is frequently required to support clinical workflow and healthcare information network (HIN) participation. An organization may integrate external services into its SOA solution to provide complete process interoperability. For example, when a patient is registered within an organization, the service may use an external service provided by the HIN to register the patient for the entire community of care. Not only is the patient's registration information synchronized, but this external communication is placed into the related workflow with little user impact, creating interoperability outside organization system boundaries.

SOA is the next step of system evolution. It builds upon previous architecture approaches while better addressing agility and effective reuse across and outside the organization. SOA provides true interoperability. Most healthcare organizations have a large portfolio of systems with redundant processing and data. SOA allows system capabilities to be selected and packaged as services that are better focused and available across the entire organization. Organizations can shift their efforts from maintaining a complex data interface strategy to creating service-oriented applications that support interoperability while more closely aligning with healthcare processes. Throughout the remainder of this chapter we explore these themes of how true healthcare data interoperability through SOA can yield an industry transformation in healthcare.

SOA for Health Information Networks (HINs)

Data integration and interoperability is a key requirement in healthcare. Medical errors that cost dollars and lives are most often the result from the lack of the right information being available in the right form at the point of care.

Worldwide, solving this problem is a key focus area for many governments and associated healthcare institutions. Healthcare information networks (HINs) are the means by which the data integration problems are being addressed. A HIN is a collaboration among the government, hospitals, specialty labs and pharmacies, as well as insurance agencies (payers) to provide a network of data exchange that builds a shared information pathway, data repositories, and application interfaces to rapidly and accurately exchange key health information across a system of healthcare.

HINs are put in place to support the following main usage models:

- Exchange of patients' electronic medical record between one care provider and another in order to get key information like the patients' medical history, allergies, persistent medical problems, and current medications and active treatments

■ Exchange of referrals between primary and secondary care providers or labs as well as the medical results of those referral visits

■ Electronic pre-authorization of treatment so that it is known quickly whether a treatment or drug is supported by the patient's insurance plan

■ Electronic claims filing and payment to increase the accuracy and speed the cash flow cycle of medical care

■ A means to electronically order and monitor consumption of prescriptions

■ A consolidated data repository of key healthcare information for legally mandated bio-surveillance activities (such as influenza or other disease outbreak)

■ A portal for the patient and healthcare stakeholders means for accessing appropriate data

Figure 7.6 gives a graphical depiction of the architecture of an SOA-based HIN.

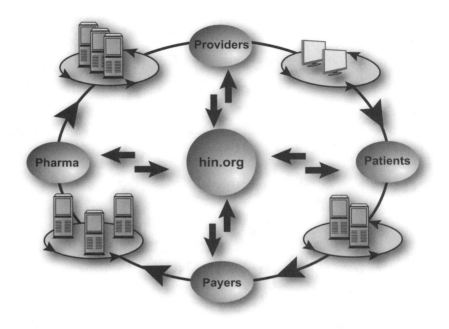

Figure 7.6   HIN Actors

Creating a Sustainable HIN

The key challenge to implementing a HIN is creating a sustainable financial model where the costs and risk to bring up the network are tolerable by the community of care and that there is a recurring source of value to justify ongoing operational costs of maintaining the network. Even in communities where the government (local, regional, or national) is providing the funding for the greater good of the community, these issues of cost, value, and sustainability are still material considerations.

Using legacy mechanisms of healthcare data integration are simply not financially feasible to implement and sustain a HIN over the long-term. If every time a new hospital, pharmacy, or government agency was brought on to the HIN a new point-to-point/broker interface is developed the following architectural and cost problem is created, which is depicted in Figure 7.7.

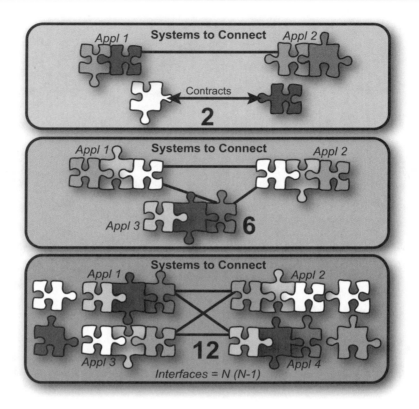

Figure 7.7 Diagram of the Point-to-Point/Broker Integration Architecture

What happens in the point-to-point/broker-based method of integration is that the number of systems interfaces grows exponentially relative to the number of participants in the HIN. A study done by Canada's Health Infoways[1] clearly shows how futile this legacy approach to integration is from a cost and sustainability perspective:

- Cost of one integration: Simple = 32,000 Canadian dollars (CAD); Medium = CAD 95,000; Complex = CAD 190,000

- 38,783 systems in Canada

---

[1] *Canada Health Infoways Integration costing – "EHRS Blueprint -> an interoperable EHR framework. Infoway Architecture Update" Canada Health Infoways Solution Architecture Group March 2006.*

- Number of types of integrations: Simple = 4,527; Medium = 20,081; Complex = 14,175
- This yields 1.5 billion system interface points
- Estimated cost is approximately CAD184 billion

This Canadian example clearly shows that establishing a HIN of scale using point-to-point integration architectures is not viable from a cost standpoint. At the time of this writing, 234 regional HINs are being put up in the USA by various state and local governments who each are spending approximately USD 2–5 million per HIN. More than 70 percent of the initial startup costs for these HINs are on the systems integration to bring the first hospitals and insurance companies on the information network. For HINs to sustain their costs over the long term, these economics must change.

Guidelines for Applying SOA to a HIN

When using SOA for HIN integration architectures, the cost of integration can be reduced significantly and a sustainable source of value to the community of care can be established. To accomplish this, the service architecture of the HIN must:

- Simplify and reduce the number of interface points to create data interoperability in the network.
- Address the architecture, infrastructure, software, and related business services as a cohesive unit.
- Be deployable within the hospital, lab, pharmacy, and insurance company as well as within the shared HIN network.
- Support legacy systems, including current and evolving standards in healthcare data representation.
- Be scalable from small to large scale healthcare organizations in terms of cost, complexity, utility, and adaptability.

The first key benefit that an SOA technique applied to a HIN will provide is to simplify the data interoperability problem. Although there are industry standards for data representation in healthcare, such as HL7, a fundamental problem with those standards is their varied interpretation in software. Therefore, the very first objective for a HIN should be to standardize the software interpretation and therefore implementation of representation and translation of healthcare data on the network. The most cost-effective way to do this is through a standardized set of core business services that represent healthcare data.

As Figure 7.8 shows, implementing SOA services to manage a standardized implementation of data representations (the "canonical data representation") reduces the number of systems interface points by an order of magnitude. Instead of each participant in the HIN and the HIN data center having to create and sustain an system interface for each participant in the network, all a participant needs to do is transform their systems representation to the one specified by the service, which defines the canonical form for the specific data being exchanged (such as patient, provider, order, referral, and so on).

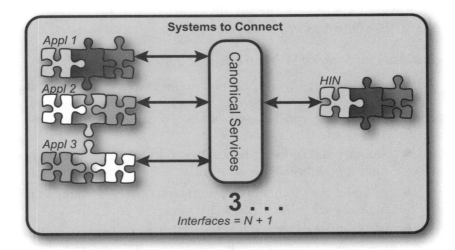

Figure 7.8   SOA Integration Architecture

This SOA, canonical-based architecture to systems integration reduces the number and cost of integration points by over 65 percent.

The canonical data representation that the SOA core business service manages establishes:

- An independent structure from any specific end-point application

- Independence (separation) of the information architecture and the technical infrastructure upon which it is implemented

- Precise message definition to assure consistent implementation

- Visibility into the data that drives business processes
- Clear definition of unique applications for a particular business transaction

Leveraging services that are built on canonical data representation allows for the HIN network to rely on a standardized software interpretation of data and therefore allows the network to support the shared instantiation and consumption of system functions by all participants of the network. This allows the HIN to provide shared services such as provider registries, medical vocabulary translation, master-person index, and record locator services on behalf of the entire community of care they represent without those services having to be deployed or duplicated in the data center of each organization which participates in the HIN. Figure 7.9 describes this architecture and some example shared services.

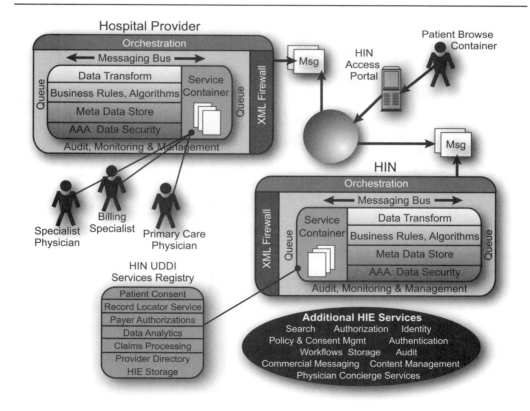

Figure 7.9   Possible HIN Service Portfolio

Using the enterprise service bus technology described in Chapters 3 and 4, both the HIN data center and each participating organization in the Health Information Network can publish and consume each others services and establish orchestrated workflows to rapidly support new business transactions and interactions among network participants. Additionally, the service container construct on the service bus architecture allows for existing, in-place clinical and administrative systems within a hospital, lab, pharmacy, or insurance organizations to be "fronted" with XML web services and participate in this architecture. This allows for realizing the benefits of SOA in an incremental and iterative fashion thereby leveraging existing technology investments. Figure 7.10 is a diagram of the service bus architecture.

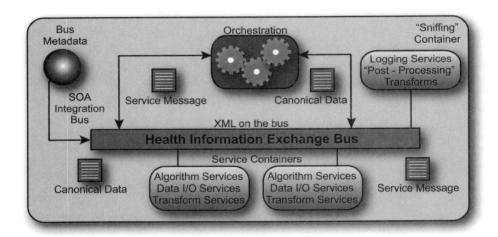

Figure 7.10   Service Bus Architecture

As seen in these examples, using SOA techniques can substantially reduce the costs of implementing a HIN in any scale. SOA also delivers features to the community of care as software services that provide a source of ongoing value beyond hosting a simple portal and database of integrated data records on patients

Extending Electronic Medical Records through SOA

So far in the chapter we have talked quite a bit about how using SOA techniques can improve the integration of healthcare information systems and substantially reduce the cost of doing so; however worldwide the average amount of automated, electronic clinical information is small.

Many healthcare organizations around the world are planning or putting in place Electronic Medical Records (EMR) systems to automate the collection, distribution, and validation of patient medical records. Although such technology has been commercially available for 30 years, the average worldwide adoption of EMRs by clinicians in their day-to-day work is less than 20 percent. Figure 7.11 summarizes the reasons for this low adoption rate and shows how SOA can help increase EMR adoption.

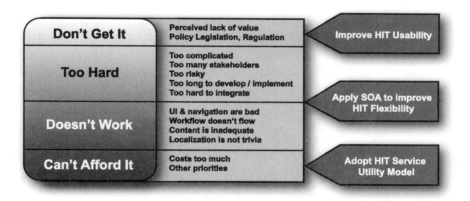

Figure 7.11   Barriers to Electronic Medical Record (EMR) system adoption

Using SOA techniques can address many of the issues described in Figure 7.11 directly.

First, many electronic medical record systems are designed to be enterprise-wide applications spanning departments and medical professions. One common side affect of this broad scope are screens with many tabs, data fields, buttons, and other user interface elements that can complicate the training and use for those whose job only requires a fraction of the functionality to complete the task at hand. An SOA-based EMR can readily support many forms of user interface because the core data and business logic functions are loosely coupled from the presentation. Therefore, the ISV developer or potentially even an IT department with sufficient engineering talent could provide specialized user interfaces by department and/or job role without having to duplicate the core processing and data validation of the EMR engine.

Second, since an SOA-based EMR is constructed as a suite of composable software services for data and business rules, workflows can be more readily customized to support individual organizational or departmental needs without having to resort to a "best-of-breed" deployment where individual departments have nearly duplicate application stacks from different vendors since one vendor supports a particular department's workflows incrementally better. Not only does it save the organizations the costs of paying for what is often the same core technology more than once, it also allows for a significant reduction in integration and sustaining costs as a common service infrastructure is reused over and over in the SOA-based EMR.

Finally, as discussed above, the SOA architecture allows for entire functions of an EMR system's or hospital's processes to be outsourced and hosted in a shared data center and consumed as a utility. Examples include the capabilities that can be offered by an SOA-powered HIN such as controlled medical vocabulary translation, master-person index services, patient record locator services, insurance verification, claims processing, and referral management. The key advantage to this is the cost of implementing and sustaining this functionality. More often than not, acquiring software functionality through the outsourced, hosted utility model (sometimes referred to as utility computing or application service provider) can be done for a materially lower overall total cost. This is due to the fact that the cost of servers, data center infrastructure, software licensing, and engineering are spread over many customers rather than being borne by each customer repeatedly, as is the case when the EMR is hosted on an internal data center. When using SOA techniques and technology, a healthcare IT organization can readily integrate internally hosted systems and technology directly alongside outsourced ones. Figure 7.12 describes this architecture.

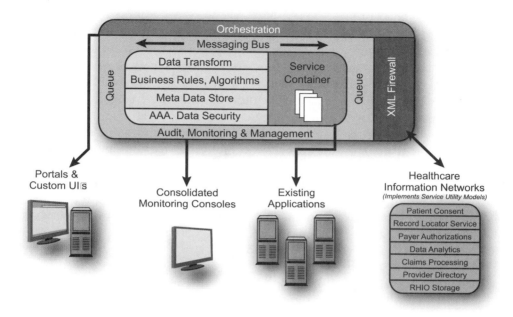

Figure 7.12 Architecture for Integrating Hosted and Outsource Applications

Building a Roadmap for SOA in Healthcare

As discussed in detail in Chapter 2, implementing an SOA technology platform and associated organizational infrastructure is not something that can be done in a single event. In healthcare, this is especially true as very few organizations have the budget or can take on the operational disruption associated with tearing out and replacing key business systems in any form of wholesale fashion.

Therefore, major administrative, EMR, and ancillary healthcare systems should first be "fronted" with service interfaces that manage highly shared data and nearly universal redundant processing. In healthcare, that involves data regarding patients, providers, orders, and controlled medical vocabulary. Key highly shared functions include things such as a Master-Person Index (establishing a common record identifier across systems for patients and medical personnel), medical vocabulary translation, and verification of patient eligibility for services via their payer policy.

The key for a healthcare organization is to focus on getting a baseline service infrastructure in place that eliminates redundant entry, storage and transformation of their highly shared data across business processes, and those highly shared functions *within* the organization first and then look to extend their reach into the community of care through Health Information Networks. This is because most healthcare organizations have a complex application landscape internally and when connecting to a HIN will need to address the architecture, technology, and business implications of providing a standardized representation of their organization's data in order to feed it to and receive it from the HIN. Also, when it comes to evaluating where to start with SOA, it is important to focus on departments and business processes where the ratio of risk, cost, and benefit are most favorable. Often the areas of the healthcare business that will derive the most benefit from SOA architecture are those that also derive the most benefit from having quality, reliable and integrated data at the point of care such as emergency, critical care, and surgical departments and their associated patient care business processes.

Given this, the following are key tasks and milestones to pursue as part of a SOA maturity model in healthcare:

- *Early Learning:* Pilot the technology and organization shifts to SOA in one department on a targeted set of highly shared data and functions (such as patients, orders, and medical vocabulary in the admissions and order processes in the ER department).

- *Re-engineering:* Extend the technology and organization investments to span departments on the highly shared data and functions as articulated above. Focus efforts on getting to organization-wide standards on this highly shared data and processing. Begin planning for HIN integration.

- *Integration:* Implement HIN integration into core systems and departments as the roadmap evolves extended service integration into ancillary and administrative systems.

- *Maturity:* A healthcare organization reaches a state of maturity when the SOA technology and organizational infrastructure permeates all major business processes, systems, and departments and supports the organizations HIN initiatives. This includes clinical and administrative systems.

As with any SOA adoption program it is critical to start in a focused, targeted area of the business and build a "snowball effect" of results both in technology and business benefit.

Key Industry Challenges for SOA and Tactics to Address those Challenges

In the healthcare industry IT budgets are far smaller than in other industries such as manufacturing or financial services. It is very common to find budgets in the range of 1.5–2 percent of revenues, which is a third to a fifth of the IT budget in other industries. This extremely tight budget situation is further compounded by the fact that these dollars not only compete with things such as personnel, service offerings and facility costs, but also other significant technology assets; namely medical devices (like MRIs, infusion pumps, and so on).

This creates a "chicken-and-the-egg" dynamic for creating an SOA adoption roadmap in healthcare. Achieving the over 40-percent sustaining system and integration cost benefits that SOA offers is sorely needed when budgets are this tight, but at the same time how do enough precious dollars get freed up to sufficiently kick-start the Early Learning and Integration phases of the SOA roadmap?

Another key challenge in healthcare is the state of technology of many healthcare IT vendors. It is quite common for EMR, integration broker, and ancillary system technology vendors to still have products in "green-screen," mainframe, and minicomputer monolithic software technology stacks. Only a small set innovators have invested to bring their software architectures and technology stacks up to the n-tier, web-based technology stacks, but at the time of this writing they remain the suppliers with the minority market share and revenue.

The key tactic to address these issues is timing and finding the right project insertion point for your organization. Intercepting the deployment of a new EMR, department ancillary system, or HIN integration project are the hot new work for many organizations and offer enormous business benefit to be implemented using SOA techniques. Through Intel's interaction with many government and private healthcare organizations as well as the ISV community world-wide we anticipate the overall market to be entering the Early Learning phase of SOA in 2007 and progressing to Maturity post-2010 lagging other industries by 3+ years, which is a pace relative to all other forms of technology adoption in this industry segment.

Summary

- The application of SOA in healthcare can substantially reduce the complexity and redundant system processing of clinical information. It can also help to simplify and reduce the cost of participation in community of care health information networks (HINs), and can improve the cost and usability (and therefore reduce the deployment risk, leading to increased adoption) of electronic medical records.

- SOA can provide a relatively inexpensive way to develop geographically independent and fault tolerant infrastructure, which is more easily upgraded than tightly bound system integrations. Availability can be increased through service redundancy.

- Proofs of Concept (POCs) can be done with relatively light resource investment, yet can provide a power tool to enlist the support of technologists and executive management.

- Due to the tight budgets in healthcare information technology, finding the right insertion project will be critical. A new SOA can build upon the momentum associated with a new EMR implementation, HIN project or organizational merger/acquisition—leveraging these inflection points can provide substantial advantage in SOA deployment.

- As with any SOA adoption program it is important to start small and build on top of incremental success. In healthcare, that means focusing on the most critical business processes where highly shared data is required and in those processes where the timeliness and accuracy are most critical. This can translate to early SOA focus on patient, provider, order, and controlled medical vocabulary data in critical care settings such as ER, ICU, and surgical.

Chapter 8

SOA in Manufacturing

All parts should go together without forcing. You must remember that the parts you are reassembling were disassembled by you. Therefore, if you can't get them together again, there must be a reason. By all means, do not use a hammer.

—IBM maintenance manual, 1925

In recent years, global competition has driven manufacturing to evolve rapidly and become more efficient and adaptable. Small variations in manufacturing costs are often the swing factor in a company's competitiveness and ultimately its viability as a competitive force in its market. In addition, manufacturing demands increased agility in the use of alternate sources for materials and components. Today's manufacturing environment must be a model of efficiency—from order management, to supply chain, to the manufacturing process itself and warehouse/finished goods delivery.

Acquisitions and mergers impact manufacturing IT too, as disparate systems must be rapidly integrated into the whole. Likewise, decisions to outsource create a rapidly changing landscape with respect to needed integration between the enterprise and external supplier systems.

SOA can enable increased efficiency by providing the capacity to select and adapt best-in-class services and focus on service quality—whether in-sourced or outsourced—to optimize the overall process for cost and needed agility. The services are readily integrated into the enterprise ecosystem through the loosely coupled and abstracted standard interfaces.

At the same time, the most competitive companies are reducing their time to market through increasingly efficient market analysis, rapid engineering development, and rapid release to production. This can give companies an edge in market presence through a rapid and agile response to changing market conditions, getting products in the channel months before a competitor can respond. SOA's ease of integration of new capabilities and services can allow a company to identify and rapidly deploy best-of-breed alternatives, gaining advantage in bringing new products to market.

The Use of SOA in Manufacturing

Manufacturing is a conservative consumer of technology, seeking stable and trusted systems on which to base production processes. SOA has been slow to penetrate the most basic functions in manufacturing, as new methodologies and architecture lead to a perception of increased risk. Manufacturing demands that systems have rock solid availability—it is unacceptable to incur business risk through deployment of immature technologies that may interrupt manufacturing processes. Reliable, time proven installations of enterprise application integration and adapters plus legacy message bus integration are deeply embedded in the manufacturing IT fabric of many large corporations after decades of hard-wired integration.

Substantial gain through any new technology must be clearly evident before it will find a place in manufacturing, where expectations are for flawless operation. Manufacturers demand minimal waste and maximum output from continuously available automation systems. This is one key challenge for installing SOA into manufacturing: meeting the challenge of low risk, high return, and high efficiency while minimizing disruption to existing systems.

Yet the time proven, rock-solid composite applications that populate the IT of a manufacturer can prove to be an impediment to the needed agility in an increasingly competitive industry. These vertically built and custom-integrated applications comprise an inflexible web of functionality composed of many moving parts, and modifications to the "machine" come at the high risk of introducing unintended consequences to the overall system. Integration of supply chain, shop floor, order management, and supporting systems was the result of long term incremental investment.

The inflexibility associated with this rigidly integrated set of applications and underlying data can, over time, increase cost of operations and decrease the responsiveness of a manufacturer. Such inflexibility runs counter to today's goal of agile and responsive manufacturing capability. SOA is increasingly sought out by manufacturers as a remedy to this inflexibility, and companies are realizing benefits beyond original expectations.

Both Johnson & Johnson, a global manufacturer of healthcare products and provider of related services, and Intel Corporation, global manufacturer of computing platforms and enabling systems, provided information on their SOA implementation efforts in support of this chapter.

Evolving from Composite Applications to SOA

If a composite-application environment is to be transformed into an SOA environment, an evolutionary and incremental approach must be taken to gradually migrate, using the crawl-walk-run gradual approach. The gradual, incremental introduction of new technology in manufacturing is required because manufacturing operations are reluctant to change, and for good reason: loss of manufacturing output can equate to loss of market opportunity and possibly revenue. An evolutionary approach with safeguards built in to ensure continued operations is needed. Figure 8.1 articulates the general strategy:

- Focus first on translation hubs to enable data to be abstracted in the environment
- Replace point-to-point connectivity with standardized messaging
- Pull common functionality out of common applications while using the application engineering refresh cycle to adapt them to the common services
- Plan and build common services to increase the re-use and assemble to order capacity in the environment

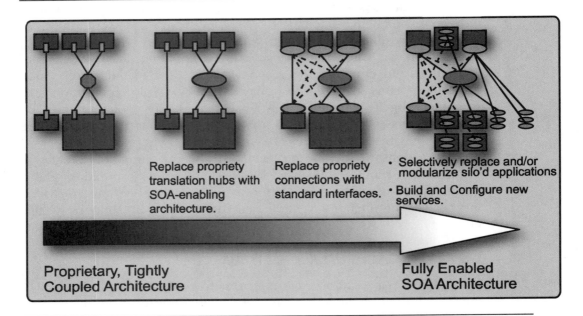

Replace propriety translation hubs with SOA-enabling architecture.

Replace propriety connections with standard interfaces.

• Selectively replace and/or modularize silo'd applications
• Build and Configure new services.

Proprietary, Tightly Coupled Architecture

Fully Enabled SOA Architecture

Figure 8.1   Transformation from Legacy Composite Application to SOA Service

The concept of assemble-to-order (which this leverages) is covered in more detail in Chapter 2. While implementation of SOA in a manufacturing environment can be a slow process, ultimately SOA is a perfect fit because it leverages manufacturing itself—in the assembly of constituent parts into a whole.

The key to evolving with minimal disruption is to introduce the new services oriented capability while allowing the existing composite applications to remain in place and functional during the transitional period. This can be done if planned carefully, without compromise to data quality or process efficiency. But the "bubble" inefficiency in doing so is also obvious: the middle stages of this evolution will require doubling-up on support; maintaining the legacy at the same time nurturing the introduction of the new SOA backplane.

Manufacturing commonly has only brief and infrequent maintenance windows available in which to make changes or additions to the environment with limited opportunity to effect changes to manufacturing related IT systems. This can mean that the logical steps to evolve the environment may take place through long iterations, and it may require years to complete the evolution. It will be an exercise in patience and persistence and a long term commitment from the organization to reach the end goal of SOA modularity and assemble-to-order efficiency. To help obtain this commitment, an SOA effort can benefit greatly from selective demonstration of SOA technology in the form of proof-of-concept implementations.

The Use of Proofs of Concept in Positioning SOA

Many organizations have used SOA Proofs of Concept (POCs) as a valued technique to demonstrate value to an organization, when there may initially be reluctance to embrace SOA methodology. The POC usually takes the form of a production simulation, with sufficient capability integrated and/or engineered to demonstrate capability (but not sufficient engineering to ensure it is production ready); in this way, a POC can provide strong evidence that that path to SOA is both viable and realizable.

Intel first executed SOA POCs in 2005, a time when IT management was skeptical of the business value of SOA. According to Don Michie, SOA Implementation Strategist at Intel, the series of POCs (a total of four) provided hard data to quantify the benefit of SOA in the areas of SOA infrastructure creation, business process adaptation, enterprise resource planning system integration, and technology integration. SOA efforts at Intel sprang from the POC results, establishing organization and technological momentum, producing results that would otherwise have taken much longer.

As an example of the benefits that can be articulated, the Intel SOA POCs were focused on specific results:

1. How can we use SOA to approach major enterprise changes?

    *   How can we use SOA to manage the upgrade of the ERP system for Accounts Payable or Order Management?

    *   How could we use the concepts of services, model/deploy/improve to make this more manageable?

    *   How can we use concepts of separation of data, rules, process and interface to enable customizations to the ERP without the same cost as custom modifications to vertical applications?

2. How do we "advertise" and "package" software services in SOA terms to IT customers?

    *   How do we know if we have too few or too many services?

- How do we describe our "base models" and "option packages" to enable and promote consumption?

3. How do we approach changes to our product life cycle and development methodology with SOA and assemble-to-order?

    - What are the organization and process implications of implementing SOA?

    - What retooling and retraining will be required to adapt to SOA development?

    - What are the transition and change management factors?

4. How will the introduction of SOA impact the management of our solutions and the automation required?

    - What changes to systems management methodology are needed to adapt to SOA based infrastructure?

    - How do we rationalize the service monitoring impact of introducing new services, and the business process automation dependencies that result?

Like Intel, Johnson & Johnson used POCs early in their evaluation of SOA effectiveness, said Aslam Handy, Chief Architect for IT. The result of the POCs was to demonstrate the potential for increased agility, and POC discoveries were consequently adopted and folded into future architectures and adopted in the enterprise. And, "by using TOGAF methodology in driving feasibility projects," Handy said, "the demonstrations of SOA technology speak very loudly."

Highly Shared Data

The management and use of data is always a key consideration in construction of IT systems. Manufacturing's enterprise architecture is often created by knitting together applications and systems based on best-of-breed capability. A natural consequence of this is a resultant lack of an integrated, holistic view of highly shared data. It is up to enterprise architects to piece together what this master data picture must be, and then to identify the technological methods to deliver the data to consuming systems and applications.

As the result of varied and distributed systems, sources of data are also distributed in the environment and the highly shared elements of that data are made available through point to point integration or through data replication. While on a case by case basis, it may have made sense to expose the data in this way, the resulting "spaghetti" of interconnections is a notorious consequence. Illustrated in Figure 8.2, the point integrations are a result of a series of tactical integration efforts absent a planned, single view of master data critical to manufacturing.

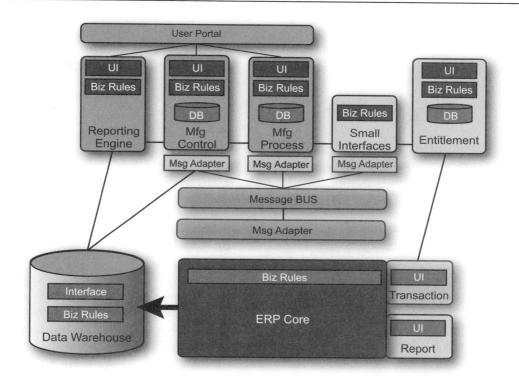

Figure 8.2   Example of Composite Applications, Interconnected Point-to-point

To attack the problem of implementing manufacturing SOA, one must first attack the problem of creating standardized views of data in areas like customer BOM, capacity, and item. For Intel, "creating services interfaces for our highly shared data services are our highest priority" for SOA business services development, Michie said.

Creating the views begins with an understanding and inventory of the sources of shared data, which are distributed throughout the manufacturing enterprise. While it may be tempting to rely on traditional mechanisms such as an operational data store (ODS) to consolidate and re-distribute shared data, SOA yields a distinct benefit in helping to ensure both availability and quality of data, sourced from multiple locations in the manufacturing enterprise.

Yield Data Example

As an example, say that yield data (used for production process control) is continually needed to feed analysis and response mechanisms and flag excursions, so that minimal material is wasted. The source of the yield data may be from any system on the manufacturing floor, stemming from equipment monitoring and stored in a localized database.

In traditional point-integrated systems, the yield data (or a transformed summary of it) may be replicated on a frequent basis to an operational data store (ODS), and/or linked into consuming systems through a series of point-to-point integrations via execution of a stored procedure or other polling activity. The fragility of this type of arrangement is notorious. Data may arrive later than desired due to batch processing, and alerts come too late. Custom-engineered point-to-point integrations are subject to irregularities that can drop or corrupt data and result in inaccurate results. What is in the ODS is not a real reflection of the yield data and decisions made on the basis of that data can be erroneous or delayed resulting in rework or waste.

In a scenario like this, SOA can do much to alleviate architectural challenges. If the origination point of the yield data were logically and physically close to the data source, confidence in data quality and timeliness could be assured. A service that sources the data can replace point integrations or extraction/load processes. SOA messaging methods such as pub-sub can be used to distribute (by publishing on a bus) yield data to all consumers of the service information as soon as it is available; caching and assured delivery can ensure that data is not compromised lost in transit. Integrity of the data is assured through the transaction envelope, and can be further secured through key based encryption.

The benefits of location abstraction, SOA routing, and pub-sub message patterns can abstract out data that originates in many locations. In manufacturing enterprises that have globally distributed centers of manufacturing, highly shared data of the same class may be originating from several locations. If the yield data in the example originated from multiple locations, the roll-up aggregation of the data could be accomplished through service interfaces between yield systems and a *yield aggregation* service, as illustrated in Figure 8.3.

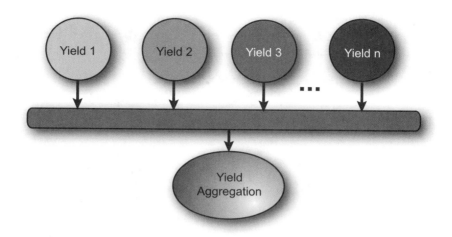

Figure 8.3   Aggregation Using SOA

With the utility provided by the yield aggregation service, a new source of yield data (from a new manufacturing line, or new factory) could contribute its data to the aggregation service with very little upfront effort. This is a because with SOA, once service providers adhere to prescribed interface format (contract and schema) and are authorized to do so, any number of service peers can communicate with zero upfront overhead to establish the communications pathways. Contrast this to traditional methods such as socket-based, PKI authenticated and hard-coded authorized data transfer mechanisms and it is readily evident how SOA can enable a manufacturing enterprise to expand and contract at the rate the business requires.

Virtual Representation of Data, and Wrapping

With the dependence of manufacturing environments on localized infrastructure, data is not centralized. Key systems in manufacturing are often defined more by organization or location, rather than by an architectural, taxonomically pure arrangement. Geographic diversity in manufacturing facilities that may be spread across the globe calls for some method of referring to the varying sources in an abstracted, virtualized way.

SOA routing and mediation techniques can help to allay this, creating a virtualized, central data view, even though the data sources themselves are distributed, as shown in Figure 8.4. While it is key that a "master" of highly shared transactional data exist, through SOA methods the delivery mechanism can be distributed even though the master reference is not.

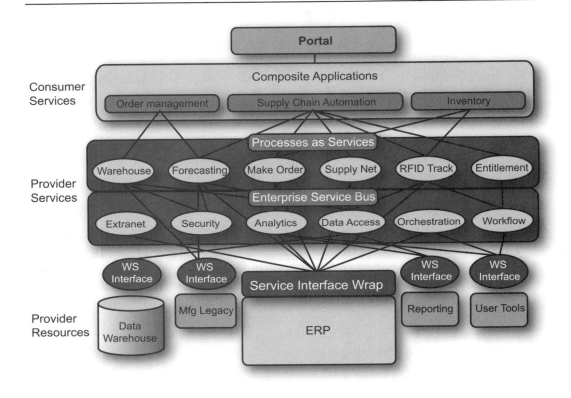

Figure 8.4   An SOA Stack for Manufacturing

Taxonomy

The ultimate goal of this transformation is to move to an environment that has all the core functions previously provided through many tightly integrated composite applications, but now decomposed and served by SOA services. An example is given in Figure 8.5.

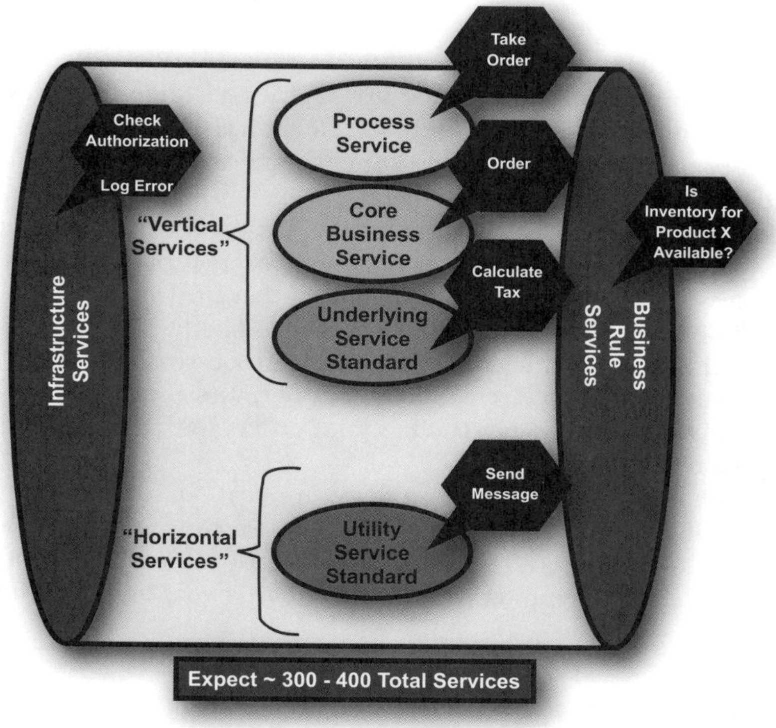

Example of Core Manufacturing Business Services

- Employee –internal, contingent, organizational relationships, plus roles & groups
- Customer
- Order – purchase, sales, service
- Location
- Physical Resource (non-people)
- Product
- General Ledger
- Incident – structured task record requiring disposition and holding history
- Document
- Event
- ACL – security access control list

Figure 8.5   Example Service Taxonomy for Manufacturing

As Figure 8.5 demonstrates, composing an inventory of services to meet existing computing needs in manufacturing while at the same time delivering the agility of SOA requires the creation of a layered taxonomy of services that build upon each other.

At the bottom of the stack are utility and underlying services that perform mostly horizontal, reusable technical functions that support a number of business operations in manufacturing such as application and end-user messaging, security functions like authentication, and common calculation functions such as calculating tax on a sales or purchase order.

The core of the manufacturing service taxonomy is the set of core business services. These are the services that provide a 360 degree view and full set of functional processing on highly shared data that are relevant in most manufacturing business processes. This includes master data lists of employee, customer, supplier, and product data as well as key transaction data types such as sales orders, purchase orders, invoices, and general ledger entries.

With this foundation of services, applications can be composed by assembling them into workflow configurable processes to do things like available-to-promise (ATP), supplier registration, yield or capacity analysis and production planning in a manner that is very agile to establish and change.

Supply Chain Efficiency

Manufacturers rely on the efficiency of their supply chain to remain competitive and in some cases retain a differentiated edge on their competition. Improvements in supply chain efficiency can result from small but significant adjustments to manufacturing materials, warehouse, or order management systems.

Also, a highly efficient supply chain, from a business point of view, is often very distributed, resulting in much collaboration with customers and suppliers of materials, manufacturing stages, logistics, and services. This often requires extending the reach of a company's ERP capability beyond the walls of the enterprise and out to all of the customers and suppliers.

Supply chains in many enterprises are comprised of woven-together applications, often with an ERP base but overall comprised of capabilities from multiple vendors or created custom in-house, creating a fragmented overall architecture.

A key problem that results from a set of ERPs and associated departmental applications incrementally woven together using EAI or point-to-point integration is that multiple transactions and data records become associated with individual logical customer and supplier entities. Therefore, extending these individual systems or individual interfaces outside the corporation is often not viable or extremely difficult to do well without encountering this problem of "multiple personality."

By implementing the SOA taxonomy described above, a company can provide a single view of product, customers, suppliers, orders, invoices, and so on, even though the implementation of that service might be stem from multiple internal systems. A properly and uniformly defined interface on core business services that represent highly shared manufacturing master and transaction data can then become the "source of truth" for applications and business-to-business integration infrastructure. Then underneath the implementation of the business service, utility services that provide routing and mediation techniques (as discussed in Chapter 4) can be used to connect and transform the structure of data to and from the appropriate internal system on a message by message basis. Also, by using the SOA technique as internal systems are incrementally upgraded or decommissioned, suppliers and customers that communicate through the core business service interfaces will be insolated from the effects of those changes.

Figure 8.6 compares the EAI and point-to-point architecture and SOA for supply chain data integration across trading entities such as customers and suppliers.

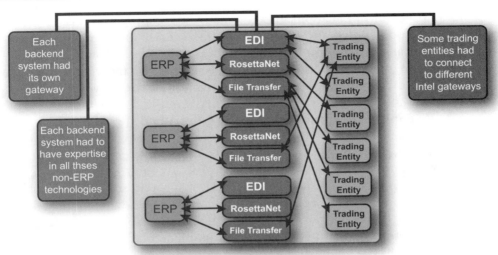

Previous Architecture

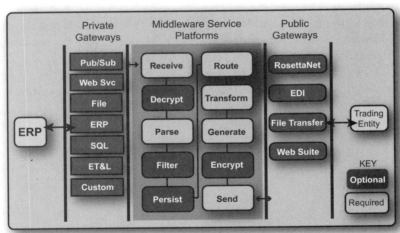

Current SOA Architecture

Figure 8.6   Supply Chain Integration

Shop Floor Service Availability

It's hard to overstate the criticality of factory production services and the services they depend on. It is unacceptable to experience loss of manufacturing capacity due to interruptions in factory automation, as would be failure to ship product on time due to automation problems.

As shown in Table 8.1, the evolved SOA-based manufacturing environment can provide relative robustness and high reliability compared to its composite application counterpart. The assembly of composite applications in their tightly integrated and stateful communications creates implicit vulnerabilities that can be avoided through basic deployment methods.

Table 8.1 Fault Tolerance Comparison of Composite Applications and SOA

Dependency	Composite Application Based Automation Characteristic	SOA Based Automation Evolved Characteristic
Critical availability of automation functionality	Applications provide single point of failure and are highly engineered to be continuously available	Redundant instances of critical services provide economical hedge for availability
Continuous flow and availability of data	Point-to-point integration creates multiple vulnerability to interruption	Data as service across a highly reliable bus protects availability
Data center system failover for business continuity and disaster recovery	Complex and expensive sustaining of replicated production environment in disaster recovery facility on cold or warm stand-by	Continuous operation of redundant services that can assume full load if other source fails

More detail regarding SOA/SOI enabled high availability was described in Chapter 4. Because of the stateless nature of SOA transactions, replica instances of services can be on-line in multiple locations simultaneously. When coupled with infrastructure-based data replication capabilities (such as those provided through storage area network providers), a very robust and fault-tolerant manufacturing automation capability can be constructed.

Additionally, systems can be architected to provide identical services in multiple factory locations, and through the use of SOA queuing, directory services and routing, provide a fully fault-tolerant way of recovering from service failure in one location by enabling service consumption between locations across a wide area network.

For example, in the previously mentioned yield aggregation service, if the aggregation service in one manufacturing site failed, the identical service in another location could pick up the load. This could be fully automatic, with transactions first being queued (by a queuing mechanism building into the SOA message bus) and routed (again, a built-in service that detects that a yield aggregation, as illustrated in Figure 8.7.

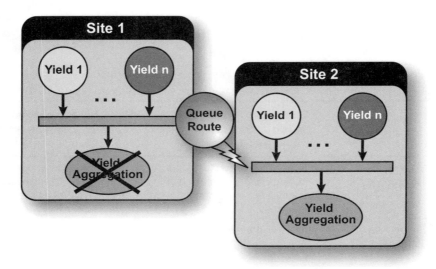

Figure 8.7   Intrinsic Fault Tolerance between Identical Services

Extranet Integration

A differentiating business characteristic in manufacturing is the ability to change sourcing at a rapid pace. This can be driven by multiple factors:

■ The need to augment internal capacity with that of external suppliers

■ The need to be able to select and switch to lower cost, including goods and services such as warehouse and distribution channels

- The need to be able to switch to lowest-cost providers of non-differentiating services (such as payroll)

A policy and identity managed extranet capability, founded on SOA, can help to enable rapid redirection to alternate, external service providers.

As illustrated in Figure 8.8, the key to this integration is a common set of policies (and policy enforcement points), and managed identities.

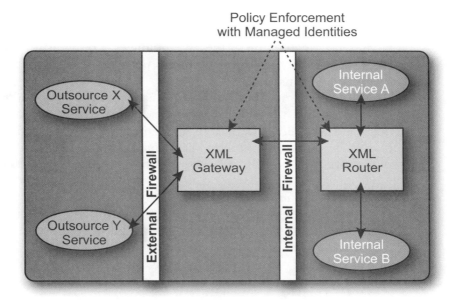

Figure 8.8   Extranet Services Integration

While the architecture in Figure 8.8 is not a mandatory one (there are many variations depending on firewall and DMZ architecture), the main point is to illustrate how creation of choke points enables consolidation of policy enforcement and recognition of identity.

Underlying this is architectural approach is the need to manage identities between companies. In doing so, a policy decision can be made to establish trust in another company's (or even individual's) identity, then allowing the flow of SOA messages through the policy control points (in the example, the XML gateway and router).

Extranet External Supplier Services Example

Consider this example: Company A has 10 systems that must be accessed by outsourced third-party providers. And further, Provider X has 30 employees who provide the actual services.

If internal account management on each of the 10 systems were maintained for the 30 employees, a total of 300 account management tasks would need to be performed in switching to Provider X. Not only would upfront account management be required, but account management maintenance would need to be performed over time. If Provider X terminated one of the 30 employees, Company A would need to quickly remove access in order to restrict that person from accessing Company A's systems.

This cumbersome and error-prone arrangement can multiply into thousands, or in the case of a large enterprise with many outsourced services and suppliers, even tens of thousands of managed accounts representing external entities. This leads not only to increasing administrative costs to maintain the accounts, but also increased business risk that errors in administration could result in unauthorized or even malicious access to information.

If identities are maintained in both Company A and Provider X and if each has the ability to cooperate in exchange of identity information, then a much lower overhead mechanism can be employed to control access. A chain of trust can be created, such that if an employee of Provider X has a valid account in Provider X's systems (that is, they can authenticate there), and if Company A *trusts* Provider X's *assertions* that a person is valid and authenticated, then that person (or that service—this works equally well for service consumers/providers across the DMZ) can access Company A resources.

Standards based Trust

In the XML services transaction based exchange of information, trust can be conveyed through standard mechanisms as WS-Trust (which is built on top of WS-Security, discussed in much more detail in Chapter 3), and assertions using SAML or other viable constructs. WS-Trust enables interoperability of security tokens (conveyed in assertions) by defining a request/response protocol by which service suppliers and consumers can request of some trusted authority that a particular security token be exchanged for another. This is how trust is effectively brokered through a transaction.

Literally, "Trust" is identified in the WS-Trust specification as

> ...the characteristic that one entity is willing to rely upon a second entity to execute a set of actions and/or to make [sic] set of assertions about a set of subjects and/or scopes.
>
> —*Web Services Trust Language,* February 2005[1]

Accordingly, if Company A trusts Provider X, it presumes that Provider X will maintain tight control of accounts and access in their domain, in particular any person/entity that has a role such that it is entitled to access Company A systems. The presumed trust between companies and suppliers would typically be reinforced in upfront negotiation of service terms and conditions.

It's clear that if a well-entrenched, pervasively adopted set of industry accepted standards and methods existed, it would facilitate a more efficient startup of a sourcing relationship and get things underway more quickly. As of 2007, this is not the case, and most deployments are from companies willing to be early adopters of the technologies. Existing standards for implying identity and asserting it—such as using X.509 certificates to establish SSL connections and implicitly, trust—are well entrenched, despite the administrative rigor and effort required to establish and maintain the relationships. However, the increased efficiency that can be realized with XML transaction-oriented trust, plus the increased rate of change in switching external/outsourced suppliers will compel increased use of these standards for greater economy and lower operations cost.

Exposing and consuming trusted services through the Internet will continue to gain importance over time. "Consumer driven healthcare models are emerging, and globalization is happening and becoming more customer-centric." Handy of Johnson & Johnson said, "Following Internet trends that push services to the 'edge' is having impact on many industry players."

---

[1] http://specs.xmlsoap.org/ws/2005/02/trust/WS-Trust.pdf

Summary

- SOA provides a fabric that can tie together disparate manufacturing services through a common infrastructure that, through vendor neutral standards, can provide a more effective and lower total cost implementation than direct connection or EAI binding.

- Key business processes can be optimized with services with greater efficiency than large vertically integrated applications, such as with supply chain management.

- Routing and transformation services in a services bus can provide rich utility to manufacturing data consumers, and using the data in-place avoids the need for expensive data aggregation. Exposing data as services can eliminate duplicate data and increase quality.

- SOA can provide a relatively inexpensive way to develop geographically independent and fault-tolerant infrastructure, which is more easily upgraded than tightly bound system integrations. Availability can be increased through service redundancy.

- Proofs of Concept (POCs) can be done with relatively light resource investment, yet can provide a power tool to enlist the support of technologists and executive management.

- Exploiting service benefits in a manufacturing extranet can shorten lead time and reduce cost of customer/supplier integration, and enable a more agile enterprise-to-enterprise interface mechanism.

- It's important to first identify the origins of highly reused master data, and commit to a common enterprise model before architecting SOA data services. While the data sources are likely distributed to many physical locations, implementation based on a common model can make a single virtual representation of master data—a necessary precursor to SOA data normalization.

- If architecting SOA into a mature manufacturing environment, expect that it will take much longer than a green-field implementation, since stability and availability of the change-adverse manufacturing environment will limit the rate of change to services orientation.

- While federated trust to manage service access between enterprises holds much promise, standards are evolving and the state of technology is not yet mature.

- While creating service wrappers around existing systems is a very efficient method to transition from vertical applications to services, it's important to stay true to a services taxonomy that represents service functions (and contract) based on where you want to go, not where you've been.

Chapter 9

SOA in Telecommunications

> *I look at what the phone company does and do the opposite.*
>
> —Craig Newmark

Telecommunications service providers have long focused on providing for the telecommunications requirements of business and consumer segments. However, the marketplace has changed dramatically over last decade. From the end user standpoint, especially in the consumer segment, convergence of IP, wireless, and POTS is driving demand for converged applications. Services such as gaming, streaming video/TV over IP, and fixed-mobile-IP convergence are driving demand for features such as location, presence, availability and voice, while demanding a simple prepackaged solution. In the large enterprise segment, the service providers are trying to move away from the number of POTS lines per customer metric to IP-based services measured by the percentage of IT spend per customer.

Addressing these changes, however, requires significant re-architecture at multiple points in the service provider's IT environment. First, we will take a look at the multiple levels of convergence that service providers are currently implementing and analyze how service oriented architecture can provide the telecom service providers the ability to create new services regardless of the underlying networks. We will take a look at the operations support services (OSS/BSS), and assess whether following SOA concepts in this environment allows for rapid rollout of new converged services with the associated billing, servicing and provisioning.

Finally, we take a look at how the adoption of service oriented architecture among the customers of telecom service providers will enable service providers to offer new value-added data services. Further we describe the changes in the central office and customer premise environment required to delivering these new data services.

SOA for Integrated Service Delivery Environment

A Service provider typically has a layered network architecture that logically looks like the one illustrated in Figure 9.1. From an applications standpoint, however, it looks more like stovepipe architecture, as shown in Figure 9.2, with different services enabled through completely separate application silos.

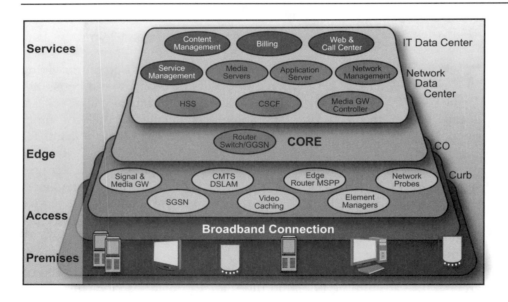

Figure 9.1   Service Provider Layer Network Architecture

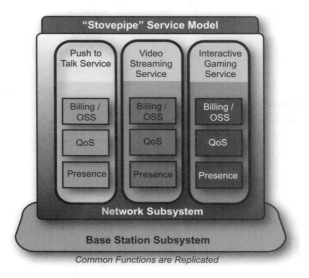

Figure 9.2   Stovepipe Service Model

As discussed in Chapter 2, while SOA technologies might offer some solutions for service providers, it is not a panacea, and definitely does not help the problem of organizational fiefdoms. The larger service providers have consolidated significantly, and many offer traditional telecommunications business, and wireless services. However, typically all three operate as independent entities due to corporate ownership, independent networks with well defined boundaries, geographic coverage, and/or due to regulatory reasons.

This structure leads to organizational barriers that limit the advantages of integrated service delivery architecture, which could otherwise offer time to market advantage in introducing new services as well as operational efficiencies in operating those services. Such structural deficiencies have provided the Internet companies (rather than the telecom service providers) the opportunities to pioneer communication services such as instant messaging and very low cost voice and video over IP.

When we refer to convergence being the key theme in telecom service providers, we are referring to the three levels of infrastructure convergence that are in progress: network convergence towards all IP, service convergence and application convergence. Discussion on network convergence from a mix of technologies to all IP is beyond the scope of this book. For the purpose of this book, suffice it say that network silos will continue to exist for a long time to come. Therefore service and application convergence becomes the key for operational efficiency and growth for service providers. The goal of service oriented architecture is to enable service providers to rapidly introduce new services at far lower costs, as the changes do not impact the network.

In wireless telecommunications, Integrated Multimedia Service (IMS) based on Session Initiation Protocol (SIP) has allowed for consolidation of voice, messaging such as short message service (SMS) and multimedia messaging service (MMS), and content such as video and music. So a wireless carrier, by adopting IMS, can offer voice, video, and data services packaged for end-user needs abstracted away from the networks. In addition to wireless telecommunications, however, the rapid spread of fixed-network broadband (such as cable and DSL) and the offering of services such as transactions, content distribution, and voice-over-IP have made IMS increasingly relevant to wire-line operators as well. Using SIP-enabled IMS therefore allows service providers to abstract applications and services from the network.

There are significant gaps, however, between this vision and reality. In order to roll out any new service, the service provider needs an associated set of back-office operations that allow for billing, provisioning, monitoring, security, managing digital rights, and so on. The IMS layer provides significant capability for feature interactions, but it does not address how interactions with the back-office should be implemented.

Let's look at services other than voice and messaging. Telecommunications service providers also deliver Internet based services, such as e-mail, Web access, and so on. These services, unlike voice and messaging, have a very light applications layer that handles all call state transitions, are not highly secure, and does not offer high quality of service. As these services are all IP-based, the OSS (Operations Support Service) environment has tended to be fairly independent of the voice and messaging based OSS environment allowing for much faster service rollout.

The next step in service convergence is the convergence of these two different class of services—the Internet based services will low security and quality of service requirements with the SIP-based services that are closer to the core telecom model of 99.999% reliability, with a very tightly controlled application plane with separate signaling, regulatory issues such as emergency calling and tight security. Offerings such as online gaming and IPTV over fiber to the home are the drivers for convergence of these two classes of services. The requirements in these lucrative services begin to look similar to telephony. Take, for example, the case of online gaming. Real-time communications is being added to gaming and the notion of latency of network and fairness becomes really important. Assuming nodes are all the same whoever gets the token faster wins the game!

Therefore, in order to create innovative applications that bundle these two classes of services, the control plane and service delivery requirements are best addressed through IMS and SOA based service delivery platforms working together, as shown in Figure 9.3.

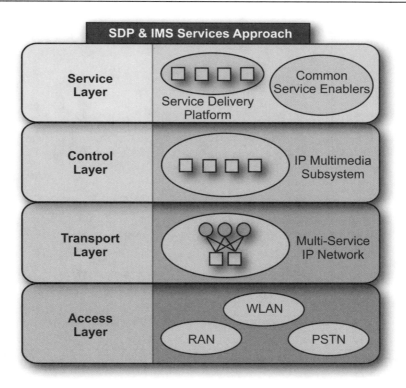

Figure 9.3   Integrated Voice and Data Service Delivery Platform and Stack

While service oriented architecture has most relevance to the service and application convergence, it needs to be noted here that some network convergence dependencies, especially concerning security, must be addressed before a service oriented architecture in a telecom service provider environment can be fully realized.

The SOA Infrastructure requirements for the telecom operator's applications have some unique characteristics as a result of the nature of the business described earlier. For example, a key requirement from the service container and the enterprise service bus is the ability to identify which services require real-time operations (such as those shown in Figure 9.4), to execute those services down the SIP stack and to execute those that do not require real-time operations down the HTTP stack. What is needed is the ability to create services over a layer of abstraction for transports, signaling and controlling.

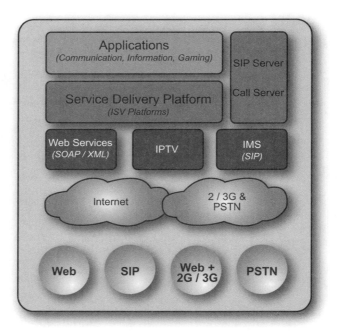

Figure 9.4   Real-time Operations

An example of how tightly coupled information can be exposed as services in the IT environment of telecom service providers is illustrated in Figure 9.5. At the bottom of the stack are utility and underlying services, which perform mostly horizontal, reusable technical functions that support a number of core business services. These services are coarse grained and provide highly shared data that are relevant to other services silos in the telecom service provider (such as across wireline and IP lines of businesses). This includes products, orders, billing, network management services, provisioning, compliance and composite services that integrate services separated over regulatory or geographic boundaries.

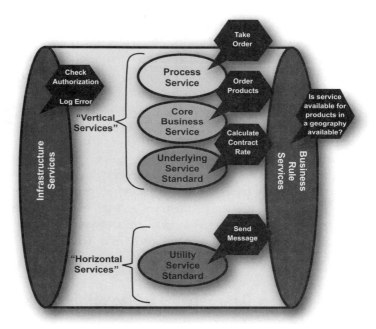

Example of Core Telecommunications Business Services

- Products – IP, POTS, Conferencing, Directory Assistance
- Order Network Management – Inventory, Order Validation, Trouble Tickets, Service Availability, Topology
- Billing – Accounting, Issue Tracking, Data
- Provisioning
- Compliance
- Composite Services – Product, Order Inventory, Network Management across geographies and products.
- ACL – Security Access Control List

Figure 9.5   Example Service Taxonomy for Telecommunications

Creating these services across product lines, and then having the ability to drive business processes by orchestrating these services across product lines, reduces the costs of bringing a customer online. For example, a field order can be issued once for all services, IP or otherwise, for cross-service provisioning at a customer location. Creation of these business services therefore is necessary, but is not a sufficient condition to be able to provide integrated data, voice, and video services of the future. For that, the problem of having an integrated service delivery environment must first be addressed.

There are multiple industry efforts underway to upgrade the OSS environment to the next generation in order to offer applications based on converged services to the customer.

Integrated service delivery is still a goal of the future for most service providers, and while SOA offers a mechanism to get there, the gaps between the SOA vision and the available infrastructure technology today continues to be fairly wide.

Outside of integrated service delivery, widespread SOA adoption in enterprises now enables telecom service providers to offer new data services in many vertical industries, which thus far have depended on specialized value-added networks. In the next section we discuss an architecture that enables service providers to offer SOA-broker services to their enterprise customers.

SOA for Business Data Services Driven off the Edge

In addition to the wireless and wire-line business for the consumer, telecom service providers also provide business data services to enterprises. While this business has thus far been limited to providing bandwidth and network security to enterprises, it is evolving rapidly to provide value to the CIO.

Service providers are trying to become trusted third-party brokers among multiple businesses. In doing so, the service providers have entered or bought into Electronic Data Interchange (EDI) value added networks (VAN) industry that has long provided trusted third-party brokering between two or more business entities to exchange critical business information. Over the last several decades the traditional EDI VAN market has been dominated by a few network operators that have offered services to nearly 50,000 private businesses in the United States alone. Several telecom service providers are attempting to enter the business of providing hosted integration services to Fortune 500 enterprises, most of which are large service provider customers, and the emergence of SOA based integration is an opportunity for these service providers to win this business.

Service Delivery Network

In order to deliver the capability similar to an EDI VAN, the service delivery network needs to be based on a managed peer-to-peer network architecture model with multiple distributed SOA proxies (service producers or consumers) at the secure enterprise network. These SOA proxies need to be managed by a carrier outside of enterprise firewall and core stateless content routing environment that we will expand upon later. The Managed Peer to Peer (MPP) model can separate the message flow (specifically, if the traffic is SOAP, the SOAP body) from the control directives (specifically, if the traffic is SOAP based, the SOAP header), sending the contents peer to peer and the control directives to a centralized stateless broker or content router as depicted in Figure 9.6. It can also send the entire payload to the logical broker for more sophisticated routing in case the core router can provide high throughput while doing deep content based routing. A simplified proxy is placed at the location of each participating enterprise. This proxy can encrypt, sign, and compress the SOAP messages before routing them either to a peer proxy or the core or the broker, and gather management information. The logical broker may be a single physical entity but is essentially a core content routing mesh that can hold all or a subset of switching rules and allow for dynamic subscription. The broker also supports a management layer to which the peers send the response time and metering information.

In such architecture, many "collaborations", defined as a set of different services belonging to different entities, interconnected via an asynchronous delivery model, can be created and effectively managed.

Although the contents of SOAP messages may not routed through the broker, store-and-forward capabilities are possible because the proxy can queue messages. By virtue of its connection to the core routing mesh, dynamic routing via the proxy to endpoints is possible. The real advantage of such an environment is for information requiring asynchronous delivery as the third party (service provider) takes over the burden of ensuring that the message is delivered and is delivered in a secure, reliable manner within a time window designated through service level agreements.

A more detailed view of the broker and a single participating enterprise is depicted in Figure 9.6. The basic concept in a service delivery network is of a collaboration among all static and dynamic subscribers and publishers of a class of messages that are made available through the service delivery network. A collaboration has a distinct contract with associated security, QoS, and reliability constraints.

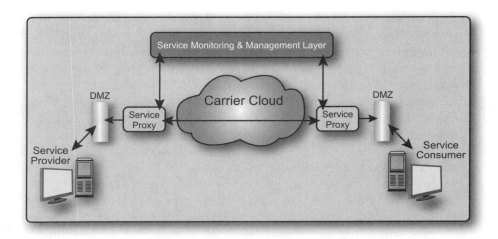

Figure 9.6   Service Delivery Networks (SDN)

The middle tier may consist of a web server, an application server, and a proxy.

The value service providers expect to offer for such customer is provided by the following benefits:

- De-coupling of endpoints
    - Publisher and subscriber endpoints can be utilizing different transport, security protocols, and data encodings.
    - Failure of one endpoint does not interact with the operation/recovery of another.
    - Publisher and subscriber are only coupled dynamically via shared topic space and subscriptions.
    - Subscription and deletions are dynamic.
- Transparency of electronic business transaction between two or more trusted or un-trusted entities

- Trust relationship between endpoint and service provider and between service providers
- Content verification and validation
- Message integrity and confidentiality in service provider network
- Non-repudiation service for both provider and consumer of service
- Reliable messaging and Quality of Service
  - Guaranteed end-to-end delivery of messages
  - Messages delivered only once
  - Timed delivery
  - Ordered delivery
- Atomic transactions

Usage Scenario for Service Delivery Network

A use case for the service delivery network application is of distribution of time-sensitive financial information such as real-time stock quotes and financial news. Such applications are much more of a pure publisher/subscriber application in which there are potentially thousands of clients that can act as both publisher and subscriber.

The data published and subscripted to falls into two major groupings:

a. Frequently generated data for which guaranteed delivery is not critical because it usefulness quickly degrades over time, such as tracking data. From the publishing client, there are "best-effort" or "best-effort with delivery list" semantics for the notification paradigm. For the subscriber, delivery within a specified window is all that really matters. The number of potential publishers and subscribers are both large numbers that can change as clients gain and lose connectivity.

b. Infrequently generated data by a small number of allowed publishers. In this use case, a large number of subscribers want to ensure the successful delivery of the data. While the data has a finite time window for its delivery, the integrity/confidentiality and reliability of delivery is critical. The publisher can utilize "guaranteed distribution with full delivery status" semantics.

Both of these applications do not require actual end client response data to be returned to the originating publisher, only potentially the status of their delivery.

Figures 9.7 and 9.8 depict the two possible scenario flows for distributing the same message to multiple subscribers and coordinating their delivery status. In Figure 9.7, the service provider core performs the aggregation of the delivery responses. This approach increases the processing load upon the service provider core but allows for the reduced overhead of reliable delivery of response data by delaying the core response message if the client delivery can be pushed down quickly.

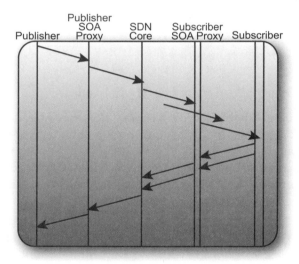

Figure 9.7   Publish-Service Data Flow with Service Delivery Network
Providing Aggregation of Delivery Responses

In the second approach, depicted in Figure 9.8, the SOA proxy is being used to perform the coordination of the delivery status. This imposes additional communication overhead upon the egress endpoint appliances for setting up a communication channel to the ingress endpoint appliance. However, it does offload this coordination and aggregation overhead from the service provider core.

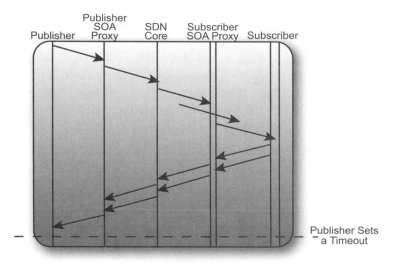

Figure 9.8   Publish-Service Data Flow with SOA Proxy Providing Aggregation
of Delivery Responses

Architecture for the Service Delivery Network

This section identifies the key issues that the architecture for a service
delivery network needs to address. These issues are grouped into the
following three areas:

> Delivery Plane: this focuses on the throughput and latency of our
> solution from a publisher generating a notification until it is
> delivered to all subscribers receiving delivery for a matching
> message. The issues associated with delivery plane include
> publication rate, message sizes, subscriber matches per request,
> subscription rule technology for subscriber matching, and routing
> domains (geographic or topic- type driven).

> Control Plane: The control plane or the service management layer
> is needed to manage the critical provisioning information for a
> collaboration among enterprise customers along with policies,
> authentication/authorization credentials, publisher information,
> and subscriber information. It needs to monitor all transactions
> for audit reasons.

Functionality: this covers what a collaboration member can do that is not part of the messaging model. It covers issues such as the confidentiality, integrity, and reliability of the data exchange, or issues such as whether the subscriber can return data to the publisher. Publisher DOS protection (contracted rates), subscription rate management, subscription rule management, publisher input schema validation, QoS management (IPv4, DiffServ code point (DSCP), 801.1p, and MPLS traffic classes.

The routing environment could be as simple as a set of identical load-balanced core routers in a simple active/active load sharing or domain divided load sharing. There is a service management layer for managing subscriptions. The basic idea is that the set of end-point proxies is where the individual applications terminate and take a service oriented flavor. The proxy handles the transport, security, and encoding mediation as well as the reliable delivery semantics. As shown in fig 9.9, the content now is in a standardized XML format that can be used to routing determination by an inner stateless network that handles the routing of input request to zero or more subscribing consumer proxies.

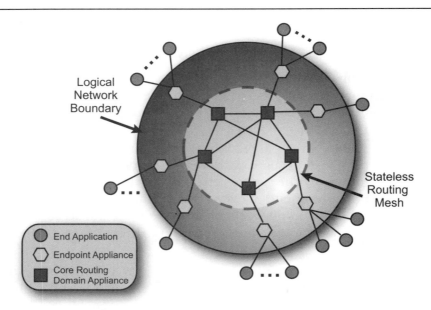

Figure 9.9 High Level Conceptual Implementation of a Service Delivery Routing Environment

Within the context of a given transaction, there are two distinct roles: provider and consumer. Providers are those enterprises that provide and host services (for example, web services) related to business functions, while consumers are those enterprises that use the particular service (such as web services) of a provider to satisfy specific business needs. It is through the communications between these network elements that a consumer's request for a particular service is satisfied in a secure and trusted manner.

Control Plane

The control plane of such a service delivery network maintains critical information and uses this information to enforce policy that governs the transactions. This control plane also integrates with the OSS/BSS environment. The control plane allows for user provisioning, business policy management and monitoring.

As depicted in Figure 9.10, the control plane consists of two major functional components: one that guarantees the secure, accountable, and highly trusted exchange of SOAP messages between enterprises; and another that controls the allocation, accessibility, and availability of system resources while maintaining end to end system performance. Both components require orchestrated communications between the distributed proxies, a centralized broker, and these colocated SOA management servers (control plane).

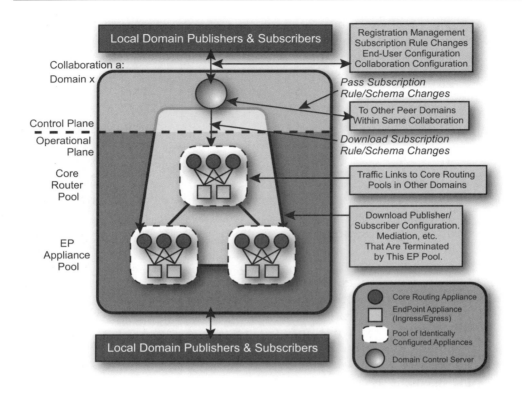

Figure 9.10   Control Plane

The control plane performs the following functions:

1. Provisioning that maps a collaboration/domain to a specific set of endpoint appliances and core router appliances.

2. Defining the collaboration share infrastructure. This is focus upon the message schema definitions and transport primitive exchange pattern that all publishers and consuming subscribers must support. This includes the potential publication of WSDL describing what a publisher can generate and a subscriber will receive to a UDDI agent.

3. Registration of publisher and subscribers with their endpoint specific processing, such as endpoint specific security, reliable delivery, transport and data encoding mediation rules/policies. This includes authentication and authorization that this

publisher/subscriber is allowed/required to perform. It also includes domain management.

4. Subscription management and routing table management. This covers the generation of routing tables from subscriber subscription requests, automatic and manual subscription removal, downloading of subscription routing tables to core routers.

The SOA management servers will typically be deployed as set of scalable, high end application servers running in regional data centers under the jurisdiction of service provider IT operations.

Key Industry Challenges for SOA and Tactics to Address Those Challenges

Industry challenges for SOA deployments in telecommunications are both structural and technical. The infrastructural build out for convergence in telecommunications (services, networks, and applications) is happening, creating fertile ground for SOA experimentation. At the same time, competition from traditional rivals, such as the cable industry, as well as emerging IT as service models such as Google, are creating cost pressures that limit the investments available for large scale SOA deployments for new services without a proven business model.

From a technology standpoint, the service providers are looking at the ISVs to provide platforms to create new revenue streams. These opportunities, especially in service delivery networks and the OSS/BSS environment, however, require additional capabilities, that do not exist in today's ISV solutions, such as ability to handle services with mixed characteristics (real-time, non-real-time).

In addition to the structural and technical challenges, however, some of the SOA challenges in our experience with service providers have been internal. Despite rapid convergence, most large service providers are still operated as different business (wireless, wire-line, enterprise) with minimal focus on driving common architecture across them. The CTO/CIO focus should be on breaking these artificial barriers down and driving a common architecture.

Summary

In this chapter we covered the application of SOA to telecommunications. The application of SOA techniques can:

- Substantially reduce the costs of deploying and managing integrated services.

- Enable service providers to generate new revenue streams through value added networks for enterprises.

- Reduce costs of operations through more flexible and reusable OSS/BSS components.

As with any SOA adoption program, it is important to start small and build on top of incremental success. It is likely that service providers have already made progress towards deploying SOA within the OSS/BSS environment and have seen the costs savings. The next steps are to use SOA to generate new revenue streams such as through the value added networks and then, as some of the underlying network infrastructure issues get sorted out, to integrated services. However, the unique requirements of service providers, especially on management, quality of service, and reliability implies that the real-world rollout of SOA will be slower than for other verticals.

Chapter **10**

SOA and Future Trends

The dwarf sees farther than the giant, when he has the giant's shoulder to mount on.

—Samuel Taylor Coleridge

XML is a big idea. Web Services takes XML one step further. It uses the generalized portable nature of XML to achieve universally descriptive interfaces and message exchange patterns. SOA, following suit, takes Web Services one step farther and applies *service orientation* to web services in an attempt to shrink the gap between technology infrastructure and business agility. It is only natural to look at this progression and ask what could be next. Which future trends have the potential to affect SOA? Which trends will engender the next step? The purpose of this chapter is to survey some of the currently emerging technology trends that have the potential to affect SOA and shape its future. Trends can be characterized as very specific pieces of technology or more ephemeral ideas, memes or points of view. Both can be very powerful in shaping the future of SOA. While it is true that almost any technology trend can be tied back to SOA in some way, we will limit this chapter to those future trends that have XML as an ingredient. The reason why comes from our assumptions about SOA in Chapter 1. That is, we believe that SOA conceived without a specific reference to XML becomes *too general*. Some of the technology trends to be examined in this chapter include the *SOA Backlash, SOA and Web 2.0*, and *SO*, the future of SOA*.

SOA Backlash: SOAP versus REST

The first trend we will look at might best be described as an anti-trend or opposing undercurrent within the SOA community. This undercurrent, called the *SOAP versus REST debate* runs opposed to a certain standards-laden version of SOA, one that is perceived as cumbersome and weighty, rather than agile. This particular undercurrent looks at the WS-* family of specifications and SOAP-based interactions in particular in a negative light. That is, WS-* is seen as a hodgepodge of complex layered technologies with no historical evidence of practical use, rife with vendor positioning. As the number of competing (and completed) web services specifications continues to grow, tension rises in direct proportion to the increasing complexity. In response to this phenomenon, a new meme has emerged that labels the WS-* family of specifications with the term *WS-Heavy* to describe its ostensibly weighty character. Complexity alone, however, is not enough to dismiss a new technology if it provides real benefits to business. What is the nature of this debate? The next few sections provide a brief outline of REST when compared to the WS-* family of specifications and tries to present both sides of the debate on equal footing. In the end, we hope to convince you that a hybrid approach is really the answer, as these two technology stacks are not mutually exclusive.

Framing the Problem

REST stands for Representational State Transfer, which is an *architectural style* derived in a doctoral dissertation by Roy Fielding in 2000. The dissertation itself is not an indictment of SOAP nor is it a position piece on why REST is superior to SOAP. Instead, it *derives* a certain abstract architectural style, called REST, from the basic web architecture of *hypermedia*, or simply put the collection of web documents and the specific interactions that have evolved from the inception of the Web. Given such a terse description, REST appears to be a theoretical model rather than a business enabler. However, if we examine REST further and follow its thread, we can understand how this simple architectural style has evolved into a vehement, nearly *religious* battle between two worldviews. At the very least, the presence of the debate appears to be slowing the growth of SOAP-based SOA interactions.

Numerous resources on the Web provide information about REST and SOAP and at times it can be difficult to tease out the fundamental pieces of the debate itself. In this section we will begin with the familiar, namely the concept of *big bus, little bus* introduced in Chapter 4 as well as the concept of *heterogeneous architecture*, which we will characterize as simply a set of enterprise software, systems, or servers all running different operating systems and protocols. For the purposes of this explanation we will begin by assuming a worse case scenario: an enterprise with both B2B (business-to-business) integration requirements and EAI (enterprise application integration) requirements. Further, even though we refer to *big bus, little bus,* we will assume here that there is really *no bus* connecting these disparate domains. Some descriptions of REST also call this scenario the *unconstrained architecture,* which means there are *no constraints* on how various pieces talk or interact with one another.

Figure 10.1 shows a representation of worst-case EAI and B2B integration problems. We are using a *shape* metaphor to denote disparate components, software, or servers. Basically, we assume that each component is different and requires custom work to make the pieces talk. If we assume a completely connected set of disparate components counting each edge twice we will approach an n^2 type of integration problem. You should note that this applies both inside the enterprise (EAI) and across enterprises (B2B). The picture shown in Figure 10.1 is a *bounded problem*—it describes an enterprise or business specific way of looking at system integration on two axes—intra-enterprise and inter-enterprise. It is also bounded in another way—by the way the businesses currently operate; surely businesses innovate, but for application integration this is generally a fixed-cost problem that *maintains* current business relationships with some return on investment and cost-savings rather than an enabler of hyper-growth. These additional enterprise and business-centric assumptions will eventually make a difference later on.

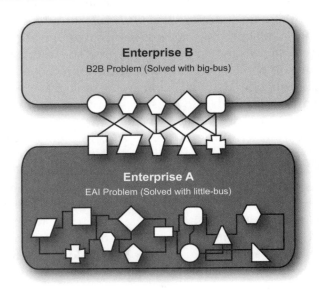

Figure 10.1   A Worst Case Scenario for Enterprise Integration

We also note that there is a *larger* version of this same problem, but it is *unbounded*—the larger version of the problem is the Internet, but more specifically, the Web itself. If we were to draw a picture of this problem, we could imagine it as an interconnected set of disparate shapes with no necessary bounds. To be clear, however, this problem is considered somewhat solved; REST looks at the example of this successful solution (which evolved using HTTP) to *derive architectural constraints* on the nature of the solution. Put another way, REST is in part an architectural style derived from those elements that made the current Web successful. Before we get to specific examples, we have to first look at the underpinnings of the theory itself. To help counter charges of undue bias, we go straight to the horse's mouth and develop a summary of REST based on Fielding's original derivation. This being said, we will not expound his entire theory, just the essential pieces to give us a solid understanding.

REST Explained

What is REST? As we have mentioned previously, it is an *architectural style* derived from the Web architecture. More specifically, it is a style derived from *constraints applied to elements within the Web Architecture*. This derived style is eventually defined with more concreteness in the form of fundamental constraints on *components*, *connectors* and *data*. In order to steer away from too much theory, we will first list and explain the five constraints Fielding thinks are important to the Web Architecture and then fully describe the three main classes of components that comprise the essence of REST. Fielding looked at the evolved Web and noted five basic properties: (a) Client, Server, (b) Client, Stateless-Server, (c) Client-Cache, Stateless-Server, (d) Uniform-Client-Cache, Uniform-Stateless-Server, and (e) Layered-Uniform-Client-Cache, Layered-Uniform-Stateless-Server. There is also a sixth optional property called *code-on-demand* but it is not important for the explanation given here. These constraints are no doubt confusing, but many of the terms used here have entered the everyday technical vernacular. What did Fielding really mean by each of these constraints? Table 10.1 provides an explanation of each constraint.

Table 10.1   Basic Web Architecture Constraints

Constraint	Properties	Explanation
Client, Server	Separation of Concerns, Functional Independence	This constraint implies that the user interface is distinct from the data storage and both can evolve independently.
Client, Stateless-Server	Session state on the client, Scalability, Reliability	Requests from the client contain all the necessary information for the server to process them. Servers can free resources to move on to the next request
Client-Cache, Stateless-Server	Network efficiency	Client side caching has the effect of eliminating some network interactions, improving efficiency, scalability, and perceived client performance
Uniform-Client-Cache, Uniform-Stateless-Server	Interface Generality, Decoupling	Components have a uniform interface that allows implementations to be decoupled from the services they provide
Layered-Uniform-Client-Cache, Layered-Uniform-Stateless-Server	Hierarchical Layers, Intermediary Support, Encapsulation	Adds the concept of layers which really means intermediaries such as gateways and proxies. These can be used to wrap legacy components or provide improved efficiency in the form of load-balancing or caching.

It is important to note that the constraints Fielding describes, which are shown in Table 10.1, are descriptive of the Web at the time (circa 2000). He tries here to capture the essence of what made the Web successful in the form of abstract constraints rather than pay homage to one set of standards or vendor technologies. This being said, there is an underlying tribute to HTTP in his abstract architectural style. Once he has laid out the constraints of the Web, he derives Representational State Transfer as a *new* set of constraints over three fundamental artifacts: *data elements*, *connectors* and *components*. We believe that the most important part of REST, its subtle core, can be found in how the *data* component is described. The next section describes these components, with special attention given to the *data elements*.

Data Elements

In the context of traditional client-server interaction, such as an HTTP GET, data is transferred from client to server. In REST terms, a *resource* is de-referenced and its *representation* transfers from the server to the client. The important observation that Fielding made (and it now seems obvious) is that links are static and can represent an invariant concept, while the representation can change over time. This idea consists in the demarcation between *resource* and *representation*. While this sounds lofty, it is exactly the same idea used when a Web site publishes a link, such as the "latest" schedule for some fictional meeting such as "http://www.foobar.com/schedule.html." We can note that there are three concepts tied to this: (a) The *resource* (*"the latest schedule"*) which is ostensibly invariant, (b) the link identifier ("http://www.foobar.com/schedule.html"), and finally (c) the actual schedule or document returned when the link is de-referenced—the *representation*. Fielding notes that *any information that can be named can be a resource*. The *resource identifier* term is used to describe the URI, but it could also have been a URN as well. So why is this resource concept important? Resources provide some familiar features such as *interface decoupling* as well as *generality* for the resource. That is, the resource can be manifested in more than one way; resources can realize one or more representations based on more specific client and server interactions, and these representations can be negotiated during the communication itself.

The second part of the data elements of REST includes the all important *representation*. This is where the term *state transfer* comes into use; Fielding looks at the Web like a giant state machine and the state transitions are initiated by and stored on the clients themselves (as the servers are stateless). Further, the *next state* of this giant state machine is considered to be captured in the representations of resources that transfer from server to client. This further implies that clients initiate state transitions of the Web in response to new state *options* that come back as server responses. It is at this point that we can begin to understand how the term Representational State Transfer (REST) becomes appropriate.

But what are representations? Representations consist of the data itself, metadata to describe it, as well as additional (optional) metadata to describe the metadata. In order to avoid getting lost a jungle of theory again, the reader can understand this simply as a message payload, a content-type, and possibly security information or routing information that is applied to the message or payload. Again, this is all still abstract, but Fielding's original thesis suggests HTTP as the model to be followed. Figure 10.2 shows a pictorial representation of the central concepts of resource and representation, and how they map to technology choices such as HTTP or even XML.

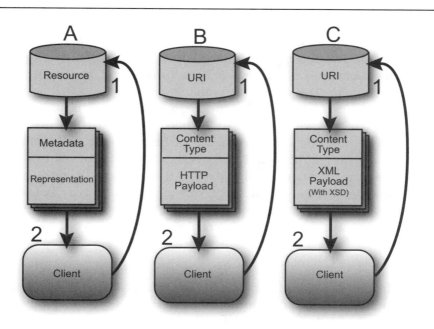

Figure 10.2   Resources and Representations in REST

Figure 10.2 shows three examples: A, B and C. In each example, a client is making a request to a server for the representation of a resource. Example A shows the representation in the abstract, the way Fielding conceived it. Example B shows the concrete implementation of HTTP with a content type to describe the payload. Finally, Example C shows another way of fitting into Fielding's framework with the use of an XML payload and an XSD, or schema definition, for the complete metadata. You should note that the last example is sometimes referred to as POX, or *Plain Old XML.*

The final two architectural pieces of REST are the *connectors* and *components.* These are less interesting because most of what makes REST important for our discussion is encapsulated in the data views just described. Connectors are the *interfaces* used by *components.* Fielding describes these as simply as client, server, cache, revolver, and tunnel. The first two are self explanatory. The third is a client-side browser cache or a web cache, the fourth is a DNS lookup library and the fifth is a tunneling protocol such as SOCKS or SSL/TLS. Each of these components has interfaces with "in" and "out" parameters. The "in" parameters consist of *request control data, a resource identifier,* and *representation.* The "out" parameters consist of *response control data, resource metadata,* and *representation.* The four components that utilize these connectors are the *origin server, gateway, proxy* and *user-agent.* Fielding notes further that some components can play a dual role as client and server (such as a proxy) and terms these components *intermediaries* within the architecture.

As noted previously, the Fielding dissertation and the definition of REST appears benign—it does not throw down any overt challenge to SOAP, nor does it appear to be solving the same problem as SOA or even SOAP. In fact, the REST architectural style appears to be a description of essential elements of the Web. If this is the case, what is the nature of this debate? Now that we have some of the theory behind us we must probe further and examine not what REST *is,* but what REST has *become;* or rather, the meme it has transformed into.

A CRUDy Central Claim

In the REST worldview, *resources* are primary. The role of HTTP is to perform one of four functions on resource concepts. These functions are POST, GET, PUT and DELETE. Described in order, POST implies the *creation* of new resource information, GET implies the *reading* of existing resource information, PUT implies the *updating* of existing resource information and DELETE implies the removal of resource information. If we look at these four HTTP request methods, we will find they map to the well-known verbs from the data storage domain: Create, Read, Update and Delete. REST advocates note that (and this is some extrapolation on the original REST model) these four verbs encompass *all we might ever want to do with resources on the Web*. If we add XML to HTTP as a payload and provide schema descriptions, we can fit a generalized cross-platform data format square inside of a proven, now nearly *ancient* technology such as HTTP. REST advocates proceed with an inductive sort of argument that builds upon the tremendous success of the Web. And here at last is where we really get to the core of the debate: *Resources on the Web can have at least two representations, (a) a hypermedia or hypertext representation for humans, and (b) a machine-readable representation for solving "web services" or SOA types of problems.* REST advocates look at the technology stack surrounding SOAP and SOA and chuckle a bit on the inside—we already have a proven, scalable technology (HTTP) that solves a nearly unbounded integration problem. If we can solve the unbounded version, this surely should apply as well to the *bounded* enterprise version of the problem. Why reinvent the wheel? The assertion of REST advocates is that the diversity of resources should be immense, but the number of *verbs* (Create, Read, Update, and Destroy) should be *scarce*. All that needs to be done can be done with CRUD, or so it is claimed. This does seem like a grand claim indeed: how can all enterprise business functions, both B2B and EAI be encapsulated in just *four* verbs? Indeed, the most common objection against REST is this perceived limitation. Before we examine this aspect of the debate further, however, we will examine a real-world example service that offers both REST and "traditional" SOAP interfaces to see how the messages manifest differently on the wire.

A Storage Service Example

The example that follows is adapted from a commercial web storage service, but the specifics have been changed to mask the actual service vendor. This example is central because this particular service offers both SOAP and REST type interfaces, which are prime candidates for looking at the similarities and differences between the approaches. The idea behind such a service is to allow web developers to store an arbitrary amount of data into keyed containers, which can then be used for retrieval at a later point in time. This particular service charges users of the service based on bandwidth of objects stored and retrieved from these logical containers. The service considers *objects* to consist of metadata and then an opaque object payload. The idea behind such a service is to provide a scalable, reliable, low-latency generic data store. You can think of this type of storage service as a building block for just about any distributed web application. Figure 10.3 summaries the basic concepts of *container, key,* and *object.*

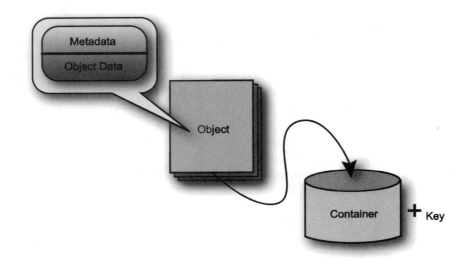

Figure 10.3 Basic Concepts for a Storage Service

In Figure 10.3, objects are stored into logical containers. The containers are named along with a key that allows the service to map from a combination of key and container name to the object itself. Further, objects also contain some metadata, which is in the form of media type information along with the octets that comprise the opaque payload. You should note that in this model, the containers can hold more than one key; in fact, one per object stored in each container. The operations allowed on these storage service artifacts are further defined as follows: (a) Container Creation, (b) Object Storage, (c) Object Retrieval (Non-Destructive), (d) Object Deletion, and (e) Key Listing. In addition to these basic operations, there are also other practical issues such as permissions (for others to read and write buckets) as well as authentication to the service itself. Other operations could also be added, but this represents a basic set for our purpose here.

So how do these operations map to real requests and responses in REST and SOAP? What do the messages on the wire look like? The first thing to remember is that with REST we are really only dealing with four fundamental operations applied to resources. This implies that REST messages come in the form of only GET, POST, PUT and DELETE whereas with SOAP, we can express the method itself within the request. Table 10.2 shows the mapping between the abstract operation name, the equivalent REST operation and SOAP method. You should note that brackets in the following table (shown in bold) denote variables that would be filled in with actual values. Also, Table 10.2 just shows the *request* side of the messages for brevity.

Table 10.2 Mapping between REST and SOAP

Operation	REST Request	SOAP Request

Container Creation	PUT /**[container]** HTTP/1.0	\<CreateContainer\>
		   \<Container\>
		      [container]
		   \</Container\>
		\</CreateContainer\>

Object Storage	PUT /**[container]**/**[key]** HTTP/1.0
	
	[object data]
	
	(Content Type is in the HTTP Header)
		\<StoreObject\>
		   \<Container\>
		      [container]
		   \</Container\>
		   \<Key\>
		      [key]
		   \</Key\>
		   \<Metadata\>
		      [content-type]
		   \</Metadata\>
		\</StoreOject\>
		
		[object data]
		(SOAP Attachment)

Operation	REST Request	SOAP Request

Object Retrieval	`GET / [container]/[key] HTTP/1.0`	`<RetrieveObject>`
		`<Container>`
		`[container]`
		`</Container>`
		`<Key>`
		`[key]`
		`</Key>`
		`</RetrieveObject>`

Object Deletion	`DELETE / [container-name]/[key] HTTP/1.0`	`<DeleteObject>`
		`<Container>`
		`[container]`
		`</Container>`
		`<Key>`
		`[key]`
		`</Key>`
		`</DeleteObject>`

List Container Keys	`GET / [container-name] HTTP/1.0`	`<ListContainer>`
		`<Container>`
		`[container]`
		`</Container>`
		`</ListContainer>`

You should note that Table 10.2 does not show complete requests, just the essence of each request. The REST requests are straight HTTP requests and the only thing omitted in the samples shown would be the HTTP headers. In this case, the headers would contain authorization information in the form of a keyed hash that identity and authenticity of the requester. Because the requests are stateless, this authorization information must be present in each request. Conversely, the SOAP requests shown are really only the SOAP body. While HTTP could also be used as the transport for SOAP, there is no guarantee that it will be, so any extra information such as authorization elements must be expressed as XML elements inside the SOAP request. Further, the SOAP example here leaves out any SOAP headers as well as any namespace declarations that appear in the body of the messages. Finally, the SOAP example also makes use of *SOAP Attachments*, specifically in the case where an object is stored at the service.

As you ponder the differences between each style of request, it should be obvious that the REST-based messages and model seems *much* simpler. It achieves the same basic functionality by riding on top of mechanisms already provided by HTTP. However, does this simplicity scale when the services become more complex? How would REST handle real world scenarios that go beyond a basic storage service? What about reliable messaging, transaction support, and asynchronous communication styles? How would message-level encryption and digital signatures be handled with REST? SOAP proponents may argue that the storage service works better as a REST architectural style simply because it is such a simple service and it already manifests itself as *create, read, update* and *delete* operations. REST proponents typically counter with observing that if we *tied down* the number of verbs, the diversity in *nouns* (or resources) will account for the additional complexity. REST proponents firmly believe that all problems in computing eventually fall into the CRUD domain, and all that must be done is the *identification* and *definition* of these resources. As we argued in Chapter 3, software complexity never really decreases, it just shifts around. Thus, if we use only four verbs, the diversity and complexity of the *nouns* must increase. This is typically done by REST proponents with careful examination of the domain and a liberal definition of what a noun can be. For example, if we were to model the relationship between *users* and *groups* with REST, we would not attempt to create nested nouns, where users fit inside groups and groups contain a set of users. Instead, we would *create* a set of singular relationships between each user and their group. Once we identify the noun as a *relationship* we can apply CRUD operations to it.

This design paradigm surely sounds elegant, and in fact it may be true. However, the time needed for this "discovery of nouns" may not be aligned with the needs of business.

Evaluating REST and SOAP

As mentioned in the previous section, SOAP proponents would look at REST architecture models and make claims that HTTP is designed well for a stateless web, but the REST architectural style doesn't account for all that is required in a full-fledged SOA. The central argument given can be characterized by pointing out additional requirements that only a SOAP framework can provide. Some of these requirements are listed as follows:

1. *Reliability:* Many verticals, such as healthcare and financial services, have strong requirements for reliable transactions. In the case of healthcare these could be long-running transactions where state must be stored over a long period of time. While it is yet unproven, SOAP does have ongoing standardization efforts to provide reliable messaging between SOAP endpoints, complete with delivery assurances appropriate for different use cases. As we have seen, REST is fundamentally stateless and currently lacks this capability.

2. *Description:* When messages are sent with REST, the de-facto standard is to make the payloads opaque or use POX (plain old XML). If we consider XML schema to be a type description language, REST does have a mechanism for describing payloads, but no *service* description language. REST proponents would argue that API descriptions are not applicable with REST because there are only four operations, but this ignores the standardization work that also includes *policy information* as part of SOA service descriptions. SOAP proponents would argue that *service descriptions* allow for richer types of messaging interactions to be universally understood and processed, rather than the standard request/response exchange pattern defined by REST.

3. *Message Level Security*: REST can piggyback easily on top of point-to-point security protocols such as SSL or IP-Sec, but it has no mechanism for persistent security properties applied to the messages themselves. If we remain in the context of POX, one could make an argument that raw XML Security standards could be used to sign and encrypt payloads, but there is no standard for where to place identity tokens in REST style messages. SOAP, by contrast, has a proven message-level security mechanism in the form of OASIS WS-Security that has a proven track record of interoperability.

4. *Publish/Subscribe*: Many business verticals rely on publish/subscribe type messaging coupled with message-level routing to publish information to a diverse number of endpoints over an application level network. The REST model doesn't directly apply to environments that use anything other than a request/response message exchange paradigm. SOAP, by contrast, has standardization efforts that allow for one-way messaging as well as topic based publish and subscribe standards. SOAP also has header mechanisms that allow portions of messages to be targeted at certain intermediary targets

As it stands, SOAP appears to be more closely-aligned with business vertical requirements and REST appears to be more closely-aligned with the nature of how the Web works. Truth be told, it would be cumbersome and weighty to use SOAP for something like the storage service if none of these additional SOAP features just described would ever be used. SOAP frameworks and the WS-* stack are often criticized for being myopic and ignoring the success of the Web. In reality, this stack of specifications is vendor designed and it is no mystery that it trades features for simplicity. The "Web" as such may have little to do with solving the *bounded* integration problem shown in Figure 10.1. In short, it is not the goal of WS-* to solve the unbounded integration problem, but merely provide business value for the here and now. As we segue into the next section, our discussion of the *unbounded integration problem* and REST will be taken up a level in terms of the Web 2.0 phenomenon. From this elevated viewpoint we look again at the relationship of SOAP and REST, but in the broader sense of SOA and Web 2.0.

SOA and Web 2.0

Considered as a precursor to SOA, the term *web service* was terrible. In the early days of web services, there was a need to continually disambiguate a "web service" from "services on the Web" as they were commonly understood. A service on "the Web" was just that, a Web site such as Amazon.com or Expedia.com, something *very* different from an XML-based, cross platform interface for application communication. As time passed, however, *web services* passed into SOA and "services on the Web" passed into Web 2.0. At last, at least in their naming, the two can finally be differentiated. There are, however, forces at play that put SOA and Web 2.0 concepts in a special relation to one another, as if they were two different realizations of a single concept. The purpose of this section is to critically examine this relationship. Specifically, we are interested in what subsets of the Web 2.0 idea are relevant for SOA, especially in terms of the practical or business level requirements.

Current predictions put SOA and Web 2.0 in a type of schizophrenic relationship: some blog pundits claim they are *convergent* while opposing theories claim they are *divergent*. In order to get to the bottom of the matter, we will have to provide an exposition of the defining components of Web 2.0 and then examine which parts or subset of Web 2.0 really bears relation to SOA in an enterprise setting. The reader may find this particular section a bit loftier than other chapters, but the trends we are dealing with have an amorphous character that tends to escape formalization.

What Is Web 2.0?

For the uninitiated, the term Web 2.0 currently refers to a cluster of concepts that characterize the direction in which the current Web is evolving. Due to this evolutionary nature, there is an inherent danger in pinning down and conclusively describing the current state of Web 2.0. It can be done, but only for a given point in time, as the Web 2.0 phenomenon is capricious and undergoing rapid change. Figure 10.4 shows our interpretation of the Web 2.0 cluster that includes what we believe are the most fundamental ideas.

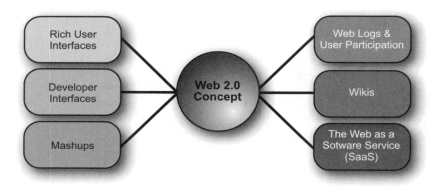

Figure 10.4   A Basic Web 2.0 Cluster Map

Compared to other descriptions of Web 2.0, our six concepts may seem minimal, and we recognize that there is much more to be discussed for a full treatment of Web 2.0. Here we aim only at its essence. The totality of Web 2.0 is difficult to grasp at once because the Web 2.0 phenomenon is really more of a social construction. The enabling technologies behind the success of the Web 2.0 phenomenon aren't necessarily new or revolutionary. In fact, the six concepts described in Figure 10.4 can be arranged by means of a derivation from emergent Web 2.0 technology memes that are themselves derived from relatively ancient technology building blocks. The term *ancient* is used half-jokingly to convey the short shelf-life of most technology (but clearly not all) standards.

You should be aware that Figure 10.5 introduces new terms and acronyms not yet discussed or defined—we will treat it as a sort of roadmap for this section of the chapter.

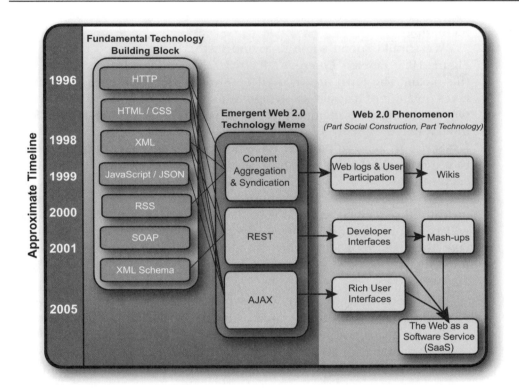

Figure 10.5   The Derivation of Web 2.0 from Memes and Technology Building Blocks

Figure 10.5 is quite busy and demands some further explanation. First, arrows represent antecedent conditions, which simply mean that the referring concepts play a central role in the derivation of the new concept. Note that the arrow styles (dotted and dashed) are included for the sake of readability. Figure 10.5 should be read backwards from right to left to see how the six core Web 2.0 concepts are composed of first emergent Web 2.0 memes, which are themselves tied back to real technology standards. The timeline shown on the left edge of the figure only applies to the left *side* of the figure—that is, to the left of the dotted line. It is shown to highlight a major difference between SOA and Web 2.0, which is that while SOA is undergoing rapid standardization that includes new technology building blocks, the major technology enablers of Web 2.0 have been in place for many years. This is the core reason why we conceive Web 2.0 as a largely social construction that innovates based not on novel technology, but instead innovative ways of using old technology.

We should spend some time and further explain the center part of Figure 10.5, labeled *Emergent Web 2.0 Technology Memes.* What does this mean? The term *meme* used here refers to a concept or word that takes on a life of its own, evolving within its domain of use. For Web 2.0, we argue that the memes that seem revolutionary, such as the REST model (as described in the previous section) or AJAX (the use of JavaScript to achieve partially refreshed pages) will pass from *new ideas* to old ones. This simply means that the architectural ideas embodied in each of these, which seem at once so new and innovative, will become the *normal way* web applications work. That is, these memes serve to unseat old perceived limitations of the Web, and once this happens they will pass into historical footnotes while new, yet undiscovered memes take their place. Each meme should be read and understood in its forward and reverse derivation. We summarize the three memes in Figure 10.5 as follows:

- Content aggregation and syndication: This implies both the primacy of user generated data and its syndication (distribution). Its major technology roots are HTTP, XML, and RSS (Rich Site Summary, or Really Simple Syndication) and it enables key Web 2.0 features such as user contributed content, the proliferation of web logs, and the emergence of Wikis as knowledge management tools. In practice, this is embodied in Web sites that provide instant feedback on articles or utilize reputation systems to rate and weigh the priority of content on a page.

- REST: As described in the previous section, this is an architectural style that has come to mean a diversity of resources coupled with scarcity of verbs (Create, Read, Update, and Destroy). As suggested in the previous section, REST allows for alternative views of the Web. Its major technology roots are HTTP, XML and XML Schema. It enables key Web 2.0 features such a developer interfaces (such as the storage service example in the previous section) that further allows for mashups. *Mashups* are web applications that draw on disparate data stores available over the Web. This meme implies the primacy of data at a basic level, whether it is user generated or not, the goal is to give web applications an easy, natural mechanism to put old data together in new ways.

- AJAX: The AJAX term originally meant "Asynchronous JavaScript and XML", but its meaning has now grown to refer to any web site with a rich user interface. Its technology roots are HTTP, HTML/CSS, JavaScript (JSON) and XML. It enables rich web applications that aim to behave like desktop (thick-client) style applications.

The Web 2.0 Endgame

According to Figure 10.5, if we look at the core concepts, three of them are shown to derive what looks to be an end-state for Web 2.0, which is software as a service. This further promotes the *web browser* from a client perspective to a status similar to the operating system. If new applications of the future run on the *"the Web"* then we can think of the Web as a new operating system and the client side browser as the operating container. This view is certainly a threatening one to traditional ISVs that conceive software in more traditional terms and it remains to be seen if this proverbial end-game will play out as predicted.

An AJAX Detour

Before we examine the deeper relationship between SOA and Web 2.0, it is useful to pause and examine AJAX in more detail as it is one of the important emergent memes of Web 2.0. As mentioned earlier, AJAX stands for "Asynchronous JavaScript and XML", but has grown to mean any web application that exhibits rich user interface design techniques. The most famous example and most often cited example of AJAX techniques is Google Maps. The key innovation here was the realization that *partial page updates* can be managed through JavaScript. That is, the old "mold" of web browser request and full-page server response or refresh was broken. It was now possible for partial redraws to occur through the use of the (now almost infamous) XMLHttpRequest object available in both Microsoft and Mozilla based browsers. This object allows a web browser to spawn additional HTTP requests in an asynchronous (non-blocking) fashion. Generally, data is passed back and forth from the browser to the server in a JSON or XML representation.

Then, JavaScript manipulation of the browser document object (DOM) can be updated in a partial manner. In short, this trick is the beginning of the browser as the next operating container for Web 2.0, and the success of AJAX relies in part on the performance of the JavaScript engine. Poorly optimized JavaScript runtime engines can wreak havoc with complex AJAX interactions, which may tax the JavaScript runtime when compared to a Web 1.0 Application. In some cases, the performance of AJAX applications across browsers can be drastic. The continued success of AJAX-type web clients will be closely tied to how well major browser vendors can optimize for this usage model.

The AJAX meme is a bit like the story of fleas at the circus that are trained to jump only a certain height with the use of an artificial boundary. This was commonly achieved by placing the fleas in closed jars of various heights. For a long time, this same type of artificial boundary existed in the form of the full-page refresh paradigm. The capability existed in the browser, but it took a social phenomenon or realization that the limit was in fact artificial. Now that this limit has been removed, we are seeing not only a flood of AJAX based web applications, but also complete *frameworks* and toolkits for building AJAX user interfaces. Some examples of AJAX-style services include Google Docs, Spreadsheet and Calendar and Zimbra Collaboration Suite. Some examples of popular Web 2.0 frameworks include Google Web Toolkit (GWT), Adobe Flex, and Dojo.

SOA and Web 2.0

We now have a characterization of Web 2.0 split into three fundamental pieces: (a) *fundamental* technology building blocks, (b) central memes, and (c) evolving concepts and predicted *end-state*. You may have noticed that SOAP is shown as a fundamental building block for Web 2.0, but doesn't seem to go anywhere, as if it were treading water in a "Web 2.0 Ocean." In reality, there are plenty of Web 2.0 style-applications that provide SOAP interfaces, and to be fair, it *could* be classified as a referring concept for *developer interfaces*. However, it is shown here as disconnected to emphasize two further points, first that the SOAP versus REST debate puts REST style interfaces (due to their simplicity) in a better position to achieve the Web 2.0 vision, and second, SOAP is really a vendor driven technology designed for enterprises rather than the smart mob of the new Web 2.0 world. Yet, despite this apparent indictment of SOAP, it appears to be connected to Web 2.0, at a basic level. Figure 10.6 shows this intersection: SOA, as conceived for business and Web 2.0 are really just realizations of the Abstract SOA Model (SOA-RM) discussed in Chapter 1.

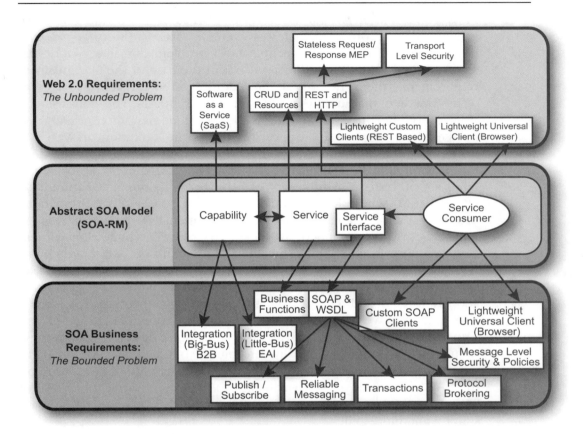

Figure 10.6   The Intersection between SOA and Web 2.0

Figure 10.6 is another busy figure, but if you focus on the middle portion, we will see the familiar abstract SOA building blocks from Chapter 1. These include *capability, service, interface,* and *consumer.* If we take each of these core concepts to their logical conclusion, tempered by either SOA or Web 2.0 type requirements, we can see how these fundamental building blocks derive Web 2.0 in the form of browsers, REST, stateless patterns, CRUD/Resources, and finally the endgame, software as a service. Similarly, if we look at the SOA business level requirements, the same fundamental building blocks derive the heavier SOAP WS-* stack really designed to address EAI and B2B business requirements. Naturally these include more "complicated" processing at the message layer such as *publish/subscribe, reliable messaging, message level security* and the need for SOA to broker or integrate with legacy style protocols such as vendor MOM (*message-oriented middleware*). You should note that both problem domains include the standard lightweight client browser, but in the case of the SOA business requirements, the browser is an indirect tool, often contacting a gateway or intermediary that initiates a series of SOAP requests. This contrasts the primacy of the browser for the Web 2.0 phenomenon, especially the mass-market, "smart-mob" aspect that drives the evolution of Web 2.0. Continuing the comparison, business requirements drive SOA to adopt business functions encapsulated within service containers, rather than a fixed set of verbs. This diversity of business functions is a natural side effect of EAI, where legacy functions take on new audiences but must maintain their original semantics and intent. Moreover, business functions are not bounded by the CRUD model, which allows them capture more concisely the meaning and intent of B2B interactions, which actually *bridges* the gap between technology and business instead of wrapping it in the elegant CRUD and *Resources* model, which is really another layer of indirection from the business perspective. You should also note that we have reintroduced the terms *bounded problem* and *unbounded problem*. The first refers to the nature of enterprise business requirements as falling generally into one of two camps (EAI and B2B), while the second implies the complete unpredictability of innovation on the Web. It is no mystery that in order for the innovative landscape of Web 2.0 to remain fertile, its core tenets and technologies will remain simpler and more agile.

What should we make of this intersection? The fact that Web 2.0 can be derived from the abstract SOA model implies a dilemma: either SOA-RM is in fact *primary* and Web 2.0 is really an SOA coupled with a mass-market "smart mob" that engenders explosive growth, or the SOA-RM model is so abstract and general that it can be used to derive just about anything. Unfortunately, both horns of this dilemma appear unsatisfactory. As we originally argued in Chapter 1, SOA-RM is general, and specific technologies must be specified in order to give it meaning. We answered this initial question by providing XML as such a building block. However, it turns out that XML is *also* a primary building block for Web 2.0. If we choose the second path and consider SOA the father of Web 2.0, we will have a social coup on our hands as the two really aim for different goals: one is a social phenomenon and the other is a business enabler. Aside from clearly different end goals, there is a social rift between the pure viewpoint represented by Web 2.0 and the businesses that aim to profit off this new natural resource. This being said, as general is it is, SOA-RM captures something essential about how software systems should model businesses in a service economy, and as far as we are *all* consumers of services, whether in the context of Web 2.0 or B2B, the core SOA-RM model appears to be deep-seeded and relevant as ever.

SO*: The Future of SOA

The bulk of this chapter aims to present a vendor-neutral characterization of future trends likely to have an impact on SOA. While not exhaustive, the two trends covered thus far give insight into the value SOA has for businesses as well as the arguments and viewpoints shared by its critics. In this final section, we will step away from a completely neutral view of the future of SOA and give some hints as to how Intel sees SOA moving beyond the purely abstract model to more holistic view. This view of the enterprise is called SOE, which stands for *Service Oriented Enterprise*. The SOE idea suggests that service orientation will be eventually be endemic not only to software, but also to infrastructure as well. As a software development trend, SOA has the potential to permeate internal software architectures. This *downward* influence of SOA is seen in architecture models such as SCA (Service Component Architecture) that describe SOA not as a solution to B2B or EAI problems, but as a model for *software architecture*.

Carrying this thread even further, we can imagine the same model eventually applying to infrastructure and operating systems. Once a component view of software becomes prevalent throughout the operating system, hardware and virtualization techniques can be used to provide finer grain control of services themselves, tied back to hardware. This allows for more complex resource allocation in the datacenter as well as finer control of individual components. This view is also closely aligned with *grid computing,* which is seen as a panacea for exploding datacenter resource costs. This view of infrastructure supporting SOA is called *Service Oriented Infrastructure, or SOI.* Figure 10.7 shows a characterization of SOE in terms of SOA and SOI.

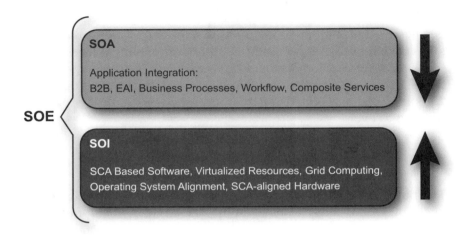

Figure 10.7   SOE in terms of SOA and SOI

Figure 10.7 can be understood as two converging trends. Considered top-down as a business driver, SOA will permeate software further, moving from an integration centric solution to a core software architecture methodology. Once this trend is in place, hardware and infrastructure can move to align with SOA to complete the final bridge between not only business and software, but business and infrastructure and *hardware*. Again, this idea must be tempered with a dose of skepticism, but if the abstract SOA model is really fundamental to business, then the realization of SOI seems to be a likely outcome.

Where do we go from here? This chapter has focused mostly on future trends that apply to SOA at a software level with Web 2.0 as the obvious contentious gorilla. SOI considered as a separate topic has not been treated here, but its component topics such as SCA, virtualization and grid computing are ripe topics for a bottom up type of treatment. Overall we believe that the core ideas of SOA, especially its importance for business, remain strong. As we have tried to show, Web 2.0 and REST-style approaches are really facets of an underlying unifying service orientation concept expressed for different audiences.

Summary

- The REST architectural style doesn't account for all that is required in a full-fledged SOA (for example, no specific definition around horizontal services such as security). The central argument between REST and SOAP given can be characterized by pointing out additional requirements that only a SOAP framework can provide. Rather than thinking of REST versus SOAP, one should consider the value the *each* brings to the table when architecting a SOA.

- REST-style interfaces with a diversity of nouns and scarcity of operations (Create, Read, Update and Delete) are often the best choice for simple services. SOAP-based interfaces should be used when the message-exchange pattern requires additional features such as reliable messaging, message-level security, more robust descriptions (WSDL), and the possibility of patterns like one-way notifications or publish/subscribe.

- While it can be argued that Web 2.0 and SOA are fundamentally different, the *service* undercurrent runs in common to both trends. For Web 2.0, the end result is SaaS (Software as a Service) and for SOA the end result is the services-oriented enterprise.

- While Web 2.0 can be characterized in many different ways, it is important to note that unlike most "new technologies" Web 2.0 is more a social construction and represents the use of existing technologies in new ways rather than truly new technology innovations.

- As SOA adoption continues, we predict a further split of the Service Oriented Enterprise (SOE) into SOA and SOI. The latter refers to hardware and infrastructure being more closely aligned with SOA over the long term, and is detailed in Chapter 4.

Chapter **11**

Conclusion

I think and think for months and years. Ninety-nine times the
conclusion is false. The hundredth time I am right.

—Albert Einstein

This book has covered a substantial amount of ground on the practical application of SOA to the enterprise with tangible examples in specific vertical industries. The first practical application discussed all the way back in Chapter 1 is that although you can think of SOA as a generic framework for approaching the design of software systems that this thinking can only go so far without application to specific technology (like XML). For each vertical industry chapter we discussed the key business challenges and how the application of SOA can address those challenges in a manner that provides substantial capability as well as a material improvement in development, deployment and sustaining costs. While each vertical industry has unique business needs and challenges for implementing SOA, common themes emerge regarding the practical application of SOA, and this concluding chapter is an examination of these themes.

Get the Foundation Right

Adopting SOA is an investment decision for your business, and like any investment the level of success is proportional to the level of planning which goes into the investment. Since SOA is fundamentally a set of software manufacturing techniques, to implement it successfully involves setting up the right organizational structure to plan, acquire, adopt, support, and continually improve a portfolio of reusable services. As discussed in Chapter 2, setting up your Enterprise Architecture, Service Procurement, Solution Assembly, and Operations organizations is the essential foundation to have material practical success in implementing SOA. Leaving in place existing organizations in silos with a focus on vertical applications, business units, and IT infrastructure might yield the creation and adoption of some reusable components but won't result in any material or long-term shift in the cost improvements offered by SOA.

In addition to the organizational investment, incremental investments in horizontal technology infrastructure will be needed, as discussed in Chapters 3 and 4. Put in place the Service Catalog for Lifecycle management in maintaining the service portfolio as well as make investments in security infrastructure, the enterprise service bus, portal, and BPM to compose those services in automated business process solutions. Finally, it is imperative to invest in an SOA monitoring and management platform for Operations, which allows your organization to effectively manage service SLAs and quickly identify and fix those services that are out of compliance.

Finally, to get the foundation right it is imperative to be proactive and consciously explicit about gaining agreement on the data definitions core business services will manage. Getting to a common data definition (in both structure and meaning) for things like Customer, Supplier, Order, and so on are necessary to generate reusable services that manage business transactions. Without that common data definition (either through internal company agreement or industry standards) it will not be possible to establish highly reusable services, but instead a mass of repeating variations on the same structures will prevail in your service inventory, sapping the cost savings out of your SOA investment.

Implement the Big Bus and the Little Bus

Throughout this book a key theme has been to segment enterprise-wide or cross-enterprise concerns from department or business process specific ones. The term we have used to describe this segmentation is *big bus* for the enterprise-wide or cross-enterprise concerns and *little bus* for the department or business process specific ones.

This segmentation is necessary to practically implement a SOA architecture at a material scale and is needed to decouple the definition, management, and ongoing operations of the overall service portfolio. This segmentation provides benefits in security, performance, operational agility, and reducing management complexity.

Pilot, Iterate, and Evolve (also Known as "Crawl, Walk, Run")

As we have discussed in nearly every chapter of the book, it is not possible for most organizations to move from the application model (either Build-to-Order or Made-for-Order) to SOA in one step. More often than not, current customer commitments and available incremental investment budgets are too constrained to implement a "big-bang" approach to an SOA deployment. As we have seen in the vertical market chapters, especially the financial services and government sectors, not all practical deployments of SOA fit a traditional definition. A key idea, and one that is of utmost importance, is not to get charmed by the grand theoretical architecture of SOA; this often leaves one in a state of paralysis in terms of actually engendering genuine change in software architectures. Instead, being *flexible* with respect to the "crawl" phase means lowering the bar for software projects to count as SOA deployments; any step in the right direction counts! Part of the power of SOA is the moniker or label it brings to fueling new projects that emphasize interoperability, standards, and a closer tie between business and software.

The recommendation is to take an iterative approach, starting with one or many pilot programs where demonstrable success can be identified and measured as well as where the results of the pilot can be used for training, technology reuse, and business justification for expanding the adoption of SOA. Once a few pilot programs are completed successfully, then making incremental long-term investments in the overall service portfolio, horizontal technical infrastructure, and associated organizational shifts are warranted. Take on the adoption of SOA one or a few business domains at a time, incrementally adding to the service portfolio but doing so in a manner that is consistent with an overall enterprise architecture roadmap discussed in Chapter 2.

The best places to start in each vertical industry and in many cases specific companies are different. Some specific examples are provided in each vertical industry chapter. There are some common themes about where to start: the best places are where cost and business agility for data or business process execution represent a significant pain point for your business. Where you need a uniform view to the reading and/or writing of data and need to substantially increase the agility by which a business process can evolve are the prime candidates for applying and realizing the value of SOA.

Keep an Eye on the Future

The IT industry is constantly evolving, no one concept or technique remains the best practice indefinitely, and SOA is no exception. As discussed in Chapter 10, REST, SOI, and Web 2.0 all represent incrementally transitional shifts in how to represent software as a service and that trend will continue.

As you make investments in the service portfolio, service catalog, and enterprise service bus, keep an eye on the future. Don't make SOAP-only investments. Stick with vendors who leverage open standards and are active in standards development initiatives. Use technology with modular representations of end-point service interface bindings and that can support the services in your portfolio that were developed today as well as a few years ago.

Finally, the concept of all computing resources providing a virtualized and extensible service interface is not that far away, and this will yield a rise in the practical use and adoption of utility computing. With SOA applied to the entire computing stack, utility computing will offer close coordination between hardware components, the applications that run on them, and the data management tools that handle provisioning, storage pooling, and a myriad of tasks that require wide-scale automation across a utility network. The utility infrastructure will be able to automatically provision and deliver resources on demand, while tracking usage for pricing and eventual chargeback. The net effect of utility computing and SOI is that the whole deployment and use model of technology shifts and now is the time to start thinking about how your organization might respond to that shift as part of your SOA deployment program.

Final Thoughts

SOA is one of the most hyped and confusing topics in IT for some time. The purpose of this book was to provide clarity to the definition and to provide specific and practical guidance on how to successfully implement an SOA deployment program in your organization. We took a complete view from the organizational and technology investments required to multi-industry specific views of how those organizational and technology investments could be applied. And finally, we reviewed the future of technology, architectures, and standards that represent relevant intersections to any SOA implementation that gets deployed now or in the near future. Thorough application of this practical guide to SOA in your environment ought to yield tangible improvements in systems agility and IT costs for your business.

Glossary

This glossary contains definitions of terms used throughout the book. Rather than provide strict definitions (which may be found in reference material), the terms used here are consistent with their overall meaning as used throughout the book. That is, they serve not only to define concepts, but also summarize the main ideas behind them as presented in each chapter. The reader should think of these as definitions with commentary.

2-factor authentication Any authentication scheme that relies on what the person has (such as a physical artifact or token) as well as what they know (such as a PIN or password).

adaptor A component that wraps a legacy system to provide a service interface. See also *container*.

application server A server capable of hosting services. Note that this term is used to mean more than a standard web application server.

assemble to order The software development process that depends on pre-assembled functional modules—services—that are readily taken from an inventory and rapidly made part of a new application.

assertion A statement regarding a service, system or user of a service. Assertions make a statement about past events, such as a particular authentication or authorization event. Can also be used to associate a set of attributes with an identity.

attack vector A possible means of attacking any system. Used in this context this system is a service, set of services, or the messages exchanged between services.

authentication A means of identifying a service, message, system (service consumer), or user of a service.

authorization A means of identifying the allowable actions for a service, message, system (service consumer), or user of a service.

business activity management Tools for monitoring the runtime state of any business process including historical trends on key performance indicators for the process. This allows the continuous improvement of business process to identify things like bottlenecks, unexpected redundant processing, open-loop control scenarios, and so on.

big bus, little bus An SOA implementation model that uses hierarchy (little busses nested under a big bus) to enable domain-specific *little bus* localized SOA implementations (which may be either custom or vendor supplied) to operate autonomously with localized standards, but integrate with the enterprise through a loosely coupled interface to the *big bus*. This model promotes both SOA agility (accommodating many SOA domain implementations) and scalability.

BPM Business Process Management. BPM systems provide a suite of tools for the solution assembly organization (as discussed in Chapter 2) to rapidly capture business process requirements at the process activity level rather than at a systems function level. BPM makes it easier for business analysts to participate in the development process, ensuring that new applications support business requirements that affect an organization's key performance indicators.

BRE Business Rule Engine. Tool for describing policies (if-then-else/case statements) that drive the decision/action behavior of activities within the business process and/or handle routing or other transaction processing decisions within a business process and associated workflows. BREs provide the means to centralize and catalog rules in a concrete and explicit way for easier change management.

build to order A manufacturing model in which all new business is effectively treated as completely new. The key characteristics of this model are that new orders are viewed as a new problem for a new customer with very unique needs that demand a customized and specialized solution. Each finished good is developed from the ground up, as if drawn on a blank sheet of paper.

business agility The desired result or goal of a close correlation between a service architecture and the changing needs of the business.

business process modeling Tools for graphically depicting the activities and flows for AS-IS and TO-BE business processes.

business process monitoring The application of monitoring and release management capabilities to SOA so that the impact of service performance and quality is clearly identified. Since common SOA services are extensively reused, performance or quality issues can have an impact on many business processes that use the common services in their "assembled" solution. Business process monitoring and governance account for the dependency of business processes on services, and services interdependencies on other services.

business processes The activity of a business or businesses working to create value.

coarse-grained services A core business or process service that is composed of other services. See also *fine-grained service*.

composite applications The end result of a successful SOA architecture. A composite application is the end-to-end as seen by the user. See also *composite service*.

composite service A service that relies on or calls out to other services to perform its main tasks.

confidentiality The means of applying data protection, such as encryption, to a message that participates in a service exchange. Can also be used to refer to encryption applied to a socket-level connection, such as is used in SSL or TLS. See also *message level security*.

container Any managed runtime environment such as J2EE or .NET that can be used to host a service or set of services.

content based routing Application level message routing centered around SOA with XML as a foundational component. Refers to XML data flows used in a service oriented architecture such as XPath routing, reliable messaging, publish/subscribe, and protocol mediation.

control plane A set of system management components that allows for signaling management and monitoring of data or voice communication. As used here, it describes the management entity needed to deploy services provided by telecommunications service provider.

COTS Commercial Off-The-shelf Software. As used here, it refers to software purchased and used with minimal modification.

crawl-walk-run An evolutionary model based on achieving phased maturity milestones. As used here, this strategy is believed to be the most reliable way to adopt SOA.

data center automation Using infrastructure services automation capabilities, the provisioning (and reuse) of resources are managed as abstracted, virtualized entities using rules- and policy-based management techniques. In this book, we identify that data center automation can be enabled through Service Oriented Infrastructure (SOI) coupled with management systems and standards (such as WS-Management).

data warehouse A collection of historical data that constitutes a summation of historical data, collected over time, providing a basis to generate reports and trending information (sometimes using data mining techniques). A data warehouse is an aggregation and accumulation of data, and as identified in this book, SOA services can feed a data warehouse from distributed services, and in addition, can provide functions such as data transformation in service form.

decoupling A technology trend that describes the separation of generalized software functions away from traditional clients or software systems into the communication path itself. See Chapter 3, specifically interface and functional decoupling.

delivery plane The components that enable data distribution for data or voice communication. Used here in reference to a telecommunications service provider. See also *control plane*.

demand trigger Provides a signal that indicates a change in provisioned resource levels is needed to fulfill a change in service level demand. An explicit demand trigger is a signal from a person or system that anticipates the need to change before any performance degradation occurs. An implicit trigger is a signal from a system that responds to changes in service capacity, adjusting service capacity up or down.

digital certificate The association between a name and a public key as vouched for by a certificate authority. Generally used to refer to a specific token type for a secure SOA exchange.

domain message bus The *little bus* component. See also big bus, little bus.

dynamic binding The ability to search for available services and bind to the interfaces in real time as the result of a decision reached within a specific business process.

EAI Enterprise Application Integration. As used here, refers to a hub and spoke model type of integration based on tight coupling. See also *ESB* and *SOA*.

EMR An information system used in healthcare to record and manage clinical information regarding a patient.

enterprise architecture The anchor-point of the SOA-based, assemble-to-order manufacturing model. This is the command-and-control function, which sets the implementation and transition plan to SOA that is used to consciously and concretely define the new organizational assemble-to-order business model and architecture. Enterprise architecture is the driver of the balanced investment portfolio and is accountable for the results associated with the architecture, investment, and governance decisions.

ESB Enterprise Service Bus. Used to denote a software component that integrates applications through the use of a bus. Often confused with SOA.

fine-grained services An atomic service that provides a single function. Collections of fine-grained services form a coarse-grained service. See also *coarse-grained service*.

fixed mobile-IP convergence A trend in the telecommunications industry that consolidates wireless, wireline, and data subscribers into a single network.

HIN A network supporting data exchange of clinical information across a community of medical care.

HL7 An industry standards body in healthcare, primarily focused on data interoperability standards development.

identity management Software that manages identities, often through the use of a standard data store such as LDAP. Identity management software can provide functions such as authentication, authorization and access control for the little-bus or big-bus portion of an SOA. SOA often relies on identity management systems as a specific service call to delegate authentication and authorization decisions. See also *assertion*.

identity normalization The act of transforming identities into a standard form before being sent across the *big bus*.

J2EE Any Java-based SOA infrastructure. While the strict definition is "Java 2 Enterprise Edition" it is generally used in the broader sense.

loose coupling The progressive generalization of communication interfaces for software systems. That is, interfaces used for communication between software systems are becoming more generic and the specific functions are represented in the data itself.

made for order A highly standardized product with a specific set of features, which, for the most part, are universally defined for all customers. This business model achieves economies of scale since the cost of a single design is spread across the revenue from multiple customers, often reducing the initial and sustaining cost of the finished good. In the case of software, this method often reduces the time it takes to deploy the software and make it usable in an IT environment.

managed peer to peer (MPP) model The architecture consisting of stateless core content routing in the center and SOA proxies (consumers or producers) or routers at the edges. MPPs are carrier managed and exist outside the firewall.

message level security Persistent digital signatures or encryption applied to messages themselves. This term is often used to distinguish from transport level security, which is transient and applied only to the communication path.

message oriented middleware General technology category that includes messaging and queuing technologies, mostly based on asynchronous delivery of messages between applications.

.NET Any Microsoft-based or branded SOA infrastructure. Also refers to the Microsoft .NET developer framework.

non-repudiation A legal concept that may be supported by a digital signature. Non-repudiation of origin implies a sender cannot later deny that a message was sent. In the context of SOA, this term is used generally to refer to authentication with a digital signature.

opaque service A type of service designed for generalized processing, divorced from the semantics of the data itself. This generally refers to services that process messages based only on structure and syntax, and not necessarily semantics. One example of this is a service that does transformation or content routing.

operational datastore (ODS) A subject-oriented, integrated, volatile, current-valued, detailed-only collection of data in support of an organization's need for up-to-the-second, operational, integrated, collective information. In this book, an ODS can be fed from a variety of services, each containing one or more data elements key to enterprise operations. Also, SOA can enable a set of scalable data services, allowing highly shared data to be made readily available to the enterprise.

PKI Public Key Infrastructure. Refers to the standards for public key cryptosystems and X.509 style digital certificates. Often considered in a negative light due to the complexity of PKI deployments, especially key management such as key revocation, rotation, and recovery.

POTS Plain Old Telephone Service.

POX Plain Old XML. Generally used in the context of REST as distinguished from SOAP to refer to a simpler, ostensibly more elegant means of achieving XML requests and responses.

resource In the context of REST, a named URI intended to be invariant. More generally, any application or document accessible on the Web (Web resource).

REST Representational State Transfer, an architectural style derived in a doctoral dissertation by Roy Fielding. The intent of REST is to model properties that made the Web successful.

secure tunnel A general term that refers to secure socket level communication between a client and server. While there are theoretically many possible protocols that can be used to implement a secure tunnel, the protocol often referred to here is SSL or TLS.

security heuristic Any action taken intended to increase the security of a system. In the context of SOA, common security heuristics include using security standards to meet a regulation, or using security standards to meet interoperability requirements. Security heuristics may or may not actually increase the security of a system; they are often used to make security arguments that ignore the security of the system as a whole.

service A real-world capability exposed through an interface. In the context of SOA, a service is defined by its interface, which defines its behavior and information model.

service assembly Function of the assemble-to-order software factory that takes services from inventory and assembles applications.

service composition A term used to describe the act of creating a service in terms of calls to other services, generally with a workflow or process model in mind.

service consumer A user of a service. In the context of SOA, the role of the service consumer generally refers to a software component and not a human user.

service contract A description of the policies, interface, and functionality of a service.

service decomposition A term used to describe the act of breaking up a service into smaller atomic services.

service delivery network (SDN) As used in the telecommunications industry, an SDN is a collaboration between all static and dynamic subscribers and publisher of a class of messages. A collaboration represents a contract with its own quality of service and security requirements.

service interface A cross-platform document that describes how a service is accessed. In the context of XML-based SOA, the service interface often refers to a WSDL document.

service adoption roadmap Plan put together to define what services are procured, in what order, and over what timeframe. Also specific decisions are made regarding where to source the services from (build, buy, outsource).

service portfolio An abstracted collection of services that is managed. For example, a collection of utility services (logging, security, routing) may constitute a portfolio. In the domain of business services, a collection of services related to a manufacturing supply chain may be a managed portfolio.

service portfolio planning The process used to plan an abstracted collection of services. The planning process takes on significance and importance as investment decisions (both financial and human resources) are made based on business needs for services.

service procurement A business process to acquire services, typically provided by third parties either as a custom developed or off-the-shelf package purchase.

service producer The provider of a service. In the context of SOA, the role of the service provider generally refers to a software component such as an application server.

service proxy A specialized service (or purpose-built software or device) that passes SOA messages bucket-brigade style, and in the process can be used for analysis or policy enforcement. Service proxies are commonly used to augment a services infrastructure for purposes of security or manageability.

service reuse A loaded term used to argue for the benefits of SOA depending on the specific stakeholder, either reuse as business agility or reuse as software re-use. In reality, a properly designed SOA doesn't distinguish between service use and service reuse. For SOA, use and reuse should be identical. See the related section in Chapter 3.

service scale-out Increasing or expanding service capacity by providing additional instances that operate in parallel. This is different from scale-up, where more capable and powerful platforms are used to increase the capability of a single service instance.

service virtualization The act of virtualizing a service endpoint, generally at a web services security gateway. When a service is virtualized, the consumer is making service calls to an endpoint that is a proxy for the actual service itself.

SOA Service Oriented Architecture. A software design practice with strong technology considerations. The authors' view is that XML is an essential foundational technology consideration.

SOA content routing Application level message routing centered around SOA with XML as a foundational component. Refers to XML data flows used in a service oriented architecture such as XPath routing, reliable messaging, publish/subscribe, and protocol mediation. See also *content based routing*, which is used as a synonym.

SOA governance process Process to review use, adoption, and exceptions to the use of the Service Oriented Adoption Roadmap.

SOA lifecycle management Process and rule set to manage the evolution of service definitions and their interfaces over the course of their life cycle from initial design to end-of-life.

SOA management Process and tools to monitor and manage the quality of the service and its adherence to its defined service level agreement.

SOA publish/subscribe A service that includes publish/subscribe style messaging that is part of a SOA. This is often closely related to SOA that utilizes content based routing.

SOA security An often cited barrier to SOA adoption. The authors believe that SOA security should be looked at in contrary terms, namely that SOA highlights existing security problems rather than causing new vulnerabilities. See the relevant section in Chapter 4.

SOA taxonomy Design of the services inventory. Specifically defining the course-grained services, which manage enterprise data and process, and their separation from fine grained services, which provide horizontal technology functions such as security, messaging middleware, and so on.

SOAP Simple Object Access Protocol. A simple XML-based envelope used to wrap service calls within an XML-based web services architecture. Often contrasted with REST. See the relevant discussion in Chapter 10.

SOE Service-Oriented Enterprise. A future trend that suggests service orientation will eventually be endemic not only to software, but also to enterprise infrastructure as well.

SOI Service Oriented Infrastructure. A future trend that characterizes enterprise infrastructure, including hardware and internal software design, as service based. One can think of this as a downward influence of SOA to lower levels of the technology stack.

stateless applications Applications for which each request from client to server must contain all of the information necessary to understand the request, and cannot take advantage of any stored context on the server. Session state, if any, is therefore kept entirely on the client while the server "forgets" the transaction once processed.

static binding Service calls that are bound at compile time, or more generally, decided a priori. See also *dynamic binding*.

tight coupling For SOA, tight coupling refers to interfaces or communication protocols tightly bound to a service. Generally, a service designed with tight coupling is the opposite of what is desired for an optimal SOA, which should be designed around loose coupling.

universal server A concept term used to describe how most servers operate today. That is, communication is done through different network ports and different transport middleware, all at different levels of interface decoupling depending on who is listening on the other end.

universal tunnel A concept model that can be used to understand service communication as a tunnel built around an accepted set of protocols and standards.

URI Uniform Resource Identifier. Used to refer to an abstract resource, either for a service endpoint or a general web resource in the context of REST.

utility computing The use of computing, storage, or networking infrastructure as an abstracted, virtualized set of resources where consumers are oblivious to the specifics of how the resources are provided. The consumption model for utility computing resembles that of utilities like electricity, water or phone service; once service standards are established by the utility and consumers adapt to "plug in," the utility can be consumed through very standard interfaces (wall plugs, hose bibs, phone jacks). In the utility model, consumers do not know or care how the capacity is supplied. Because some margin of unused capacity is always available, it has the advantage of very low marginal cost (in time and money) to acquire resources needed to fulfill a capacity. It also lends itself to a consumption-based charge model for services provided.

value chain The set of business processes, applications, and data that constitute an end-to-end representation of a company's products and/or services. Value chain may include design, order taking, manufacturing, service delivery, supply chain planning, order-to-cash delivery of services or goods. Not included in the value chain include supportive functions that enable the company but in themselves don't directly add to the value of goods or services.

virtual infrastructure management Management of infrastructure that has been virtualized; for example, the provisioning and monitoring of virtual machine "guests" as provided by a hypervisor. Other managed virtualized infrastructure can include mass storage and network.

VoIP Voice over IP. One of the driving technologies for converged networks in the telecommunications industry.

weakest link property The property that states the overall security of any system (including services within the context of an SOA) is only as strong as its weakest link. This property is often ignored when the security of a system is claimed to be increased through the use of a specific standard or the meeting of a certain regulation.

web security The overall security of a web application. Refers to the general class of attacks that focus on exploiting weaknesses in web servers and web browsers.

web service A service designed around web-based protocols and XML, specifically HTTP and SOAP.

web services security gateway A device (typically an appliance or server) that proxies communication between service producers and consumers for the purposes of offloading expensive XML and web services security processing, such as XML Security and WS-Security. web services security gateways also provide content attack prevention for content-borne threats.

workflow automation The automated movement of business processes or tasks through a work process. This includes both the sequenced automation of services, applications and data, and it can include human interaction at junctures that require it.

WS-* A term used to refer to the collection of numerous web services standards. Often used to denote the fact that there are seemingly too many standards in the space of XML based web services.

WS-heavy A term used to refer to the collection of numerous web services standards, but in a negative light that refers to the collection of standards as too onerous and complex for real-world use.

WS-I An open industry organization chartered to promote web services interoperability across platforms, operating systems, and programming languages. Symptomatic of the increasingly general nature of web services security standards that require even further profiling and constraints to be practically used. Even though WS-I doesn't create standards, the profiles they create are viewed as standards that are either supported or unsupported by vendor products.

XML eXtensible Markup Language. The authors believe that XML is a foundational element to SOA.

References

This section mentions the various reference materials used throughout the book, either directly or as an influencing factor. Reference material includes specifications and standards, complete books, or just noteworthy Web resources.

[1] "What is Windows Communication Foundation". http://msdn2.microsoft.com/en-us/library/ms731082.aspx.

[2] [ITU-T Recommendation X.509][2] (2005): Information Technology - Open Systems Interconnection - The Directory: Authentication Framework, 08/05.

[3] Check 21 Act. Public Law 108-100

[4] D. Eastlake, J. R., D. Solo, M. Bartel, J. Boyer, B. Fox, E. Simon. XML Signature Syntax and Processing, W3C Recommendation, 12 February 2002.

[5] Distributed Management Task Force (DMTF), Inc. http://www.dmtf.org/home

[6] Federal Information Processing Standard (FIPS) for the Advanced Encryption Standard, FIPS-197. November 2001

[7] Google Web Toolkit. http://code.google.com/webtoolkit/

[8] GSM 03.40, Technical realization of the Short Message Service (SMS)

[9] JSR 208 - Java Business Integration (JBI). http://jcp.org/aboutJava/communityprocess/final/jsr208/index.html

[10] JSR 914 (JMS 1.0 and 1.1).
http://www.jcp.org/en/jsr/detail?id=914

[11] Krafzig, D., Banke, K., and Slama, D. 2004 *Enterprise Soa: Service-Oriented Architecture Best Practices* (The Coad Series). Prentice Hall PTR.

[12] OASIS Reference Model for Service Oriented Architecture (SOA). http://www.oasis-open.org/committees/tc_home.php?wg_abbrev=soa-rm

[13] OASIS Security Services (SAML) TC. http://www.oasis-open.org/committees/tc_home.php?wg_abbrev=security

[14] OASIS UDDI Specification. http://www.oasis-open.org/committees/tc_home.php?wg_abbrev=uddi-spec

[15] OASIS Web Services Reliable Exchange (WS-RX). http://www.oasis-open.org/committees/tc_home.php?wg_abbrev=ws-rx

[16] OASIS Web Services Secure Exchange (WS-SX). http://www.oasis-open.org/committees/tc_home.php?wg_abbrev=ws-sx

[17] OASIS Web Services Security (WS-Security). http://www.oasis-open.org/committees/tc_home.php?wg_abbrev=wss

[18] Organization for the Advancement of Structured Information Standards (OASIS). http://www.oasis-open.org

[19] RFC 2045. MIME Part One: Format of Internet Message Bodies.

[20] RFC 2246. The TLS Protocol Version 1.0

[21] RFC 2617. HTTP Authentication: Basic and Digest Access Authentication

[22] RFC 3031. Multiprotocol Label Switching Architecture

[23] RFC 791 – Internet Protocol

[24] RFC3261. SIP: Session Initiation Protocol

[25] Roy T. Fielding, "Architectural Styles and the Design of Network-based Software Architectures", PhD thesis, UC Irvine, 2000

[26] SCA 0.96 specification.
http://www.osoa.org/display/Main/Service+Component+Architecture+Specifications

[27] SOAP Messages with Attachments. W3C Note 11 December 2000. http://www.w3.org/TR/SOAP-attachments

[28] The 3rd Generation Partnership Project (3GPP).
http://www.3gpp.org/About/about.htm

[29] The Extensible Stylesheet Language Family (XSL).
http://www.w3.org/Style/XSL/

[30] The Open Group Architecture Framework.
http://www.opengroup.org/architecture/togaf8-doc/arch/

[31] The OpenSSL Project. http://www.openssl.org/

[32] Tim O'Reilly (2005-09-30). What Is Web 2.0. O'Reilly Network.

[33] UML Specification v. 1.1 (OMG document ad/97-08-11)

[34] W3C Recommendation, "XML Path Language", 16 November 1999

[35] W3C Working Draft, "XML Encryption Syntax and Processing," 04 March 2002.

[36] Web Services Description Working Group.
http://www.w3.org/2002/ws/desc/

[37] Web Services Interoperability Organization (WS-I).
http://www.ws-i.org/

[38] World Wide Web Consortium. http://www.w3.org/

[39] WS-BPEL 2.0 specification (OASIS standard). http://www.oasis-open.org/committees/tc_home.php?wg_abbrev=wsbpel

[40]National Information Exchange Model
http://www.niem.gov/

[41] Slaski, B., & Coleman, G. (n. d.). *Accelerated information sharing for law enforcement (AISLE) using web services*. Mclean, VA: Advanced Technology Systems and Madison, WI: Wisconsin Crime Information Bureau.

[42] Coleman, G 2006 Symposium on Justice and Public Safety Information Sharing

[43] Federal Enterprise Architecture
http://www.whitehouse.gov/omb/egov/a-1-fea.html
Global Justice XML Data Model
http://www.it.ojp.gov/jxdm/

[44] Canada Health Infoways Integration costing – "EHRS Blueprint -> an interoperable EHR framework. Infoway Architecture Update" Canada Health Infoways Solution Architecture Group March 2006.

[45] Financial Information eXchange
http://www.fixprotocol.org/

[46] Financial products markup language
http://www.fpml.org/

[47] Web Services Interoperability Organization
http://www.ws-i.org

[48] Advanced Message Queuing Protocol
http://www.amqp.org/

[49] 'The IMS'; Miikka Poikselka, et al; ISBN 0-470-87113-X

White Papers

[50] White Paper, IMS Architecture & Validation Laboratory – Intel

[51] White Paper, BEA WebLogic Service Delivery – BEA & Intel

[52] SIP for Dummies – Avaya

[53] Service Orchestration of Intel-Based Platforms Under a Service-Oriented Infrastructure – Intel Technology Journal Volume 10 Issue 04 Published November 9, 2006
http://www.intel.com/technology/itj/2006/v10i4/2-service/1-abstract.htm

Index

Continuing Education is Essential

It's a challenge we all face – keeping pace with constant change in information technology. Whether our formal training was recent or long ago, we must all find time to keep ourselves educated and up to date in spite of the daily time pressures of our profession.

Intel produces technical books to help the industry learn about the latest technologies. The focus of these publications spans the basic motivation and origin for a technology through its practical application.

Right books, right time, from the experts

These technical books are planned to synchronize with roadmaps for technology and platforms, in order to give the industry a head-start. They provide new insights, in an engineer-to-engineer voice, from named experts. Sharing proven insights and design methods is intended to make it more practical for you to embrace the latest technology with greater design freedom and reduced risks.

I encourage you to take full advantage of Intel Press books as a way to dive deeper into the latest technologies, as you plan and develop your next generation products. They are an essential tool for every practicing engineer or programmer. I hope you will make them a part of your continuing education tool box.

Sincerely,

Justin Rattner
Senior Fellow and Chief Technology Officer
Intel Corporation

**Turn the page to learn about titles
from Intel Press for system developers**

Applied Virtualization Technology

Usage Models for IT Professionals and Software Developers

By Sean Campbell and Michael Jeronimo
ISBN: 0-9764832-3-8

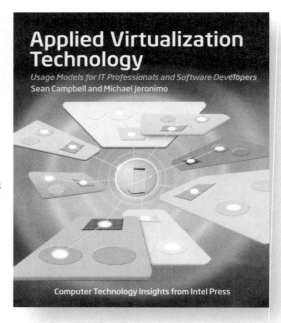

Server and desktop virtualization is one of the more significant technologies to impact computing in the last few years, promising the benefits of infrastructure consolidation, lower costs, increased security, ease of management, and greater employee productivity.

Using virtualization technology, one computer system can operate as multiple "virtual" systems. The convergence of affordable, powerful platforms and robust scalable virtualization solutions is spurring many technologists to examine the broad range of uses for virtualization. In addition, a set of processor and I/O enhancements to Intel server and client platforms, known as Intel® Virtualization Technology (Intel® VT), can further improve the performance and robustness of current software virtualization solutions.

This book takes a user-centered view and describes virtualization usage models for IT professionals, software developers, and software quality assurance staff. The book helps you plan the introduction of virtualization solutions into your environment and thereby reap the benefits of this emerging technology.

Highlights include:

- The challenges of current virtualization solutions
- In-depth examination of three software-based virtualization products
- Usage models that enable greater IT agility and cost savings
- Usage models for enhancing software development and QA environments
- Maximizing utilization and increasing flexibility of computing resources
- Reaping the security benefits of computer virtualization
- Distribution and deployment strategies for virtualization solutions

Enhance security and protection against software-based attacks

The Intel Safer Computing Initiative
Building Blocks for Trusted Computing
By David Grawrock
ISBN 0-9764832-6-2

With the ever-increasing connectivity of home and business computers, it is essential that developers understand how the Intel Safer Computing Initiative can provide critical security building blocks to better protect the PC computing environment. Security capabilities need to be carefully evaluated before delivery into the marketplace. Intel is committed to delivering security capabilities in a responsible manner for end users and the ecosystem.

A highly versatile set of hardware-based security enhancements, code-named LaGrande Technology (LT), will be supported on Intel processors and chipsets to help enhance PC platforms. This book covers the fundamentals of LT and key Trusted Computing concepts such as security architecture, cryptography, trusted computer base, and trusted channels.

Highlights include:

- History of trusted computing and definitions of key concepts
- Comprehensive overview of protections that are provided by LaGrande Technology
- Case study showing how access to memory is the focal point of an attack
- Protection methods for execution, memory, storage, input, and graphics
- How the Trusted Platform Module (TPM) supports attestation

In this concise book, the lead security architect for Intel's next-generation security initiative provides critical information you need to evaluate Trusted Computing for use on today's PC systems and to prepare your designs to respond to future threats.

Managing Information Technology for Business Value

Practical Strategies for IT and Business Managers

By Martin Curley

ISBN 0-9717861-7-8

Managing Information Technology for Business Value is Martin Curley's call for IT and business managers to reformulate the way they manage IT. Curley's argument is based on evidence, from his work at Intel and with other leading enterprises, that IT investments can and should be linked directly to enterprise business indicators.

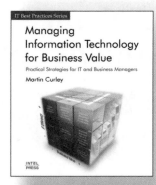

66 *Curley offers practical advice and insights ... required reading for all IT executives.* 99

Prof. Paul Tallon,
Carroll School of Management,
Boston College

Measuring the Business Value of Information Technology

Practical Strategies for IT and Business Managers

By David Sward

ISBN 0-9764832-7-0

In today's fast moving competitive business environment, companies increasingly demand that IT investments demonstrate business value through measurable results. Expanding on concepts offered in Martin Curley's *Managing IT for Business Value*, David Sward explains how business value programs are established, measured, maintained, and governed, providing a blueprint for evaluating IT investments and equipping the reader with the tools required for success.

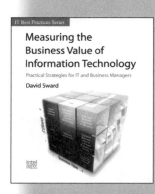

A customer-focused approach to determine the business value for any IT investment

● *Multi-Core Programming*
Increasing Performance through Software Multi-threading
By Shameem Akhter and Jason Roberts
ISBN 0-9764832-4-6

Developers can no longer rely on increasing clock speeds alone to speed up single-threaded applications; instead, to gain a competitive advantage, developers must learn how to properly design their applications to run in a threaded environment. This book helps software developers write high-performance multi-threaded code for Intel's multi-core architecture while avoiding the common parallel programming issues associated with multi-threaded programs. This book is a practical, hands-on volume with immediately usable code examples that enable readers to quickly master the necessary programming techniques.

Discover programming techniques for Intel multi-core architecture and Hyper-Threading Technology

● *The Software Optimization Cookbook, Second Edition*
High-Performance Recipes for IA-32 Platforms
By Richard Gerber, Aart J.C. Bik, Kevin B. Smith, and Xinmin Tian
ISBN 0-9764832-1-1

Four Intel experts explain the techniques and tools that you can use to improve the performance of applications for IA-32 processors. Simple explanations and code examples help you to develop software that benefits from Intel® Extended Memory 64 Technology (Intel® EM64T), multi-core processing, Hyper-Threading Technology, OpenMP†, and multimedia extensions. This book guides you through the growing collection of software tools, compiler switches, and coding optimizations, showing you efficient ways to get the best performance from software applications.

❝A must-read text for anyone who intends to write performance-critical applications for the Intel processor family.❞

Robert van Engelen,
Professor,
Florida State University

Special Deals, Special Prices!

To ensure you have all the latest books
and enjoy aggressively priced discounts,
please go to this Web site:

www.intel.com/intelpress/bookbundles.htm

Bundles of our books are available,
selected especially to address the needs
of the developer. The bundles place
important complementary topics at
your fingertips, and the price for a
bundle is substantially less than
buying all the books individually.

About Intel Press

Intel Press is the authoritative source of timely, technical books
to help software and hardware developers speed up their development
process. We collaborate only with leading industry experts to deliver
reliable, first-to-market information about the latest
technologies, processes, and strategies.

Our products are planned with the help of many people in the developer
community and we encourage you to consider becoming a customer advisor.
If you would like to help us and gain additional advance insight to the latest
technologies, we encourage you to consider the Intel Press Customer
Advisor Program. You can register here:

www.intel.com/intelpress/register.htm

For information about bulk orders or corporate sales, please send e-mail to
bulkbooksales@intel.com

Other Developer Resources from Intel

At these Web sites you can also find valuable technical information
and resources for developers:

developer.intel.com	general information for developers
www.intel.com/software	content, tools, training, and the Intel® Early Access Program for software developers
www.intel.com/software/products	programming tools to help you develop high-performance applications
www.intel.com/netcomms	solutions and resources for networking and communications
www.intel.com/technology/itj	Intel Technology Journal
www.intel.com/idf	worldwide technical conference, the Intel Developer Forum

Intel
PRESS

6173-0134-3336-4549

If serial number is missing, please send an
e-mail to Intel Press at **intelpress@intel.com**

IMPORTANT

You can access the companion Web site for this book
on the Internet at:

www.intel.com/intelpress/soa

Use the serial number located in the upper-right hand
corner of this page to register your book and access
additional material, including all code examples and
pointers to development resources.